MW00398407

First published in the United Kingdom
in 2023 by Rocket 88, an imprint of

Essential Works Limited
40 Bowling Green Lane
London ECIR ONE
United Kingdom

All interviews and text compiled by Dave Everley

Classic Edition: 9781910978986
Signature Edition: 9781910978993

Printed in Czech Republic

rocket88books.com

LIFE...? AND NAPALM DEATH

Shane Embury

This book is dedicated to Ann and Thomas Embury –
you did the best you could, and I hope I made you proud.

Sending thanks, love, and Blessings of the Universe to:
Dave Everley for helping me write this book and spending
endless hours deciphering my Shropshire slang, Madoka
Embury and family for their love and patience, Sarah
Embury, my Napalm Death family for their friendship and
love, Dan Tobin, Carl Stokes, Russ Russell, Kevin Sharp,
Simon Efemey, and all at Rocket 88 for doing this.

Life is to be lived and loved.

Shane ND, June 2023

Contents

Introduction

It's always hard to know what to say when you're talking about yourself, and how honest you should be. The last thing I want with this book is to upset anyone, but I also want to present myself as truthfully as I can.

This is my story and how I remember it, warts and all. Other people will probably have different memories, good and bad, but I don't feel the need to hide anything that might seem embarrassing, or the darker side of my character. Have I done stupid things? Yes, plenty. Do I have any regrets? Only one: that I didn't join Napalm Death when Nik Bullen first asked me to in 1987, when they were between the recording of *Scum*'s 'A' and 'B' sides.

It made sense at this point in my life to document everything as honestly as I can. A lot has happened in the last few years – there's been a major pandemic, my mom passed away, I've stopped drinking and started again and ended up in hospital in great pain because of it – and all these things have affected me in different ways. So, this book represents a step forward for me. I'm looking backwards, but I'm looking ahead as well. This is me re-evaluating what's been important in my life and is still important as I move forward.

This is what it is.

Shane Embury, 2023

1967

66 I was born on 27 November, 1967, in Broseley, Shropshire. It's a tiny village on top of a hill overlooking a place called Ironbridge, which is the birthplace of the industrial revolution. Charles Darwin was born in Shrewsbury, which is about 16 miles up the road, and Tolkien based part of *The Lord Of The Rings* on the area. That's pretty good company to be in.

Broseley was a nice place to grow up, but it was quite insular. My whole family were all from Broseley and the surrounding villages. Everybody knew everybody else's business back then. When Napalm started taking off and we did a couple of TV shows, people would come up to my mom and say, "I saw your Shane on the telly last night." Of course, my mom loved it.

I grew up in a totally working-class family: me, my sister, my mom and my dad. My mom's name was Ann-Lilian. She was a big music fan and the radio was always on in our house back in the day. The Beatles, Tom Jones ... she loved all that. She was really encouraging. When I was a bit older, she'd let me blast out music in my bedroom or watch *Hammer Horror* movies. All of which shaped what I'd do later in life.

My mom always used to tell me that she liked Napalm's music, and I'd think, "Is she having me on?" But there's one thing that really sticks in my mind about her from when I was a teenager that makes me think maybe she did.

There was an Italian band that I liked called Bulldozer. They were around in the early-to-mid-80s, and they were really heavy for their time. One day I came home from school and could hear their album playing. I'm thinking, "What the hell's going on here?" So I walked upstairs and my mom is sitting in my room with Bulldozer blasting out at full volume.

"What's happening, mom?"

"The neighbour is pissing me off, so I put this on."

"What, you randomly picked this one out and put it on?"

"No, I like this one."

"Wait, so you actually chose the Bulldozer album? It wasn't just the first one you came across that you pulled out to wind up the neighbours with? Are you serious?"

I'm not sure if I believed her, but I was impressed.

My mom came to a few Napalm Death gigs over the years. When Mitch Harris, Napalm's guitarist, joined the band in 1989, she was bouncing around at the front. My dad was there too. He was downstairs having a pint.

My dad, Thomas, worked for a company called GKN Sankeys, who made tractor wheels. He worked in the factory on the assembly line, and he'd tell me about how they all used to spend their days throwing these huge wheels around.

He was a typical 70s father. He wasn't ultra-strict. He never hit me, which a lot of parents did to their kids back then – they'd give them a clip across the ear if they were misbehaving. But me and my sister definitely had to do things his way. You'd come home from school, have your tea and that was it – upstairs you'd go.

He had a tough upbringing. He didn't know his real father and he wasn't really wanted by his mom. He left home at 15 or 16 and joined the army. He was stationed in Germany so he never saw conflict, but I think that provided a home for him. He was quite a royalist, he really liked the Queen, and he'd talk about the army a lot: "Army this, army that." Even when I was a kid, I was thinking, "There's no way I'm joining the army."

Like for so many kids of my generation, it was hard to get close to my dad. He would have been 22 or 23 when they had me, and to be fair to my dad, he was working a lot. He always meant well, but there was a bit of distance – he'd be up the pub on a Friday and the weekends.

When he came back to the UK, he was still searching for the camaraderie he got from the army. I think that's what he got from going down the local club. I imagine the fact that they had me when they were fairly young was stressful, too. As a father now, I can relate to the stresses that he probably had, and I'm much older than he was at the time.

If I inherited any musical genes, it would have been from my dad. He'd been in the brass band in the army, playing the tuba. At home, he'd sit in the garden and listen to brass band music, which drove me nuts. My mom would make fun of it: "All he listens to is his army music." Weirdly, years later, I can hear its influence creeping in with some of the soundtrack music I'm doing now. It's funny how things work out.

Money was tight for the family. My mom and dad had arguments about it, in the same way a lot of working-class parents did. They got on well, but money was an issue. As I got a little older, I heard them talking about their worries, and you can't help taking that onboard. They both drank and they both smoked, but that's what people did. You could say it was a waste of money, that they should have spent it on something else, but I think they wanted the escape.

We didn't have nurseries or pre-school back then, or if we did, they certainly didn't exist in Broseley. Because of the money situation, my mom had to work as well, so I spent a lot of time with my grandmother, who lived just down the road in Broseley. I pretty much grew up from the age of five or six at my grandmother's.

My nan's name was Violet, which is the middle name of my daughter. She came from a pretty big family – she had six or seven sisters and six or seven brothers. They were the Marstons; I'm not sure if they're related to the Marston family of beer fame (maybe I should ask, see if I can get a family discount). My grandad would be down the local pub a lot, so my nan was always around the house.

My nan was great. I've always been a big guy, and she'd encourage me to eat even back then. I'd have something to eat at home then go round my nan's. She'd say, "Have you had your tea?" and I'd say, "No." So I'd have another one. That's just the way I was. A greedy little bastard, basically.

I reckon it was at my nan's that I first knew I wanted to be a musician without actually realizing it. She had these buckets, and I used to hit them – just bash the hell out of them. She always had to buy new ones, because I kept breaking them: "Shane's fucked my buckets again." She used to call me "Schimtar", which is a strange word. I think it was the name of the local crackpot.

I wasn't a lonely child, but I enjoyed being on my own. I liked solitude, even from an early age. I think that stemmed from spending so much time at my nan's. I was left to my own thoughts and imagination, which wasn't a bad thing. In a lot of respects, it probably defined who I became later in life.

My grandad was a little bit of a standoffish kind of guy, but I got on fine with him. Years later, I remember Danny Herrera, Napalm Death's drummer, taking him out on the piss one Sunday afternoon. I warned Danny, "Be careful, he can drink, don't let the age fool you." And Danny said , "Your grandad's an old man, I'll be ok." And of course, my grandad wiped the floor with him. He'd got Danny on the whiskey at two in the afternoon. Danny said, "I can't believe it, your grandad tried to kill me!" I did warn him…

The other important person for me growing up was my Uncle Charlie, my mom's brother. He'd been in the navy, and he had the tattoos to prove it. He was an amateur boxer, and he loved fart jokes and that kind of thing. When you're a kid, that stuff is impressive. Shropshire's quite a rural county, and there was lots of countryside around Broseley back then, lots of green fields, and he'd take us out on rambles. He was really free-spirited, which is something I admired. My mom always said to me, "I see him in you all the time."

I don't want to make it sound like it was an unhappy childhood. It was a really happy one for me. I think my mom and dad had their ups and downs, but that's marriage for you. Being married, I know that now – it's a test, and it can trip you up if you're not careful. I think my mom especially had to be pretty strong. I like to think I've inherited a bit of that strength from her, but I'm not the person to ask about that.

I still go back to Broseley quite a bit. It's changed, but not that much. When I think about that kid banging on his nan's buckets, it amazes me just how things turned out.

The 1970s

When I was growing up in the late 60s and early 70s, *Top Of The Pops* was a huge thing in our house, like it was for so many people at the time. This was years before MTV, and it was the only place you could actually get to see your favourite bands on the telly. We'd watch it together as a family. You'd get "What's this rubbish?" from my dad, but my mom was into a lot of the things that were on there.

Top Of The Pops was my first real introduction to music – and to heavy music, too. Led Zeppelin's 'Whole Lotta Love' was the theme tune (even if it wasn't the original version). Sweet, Slade, Queen… they were all on there, and it made an impression.

The first record I ever got was a Slade single, 'Gudbuy T'Jane'. There was a shop in Broseley that sold bicycles and records, for some reason, and my mom would go in and buy me a different single every week. I loved Sweet, but I really loved Slade. The way they looked, the way they sounded, the loud, crazy-shaped guitars… they were just larger than life. I knew they were from Walsall, which isn't a million miles away from Broseley, although at that age it might as well have been Timbuktu.

I got to meet Slade guitarist Dave Hill years later at the *Kerrang!* magazine awards. I was looking around the room and I clocked him: "Fucking hell, it's Dave Hill!" He was a lovely bloke, very down-to-earth, though I'm not sure what he made of the bass player from Napalm Death telling him how much he loved his band. (Years later, I got to go to John Peel's house after he died, and he had all the Slade records there, which shows what brilliant taste in music he had.)

The other big influences on me as a kid were horror and sci-fi. I was big on *Hammer Horror* movies. My mom and dad would occasionally go to the local social club, and my auntie and uncle – who weren't actually related to us, they were our next-door neighbours – would let me stay up to watch the Hammer movies. *Curse Of The Werewolf* with Oliver Reed, *Curse Of Frankenstein* with Christopher

Lee, *Dracula: Prince Of Darkness*, *The Gorgon* – they were tame compared to a lot of the stuff that's around now, but when you're a young kid, they're terrifying and brilliant.

I loved the classic old Universal movies from the 1930s too, things like *Dracula*, *Frankenstein* and *The Wolfman*. Me and my mom would go to the corner shop, and I'd buy packs of bubble-gum that came with the Universal Monsters horror cards in them. I'd toss the bubble-gum and keep the cards to trade with my friends.

That stuff has stuck with me, maybe more than I sometimes realize. I can't always help my daughter with her homework, but I can tell her who directed the 1931 *Frankenstein* movie. And a lot of my chord structures when I write music have the same notes as the music on *Hammer Horror* films. It's not deliberate, it just soaked into my brain at a young age.

Then there was *Doctor Who*. Looking back on those episodes now, the sets are wobbly and the effects look pretty dated, but there was something otherworldly about it – this guy hopping through time, going from planet to planet, taking on all these weird and wonderful monsters. That's every kid's dream, right?

Jon Pertwee and Tom Baker were my Doctors. I loved Tom Baker so much that my nan knitted me a proper, 14-foot scarf just like the one his Doctor had on the show. I was obsessed with the Daleks. My mom always said she could hear me coming home from school before she could see me, because I'd be shouting, "Exterminate! I am a Dalek!" Even now, I still love them. In the middle of the pandemic, I was sitting there making music for one of my side projects and I thought, "I need some Daleks." So I went and spent £150 on a pair of big Daleks. What can I say? I'm a geek when it comes to that stuff.

It wasn't just *Hammer Horror* and *Doctor Who*. I used to watch old musicals with my grandmother – *Singing In The Rain*, and anything with Fred Astaire. I'd watch tv shows like *The Professionals* and *The Saint*, and I'd record the theme tunes on cassette. Looking back on it now, it could explain why I like so many different kinds of music today – I just took it all in without realizing it.

I think movies were an escape for me. I was never a lonely child, but I was solitary, and even as an adult I'm a bit of an escapist, which is good and bad. It's good because it takes you away from the problems life can throw at you and lets you create a space in your own head. But it's bad for pretty much the same reason – it means you sometimes end up avoiding the problems that need dealing with. I think I've got better with that over the years, even though I still have no problem spending £150 on a pair of Daleks.

As much as I liked all that stuff as a kid, I found my footing with heavy metal. I can't really say what the stepping stones that got me there were. Like most kids whose tastes are still forming, I was into lot of different kinds of music – chart music, the Bee Gees, even a bit of disco. I remember the Sex Pistols coming out and thinking, "Whoah, what's this?" I was only 10, so I was a bit too young for punk, but it made an impression.

Even at that age, I think I was the kind of person who was looking for the next thing that was faster or heavier, and I came across a lot of the bands I loved through *Top Of The Pops*. I remember seeing videos for Black Sabbath and Thin Lizzy, and Judas Priest's 'Taking On The World' – they had the full-on leather regalia, the Flying V guitars. AC/DC, Saxon, Rainbow – there was this whole world that I was just discovering.

I wasn't the only person thinking like that in Broseley. There was a kid named Mitch Dickinson and as I was getting into Sabbath and Priest and AC/DC, so was he. The two of us would quickly become partners in crime.

I met Mitch's brother Paul first, though. We were in the same class at school, and we both loved *Hammer Horror* movies – we used to sit there drawing pictures of Christopher Lee. I'd bumped into Mitch, who was a couple of months older than me, but only met him properly through Paul.

Mitch lived with his mom right in the middle of the village square, and I spent a lot of time at their house. We loved the same kind of music and similar films, and our friendship grew from there. We'd hang out and talk about movies and music, and just imagine stuff. When you're kids growing up in a village where there's not much to do, your imagination is everything.

Back then there was a mail-order company called Britannia Music Club. You could pick three albums at a time and get them sent to you. I picked Thin Lizzy's *Jailbreak*, *Killing Machine* by Judas Priest and Black Sabbath's *Never Say Die*, which is an album I still love to this day. Mitch and our other friend Wayne Aston got some albums from there too, and we'd exchange records and tape them.

My record collection was helped along a bit by Mitch in another way. He'd go into Birmingham and pinch albums from shops without paying for them. I'd say to him, "If you're going to do it again, can you get me this one?" I had all the Deep Purple albums, all the Rainbow albums. What can I say? Money was tight back then.

A few of us formed a little gang. We once had an infamous head-banging competition to the Rainbow song 'Stargazer'. Four of us wanted to see who could last until the end of the track, which lasted nine minutes. I won that one, of course. There really wasn't that much to do in Broseley in the late 70s.

Being a metal fan in a place like Broseley wasn't always easy. Small villages have a very particular way of thinking, and if you look different you really stand out. As we grew older and got more into metal, we started getting strange looks. People would want to fight purely because we had long hair and a denim jacket.

I had experiences of bullying as a kid. Kids who were "different" were picked on, and it sometimes seemed like I was a target. Maybe it's because I was a bigger kid, or maybe it's just because the stuff I was into was "weird" – horror movies or metal or whatever. If there was a kid who was big or fat on the TV, they'd call you that. It does get to you after a while, and you end up avoiding those people.

The bullying was fairly low level in primary school, but one time in secondary school, when I was 13 or 14, this kid got pretty aggressive with me. He tried to tie me to a tree, which I suppose sounds funny but it's pretty upsetting. He was also bullying Mitch, who was a skinny kid, but could be pretty feisty. I wasn't – even though my uncle was an amateur boxer, I've never been into fighting.

That's when me and Mitch started thinking, "These people are arseholes, fuck 'em." I can't say I was always in lessons when I was meant to be. We'd sign in on the register then just walk out again. We'd walk back through the woods and start messing about on boats that were on the lakes in there. Or we'd just think, "Fuck it", and go to Mitch's house while his mom was at work, and play on his Commodore 64 and listen to Rainbow. That was our thing, fuck everybody else.

Bullying does have an effect on people at that age. I can still feel that effect today, to be honest. One day not so long ago, I was in a really good mood, trying to get my car into a parking space up outside my house. I must have been taking a bit too long, cos this guy in a car behind me pulled his window down and said, "Move, you fat bastard." I just burst into tears.

Maybe that's a weird reaction for a grown adult to have, but that stuff still plays on my mind. You look at your past, and things like bullying and feeling like an outsider, and it does shape who you are, not just in your music but also in your friendships and relationships.

I've thought a lot about that. I sometimes wonder how it might have shaped me as a person and what I went on to do with music. It's that idea of someone doing something to prove their worth to other people. I was always told at school: "You're never going to be successful, you're wasting your time with this music thing." Perhaps there is an element of showing people that I've made my mark. It's a cliché, but there's some truth in every cliché.

The other side of that is that some people don't have to justify the reasons for doing what they do. They do it for the pure enjoyment of creating. When I came across the punk and underground metal scene a few years later, I felt at home because nobody was talking about what was right and what was wrong in terms of what people were doing. For me, it was as simple as, "I want to make music, I want to create something." That's what I always wanted to do. Ever since I was a kid, I've been on this quest to be in a band and play music.

EYE WITNESS: SARAH WRIGHT

Shane's sister

The first time Sarah Wright – née Embury – heard Napalm Death, she didn't know what to make of them. It was the late 80s and Sarah's big brother Shane was their bassist. The siblings' musical tastes were poles apart. Shane was immersed in the subterranean world of metal, punk and the more experimental wing of indie music. For Sarah it was all about the pop bands of the day: A-ha, Erasure and their ilk.

"I couldn't understand a word they were saying at all," says Sarah of her first encounter with her brother's band. "It was just shouting. It's still just shouting, even now."

Seven years separated the two of them. According to their mother, Ann, the young Shane was unimpressed at having a new sister. "Apparently when I was brought home, he said, 'Take her back, I want a brother,'" says Sarah.

Despite that initial disappointment, the pair were close growing up. "We never really argued," says Sarah. "Shane was closer to mom than I was. I was closer to my dad. It was a typical boy–girl thing."

Heavy metal factored large in Shane's life for as long as Sarah can remember. "His bedroom would be full of Black Sabbath and heavy metal stuff," she says. "At one point, he had a goat's skull in a bucket in there, just floating. I've no idea where he got it."

As she explains, Ann and Tom Embury were happy to indulge their son's passion for loud music, even when he decided to take up drumming after joining his first band, Warhammer. "They let him get on with it," says Sarah. "He had his drumkit at the back of the lounge. There were dips in the carpet from where he used to sit there playing. The neighbours weren't very happy, but mom would just tell them to bugger off."

She remembers Shane being a self-contained teenager, happiest losing himself in music, whether listening to it or playing it. "He wasn't really an extrovert," she says. "He had a few friends at school, but there was a bit of bullying because he was a bigger kid. Scratch the surface and he's quite an insecure person. You look back at old interviews and he was always at the back, not speaking."

The age difference meant the Embury kids rarely socialized outside the house growing up. At home it was a different matter. "He was really good at art," says Sarah. "He drew album covers all the time. He'd do my art homework for me and I'd go in and get A+. Then I'd do it myself and get a D."

Shane's appearance – denim jacket, heavy metal patches, masses of hair – marked him as an outsider in their hometown, drawing unwanted attention from some of Broseley's other inhabitants. "He never went out at home when he was of drinking age, because he could never be bothered with the flack of it all," says Sarah. "I think that's one of the reasons he moved to Birmingham. I remember sitting in the lounge crying because he was leaving home."

Napalm Death may have baffled Sarah when she first heard them, but having a brother in a band – especially one who had appeared on a BBC Arena documentary – gave her a certain cachet among her schoolfriends. With hindsight, Shane had been preparing for fame – or possibly notoriety – long before that. "He was always practising his autograph on the back of my dad's newspaper. Any bit of blank space and he'd scribble it on there. I watched him do it so many times. A few years ago, we were at one of his gigs and there were young fans who wanted albums signing. I said, 'Oh, I can do that for you', just because I'd seen him do it so many times."

The first time Sarah saw Napalm Death live is lost to memory, although she does recall that, "There was a wheelie bin absolutely full of alcohol in their dressing room."

The Embury family would travel to nearby Wolverhampton or Birmingham whenever the band were playing a show. "Mom and dad would drive us over," says Sarah. "I usually ended up on crowd control with my mom, because otherwise she'd end up in the moshpit. Shane would say, 'You know she's going to get something chucked over her – you've got keep her away.' But they were both really proud of him. They'd wear the T-shirts. Dad would aways have a vest T-shirt on. And they were always really protective of him, especially mom. Whenever he'd get heckled, you could see her hackles rising. I'd tell her, 'Mom, this is what they do, it's just part of it.' And she'd say, 'If they say anything nasty about my son, I'm going to kill 'em.'"

Whereas Shane hadn't been a big drinker when he was living at home, he developed a taste for alcohol after joining Napalm Death. Sarah noticed this whenever he paid one of his regular weekend visits home. "One time he came back from Ironbridge drunk, put the gas cooker on and passed out on the floor in the kitchen. "There was no flame, the whole place stank of gas. I turned it off and tried to drag him upstairs. The size he was, it wasn't happening, so I had to leave him there."

As the years progressed, Shane's alcohol intake sometimes gave his sister cause for concern. "I always worried about him," she says. "Being in a band isn't always a good environment for a healthy lifestyle, especially when you're not supposed to drink. When he ended up in hospital in Germany in the early 2000s, that was hard to deal with. And he did go off the rails a little bit after our mom died. I still worry about him. He's not getting any younger, none of us are."

Napalm Death's music may still be several notches too loud for her, but Sarah remains proud of her brother's achievements – especially his less aggressive Dark Sky Burial project. When she attends Napalm Death shows now, she can still see the shy kid with the Black Sabbath posters on his wall and the goat's skull floating in a bucket. "Even on stage, he's happier in the background. He's not the singer or the drummer. What he does is really important, but he doesn't have to be in the spotlight to do it. He's still that quiet, insecure kid getting lost in his music."

1981–1983

66 I've played over 5,000 gigs with Napalm Death, and I've got the tinnitus in both ears to prove it. Even after all this time a great show can make you feel brilliant, but there's nothing like the magic of your first gigs as a kid.

I can't remember exactly what my first concert was – it might have been Tygers Of Pan Tang at the Birmingham Odeon or it might have been AC/DC on the 'For Those About To Rock' tour. I remember reading about AC/DC's PA spec and shitting myself: "It's going to be so loud, it'll blow my head off." Of course, I ended up at the back, which was massively annoying. But AC/DC didn't fuck about onstage. There was hardly any talking, they'd just smack straight into every song.

There was a real excitement to going to gigs back then. You'd see adverts for shows in the back of *Kerrang!* magazine, order the ticket and get it delivered in the post. It's so much easier now with the internet, but maybe some of that excitement has been lost. It was a trek to get from Broseley to Birmingham or Wolverhampton in those days. Me, my friend Wayne Aston and a guy named Mike Clarke, who was a little bit older than us, would get the coach. Or, if there was space in someone's car, we'd all pile in and head down there.

I saw loads of great bands back then, and missed a few too. I was supposed to go to see Ozzy play on the 'Diary Of A Madman' tour in 1981, but he cancelled because of flu, or at least that was the official reason. I was devastated because *Diary Of A Madman* is one of my favourite albums. This was right before his guitarist, Randy Rhoads, died in a plane crash – I never did get to see that line-up of Ozzy's band play, which I'm still gutted about.

Gigs were pretty special when you didn't know the intricacies involved in actually putting a show together. Even the dry ice smelled different – it was sweet, somehow. And I'd always come home from gigs back then with my ears ringing for three or four days and my neck aching from headbanging. I'd sit in class at school and not really pay attention to what the teacher was saying.

At that time, I was always looking for the next faster, heavier and nastier band. Magazines like *Sounds* and *Kerrang!* would do their lists of the 100 Greatest Heavy Metal Songs. I'd read them and think, ".38 Special? That doesn't sound very heavy to me." But then I started reading about this band Venom.

They were three guys from Newcastle who looked like a gnarlier, more Satanic version of Motörhead. They had long hair and leather trousers, shades and inverted crosses. They were pretty much the perfect band for a 14-year-old headbanger like me. The legendary journalist Geoff Barton had lost his mind over them in *Sounds*. Their debut single 'In League With Satan' had come out on Neat, which was this brilliant British record label. They were definitely something I needed to check out as soon as I could.

There was a record shop in a place called Wellington, a few miles from Broseley. The guy who ran it had all the regular rock and metal releases, but he'd get in stuff that was a bit more under the radar. I walked in and there it was: Venom's debut album *Welcome To Hell*, £3.99. I thought, "I'm having that."

While I'd read about Venom, I'd never actually heard them. I had an idea of what they might sound like, but I wasn't exactly sure. So I couldn't wait to get home and put the record on. My dad was in bed because he'd been working nights, so I had to listen to it on headphones. But as soon as the opening song, 'Sons Of Satan', started blasting out, I knew it would be good. It sounded like a fucking concrete mixer. I thought it was the most amazing thing ever. Now, Motörhead were abrasive and heavy, but this was something else. There were absolutely no smooth edges – it was as raucous as hell, pun intended. And the imagery was just as extreme for the time – lots of inverted crosses. When you got into Venom, you were making a statement. I remember some religious guy knocked on our door once, saying, "Come to Jesus." I just showed him the *Welcome To Hell* sleeve. He didn't look happy.

After school when we were bored, we used to go down to the graveyard and blast out our music. I had a cassette with Venom's 'Black Metal' on one side and 'City Baby Attacked By Rats' by GBH on the other, and we had this boombox which was abnormally loud for some reason. We'd play those records at maximum volume.

People would come over to see what was happening and we'd ignore them. Weirdly, the vicar never told us to turn it down or chased us off. Maybe he was too scared to come out. I was never really into the occult as such, though, it was more the imagery. I think it was more an extension of not wanting to fit in: this band coming out of the blue, singing about Satan and whatever was attractive at that point in my life. I know now that Venom were tongue in cheek, but I didn't know that at the time.

Venom were a bridge to so many other things that would shape me. Mitch's step-brother was into punk bands like The Exploited, Dead Kennedys and Discharge. He'd say, "If you like Venom, you might like this...", and he'd put on *Hear Nothing See Nothing Say Nothing* by Discharge, who sounded like a punk Venom. For someone like me, who was always looking for the next extreme thing, it was brilliant.

Ironically, my sister got married at that church years later. One of my other bands, Lock Up, had just played the Wacken festival in Germany, and I'd only just made the wedding by the skin of my teeth. I'm standing there, red-faced and hung over, shaking the vicar's hand, wondering whether he'll recognize me from the days of hanging out with my mates in the graveyard, blasting out Venom. He didn't say anything, but I like to think he remembered it.

That period is really influential on an 80s-influenced thrash project I started recently. It's based on us at that point: one of the titles I've got for it is Slamming In The Graveyard. There's a bit of nostalgia there. I think I just want to connect with my 14-year-old headbanging self. When I speak to people in bands I know around the world, we all have similar experiences – being rebellious teenagers. It's a universal thing.

There's another reason why that period of my life is so important to me. That was when I started getting involved in the tape-trading scene.

The tape-trading scene was like a primitive social network. You'd send off tapes and letters of your band, and whatever tapes by other bands you'd got that week, and you'd get tapes and letters back. Metallica became famous through the tape-trading scene – their demo *No Life Til Leather* had been passed around by everybody.

I'm sure it's hard for kids who have grown up with everything at their fingertips on the internet to get their heads around just how important it was. Metal magazines in the 80s very rarely covered underground music, if at all. Metallica would get mentioned, and Slayer and maybe a band like Exodus. But there was a whole layer of metal and punk bands beneath them that weren't getting written about. That was the stuff I was interested in – the more extreme, out-there stuff that most people didn't know about. And we found out about it through tape trading. At one point, I was getting 30 tapes a week. I got tapes from bands who became really well known in the metal scene later on, like Possessed from San Francisco, and Death, who had just moved from Florida to the Bay Area. No one knew those bands at this point. It was ours. It was special. To be honest, it turned you into a bit of a snob: the more obscure the band, the better.

There were tapes you just had to have. Possessed would play at Ruthie's Inn, which was this famous venue in San Francisco, every weekend. I always had to get hold of tapes of the gigs in case they played a song that hadn't been released anywhere else. The sound quality wasn't great, but that didn't matter. Tapes would come in the post, you'd listen to them, then add them to the list you had to trade with people around the world.

Some of the things I got through tape trading have really stuck in my mind, like the tape of the band Crumbsuckers from New York featuring their very first singer, way before their first album came out. They did this mad cover of the theme to the kids' TV show *Inspector Gadget*. There's loads of stuff I can't remember these days, but for some reason I can remember that.

There were so many bands that are totally unknown now, and loads that were pretty unknown back then, too. I loved Slayer and Exodus and those bands, but you'd try and find the most obscure stuff you could. One of my favourites was this amazing hardcore band called Damage from New York. They had two bass players and recorded a couple of live albums at CBGBs. There was another band from LA called Arch Enemy – not the same Arch Enemy that's around now. They only did one rehearsal tape, which me and Bill Steer, who was Napalm Death's guitarist when I joined, both loved.

Years and years later, I met their guitarist. He came up to me and said, "Hey, I'm such-and-such from Arch Enemy". I was, like, "Wow, that's a blast from the past."

That was the thing about tape trading. Having tapes and hearing new music was important, but so was forging friendships. I got to meet so many people through the scene. I used to trade with people from all over the world – New York, LA, Japan. A guy from Ireland sent me a tape of this band from LA called Terrorizer, who I loved. I started writing to their guitarist, Jesse Pintado. Jesse lived in LA, and I used to call him and wake him up because I always forgot about the time difference. Everybody calls everybody "fool" over there: "How you doin', fool?" It'd be 4 o'clock in the morning there when I called. He'd pick up the phone: "How you doin', fool?"

My mom wasn't very happy about me using the phone to call people in America because it cost a fortune, so she put a lock on the phone. I managed to crack that pretty easily. I worked out you could tap the numbers out on top – if you wanted a 1, you tapped it once, if you wanted a zero, you tapped it 10 times. She'd get the bill in and go ballistic: "How the fuck are you calling people when I've got this lock on it?" (A few years later Jesse moved to the UK and joined Napalm Death.)

I got to meet a lot of these people when Napalm Death finally toured America. I met the guys from Deceased and Cryptic Slaughter, and Oscar from Terrorizer. Nicke Andersson, who was the drummer in the Swedish band Entombed, wrote to me because he loved my band Unseen Terror. When we eventually met, he said: "You never wrote back to me, did you!"

"Ah, sorry mate, I completely forgot!"

I was a kid from Broseley. The tape-trading network made me realize there was this bigger world out there, and that I was connected to it. I just hadn't stepped out of the door yet.

1984–1985

 Every kid who's spent hours headbanging to Rainbow and Venom in their bedroom dreams of having their own band. For me, that first band was Warhammer.

Warhammer formed in 1984, but we'd talked about being in a band for a long time before it actually happened. We'd come up with names we'd call ourselves, the stage sets we wanted, the lighting show, even the explosions. Bands like WASP were coming out, with pyro and codpieces and throwing raw liver at audiences. I remember Venom saying they needed to play some shows because they'd already spent a load of money on pyro. I thought, "Excellent! That's what I want!"

There was no actual plan to become a musician. We just sort of sat there and it happened. It was originally me and my friends Wayne Aston and Mike Clarke (Mitch Dickinson joined us a bit later). We'd all got guitars at one point or another, so of course everybody wanted to be the guitarist. I had this cheap thing, but I didn't really take to it. I could string together a few simple riffs, but that was it. Wayne was already playing guitar, and Mike ended up playing bass and singing, so I said, "Well, I'll play drums then."

I'd always liked hitting things, going right back to my nan's buckets of course. The only problem was that I didn't actually have a drumkit. I plucked up the courage to ask my grandad if I could borrow £100 from him to buy one, and I was shitting myself, because he was quite a standoffish man. But he gave it to me. And he never, ever, asked for it back.

I never bothered with drum lessons. I just listened to my Slayer and Venom records and thought, "How do they play so fast?" My kit was set up in my parents' living room, behind the sofa – couch, TV, drumkit in the corner. I could only practise at certain times because it was so loud. The neighbours on one side were fine. The neighbours on the other side, who were actually my dad's friends, were always complaining. I'm not surprised, in fairness…

It was Mike who suggested the band's name. He was into Games Workshop role-playing stuff, which is where the name Warhammer came from. That wasn't my scene, mainly because I couldn't afford to play it – it seemed like you needed to buy a lot of rule books and models of orcs. We had other cheesy names – I think I might have come up with 'Hellrat' – but Warhammer was the best, so we went for it.

A lot of new bands did covers, but we wanted to do our own songs. Slayer, Venom and the Swedish band Bathory were our unholy trinity. We ripped off a Bathory riff for our song 'Carnal Lust'. We ripped off Slayer's 'Necrophilia' for another song.

We rehearsed in a place called the Bladen Social Club. It cost us three quid a week and it was like something from the TV show Phoenix Nights – you half expected to walk in and find Creme Brulee playing. There was a signing-in register and a bar and a room where people had discos on a Saturday night. It also had a big stage where we'd set up the drums and start bashing things out. God knows what people next door thought: "What the hell are those noisy bastards doing?"

Weirdly, there was a buzzy little scene going on around Telford and Ironbridge. The three big local bands were Southern Cross, Wolf and Spellbound, and they'd play a pub called The Swan in Ironbridge. That's where I met all those guys. Carl Stokes, Spellbound's drummer, covered his kit in leather, which was pretty impressive. He ended up going on to drum with the band Cancer, and I'm still good friends with him today – he's done stuff with my side project Dark Sky Burial.

Warhammer made a six-track demo, *Abattoir Of Death*. We recorded it on 30 November 1985 in Shrewsbury for £50. We didn't really know what we were doing, but it felt like we'd made something of our own. The funny thing is, me and Mitch went down to London to see Anthrax and met a kid named Lee Dorrian in Shades, which was this great metal record shop in Soho. Him and his friend were headbanging to Metallica's 'Ride The Lightning'. We got talking and I said, "I'm in a band called Warhammer." And he went, "What? You're in Warhammer? Fucking hell, I've got your demo!" I was gobsmacked. A year or so later, we were both members of Napalm Death.

People keep asking if the demo is ever going to come out properly. Lee was going to release it on his label Rise Above a few years ago, but Wayne and Mike got a bit precious about it and didn't want to put it out. OK, fair enough. I do want to put it out some day, though. We'll see.

Warhammer got to play a couple of proper gigs in December 1985, but the funniest gig we played was in my parents' living room one Saturday afternoon. My dad was up at the social club and I don't know where my mom was. A few mates came over, and we pushed the sofa out of the way and plugged the mic in through a practice amp. We were playing at Slayer speed, and it was chaos. The neighbour was in bits: "They've been playing for 20 minutes." The bollocking we got was hilarious.

Warhammer fell apart in early 1986. Me and Mitch were heavily into the tape-trading scene, getting into really fast underground music like DRI, the punk band from Texas, and Crumbsuckers. We wanted to play faster stuff, but the other guys went: "Hmmm, we're not into this." I was trying to tell them that there was this whole scene out there that we could fit into, but I think they just wanted to do something other than Warhammer.

There was no big bust-up, but that was it. I was devastated. My first band was over. But there was a silver lining. Around the same time as Warhammer fell apart, me and Mitch had discovered a new band from down the road in Birmingham who sounded way louder and way more extreme than anything we'd heard before. The band's name was Napalm Death.

1986

66 The first time I ever saw Napalm Death was at the Mermaid pub in Birmingham. It was 22 March 1986, and it's no exaggeration to say that night changed my life forever.

Mitch had met this guy in Brum a little while before. The guy had seen Mitch's backpack with a Siege patch on it and come over to talk to him. He said his name was Justin Broadrick and he was the guitarist with a band named Napalm Death. He told Mitch his band were playing at a pub called The Mermaid soon, and he should come to the show.

Napalm Death had already been going since the early 80s. They'd started out as an anarcho-punk band. Two of the original members were Nik Bullen on bass and vocals and Miles Ratledge, who everyone called Rat, on drums. Justin had joined a few years later. There'd been a lot of line-up changes even by that point, and I think they might have split up and got back together a couple of times.

I didn't know any of that when Justin invited Mitch to the show. I'd never even heard the name Napalm Death before, but it sounded like the kind of thing I'd like, so me and Mitch decided we'd be up for going to see them.

The Mermaid was this Irish pub in Sparkbrook in Birmingham. Downstairs, it was a normal boozer, but it had a room upstairs that had punk gigs on all the time. It was the kind of place where you'd pay £1.50 to see seven bands. Chumbawamba played there years before they had a big pop hit with 'Tubthumping'. Bands like Swans from New York played – I didn't see them, but apparently they were so loud that plaster was falling from the ceiling. Reggae bands used to play there too – there was a real mix.

I remember the journey vividly. We got the bus from Ironbridge to Birmingham, then we got the Number 6 to The Mermaid. We'd been to gigs before, but this was a bit different – it was like stepping into another world.

To be honest, I was a bit worried about going to a place like The Mermaid. There had been a lot of tension between the punks and the metalheads back in the late 70s and early 80s. It was a real tribal thing. You'd hear tales of gigs where they'd get into fights with each other, and I didn't know what was going to happen. All these images flash through your head: "Will I get beaten up?" The first thing I noticed when we stepped through the door was that me and Mitch were the only metalheads in there. There were punks everywhere, drinking cider that cost 50 pence a pint, sniffing glue. Some of them had piercings and tattoos – all kinds of wild people. I'd never seen that kind of stuff before.

Rat – Miles Ratledge – was dancing in the pit when Napalm came on, and he was shaking his hands like The Joker, with this mad look on his face. I'd never seen anyone dance like that before. The way the punks were moving to the music was completely different to the kind of air-guitaring and headbanging we did. The Napalm Death show that night was amazing. They instantly became my favourite band. I was a fan of the Swiss trio Celtic Frost, who made this kind of slow, primitive metal noise, and I loved an underground American hardcore punk band called Siege, who played faster than anyone else at that time. With Napalm Death, here was a band who sounded like both – Celtic Frost when they played slow and Siege when they played fast. It was the perfect combination.

That was also the night I met Mick Harris, Napalm Death's drummer at the time and a friend for more than 35 years now. Mickey's always been a really hyper, in-your-face character, and at The Mermaid he came out of the blue and jumped on me. He must have been intrigued by the way I looked – nobody else there was wearing a bleached denim jacket with 'Thrash 'Til Death' on the back.

Mickey Harris and I became really good friends really quickly. I was 18 and still living in Broseley, so I'd travel down to Birmingham and stay at Mickey's parents' house, where we'd play records and tape trade and just talk about music.

At the time, I was working in a place called Hornsey Gates, a steelworks, and I hated it. They'd already threatened to fire me because

I took off to go and see Celtic Frost in London one day without telling anybody. I tried my best to buckle down, but it just wasn't happening. Eventually I said, "Fuck it, I'm not doing this anymore."

I told my dad I was jacking it in. He said, "Why are you quitting?"

I said: "Because I'm going to hang out with Mickey Harris in Birmingham. It sounds like more fun to me."

So I quit. I packed in work and went on the dole and spent my days hanging out at Mickey's mom's house, just goofing around. Mickey is one of the funniest and most eccentric characters I know. He was a total livewire, especially back then. I was at his mom's house once when he was ironing his clothes. Something went wrong with the ironing and he suddenly started swinging the iron around like a lasso. And then he let go of it and it went flying down the garden and hit the garage. He turned to me and said, "Shane, we've got to get the 35 bus into town."

"Why, Mickey?"

"I gotta buy my mom a new iron."

Mickey was a real piss-taker as well. It used to wind some people up, but I didn't mind it, at least most of the time. He would always take the piss out of my hair, my appearance – it was like being back at school. There was a kids' TV show in the 70s called *Double Deckers*, and one of the characters was this large kid called Doughnut. Mickey would call me "Doughnut". I can laugh about it now, but it got to me sometimes.

Occasionally I'd snap. I'm not a violent person, but I'd threaten him. I remember once he said something and I left a really angry message on his voicemail. I can't remember what it was, but it was enough to wind me up. I was probably a bit sensitive back then. I think maybe I still am.

But mostly me and Mickey had a mad friendship, and it was through him that I got to know the rest of Napalm Death. I'd go to see them practice, and I ended up sitting in on the recording of their debut album, *Scum* – or at least the first side of it.

Scum is a weird album, in that the original Side A and Side B were recorded by two different line-ups nearly a year apart. The reason for this was that the A-side was originally supposed to have been part of a split LP with a band called Atavistic released on Manic Ears

Records, but for some reason that didn't happen. Napalm ended up recording it and sitting on it for months.

The line-up on Side A of *Scum* was Justin Broadrick, who had invited me and Mitch to see them play at The Mermaid, on guitar and vocals, Nik Bullen, who had founded Napalm Death in the early 80s, on bass, and Mickey on drums. Mickey was still in the band when they recorded Side B of *Scum* in 1987, but Justin and Nik had gone by that point. They'd been replaced by singer Lee Dorrian, guitarist Bill Steer and bassist Jim Whitely, who I'd end up replacing the following year.

I remember the session for the A-side of *Scum* vividly. It was an overnight session at Rich Bitch studio in Birmingham. Digby Pearson, who ran Earache Records, was there, along with some of the guys from the band Head Of David – who Justin Broadrick left Napalm shortly afterwards to join.

They started recording at 9 or 10 at night and went through to 6 o'clock in the morning. At one point Mickey and Nik got into an argument about something or other. Mickey liked an argument, and Nik was quite stubborn. I remember telling Justin his second guitar track was out of tune, but they weren't having it: "No, it sounds cool." I was right though.

I already knew some of the songs that appeared on the first side of *Scum* just from being around Napalm. They were originally a lot slower, but Mickey joined the band and sped everything up. 'You Suffer' is one of the most famous Napalm Death songs, partly because it's only 1.3 seconds long. The lyric is just: "You suffer/But why?" But before they recorded it, it was longer: "You suffer/But why?/Because you're fucking stupid." It was still only six or seven seconds, but I guess they felt even that was too long.

The song 'Scum' has changed a bit too. It begins with a bass intro, which is the version everybody knows. But it originally started all at once – guitars and bass. For some reason they decided to cut the guitar out.

I had a copy of the A-side of *Scum* way before it became an album, and I used to tape-trade it with my friends. They'd hear it and go, "Fucking hell, who's this?" People hadn't really heard anything like it before – this mash-up of crustpunk and filthy metal that would come to be known as "grindcore".

Even now, Napalm Death get called a "grindcore band". I don't hate that description, but there's so much more to what we do than that. Plus people misunderstand what "grindcore" really meant.

I might be wrong about this, but my memory is that Mickey Harris invented the term "grindcore". Mickey had a funny way of saying if he liked something. He'd go, "This kills", or "This grinds". He's got his own dictionary, and sometimes I have no idea what he's talking about. Mickey came up with the word "grindcore" to describe music that had this heavy, distorted, pulsing bass. Stuff like Swans on their early records – it sounds like someone's taking a bonesaw to your skull. It was never about how fast you played. When I hear people go, "Grind is about speed, it's about politics", I think, "No, you're missing the point."

Back then, I was still just some kid in the crowd at these shows anyway. The Mermaid, where I saw Napalm for the first time, was the scene of some amazing gigs. The biggest band I saw playing there was DRI. One of the craziest shows was Extreme Noise Terror, who had come up from Ipswich on a coach with loads of their mates. I remember standing there with Mickey, watching all these punks piling off the bus with all kinds of mohicans. It was like the Addams Family on crack. As it happens, one of Extreme Noise Terror's singers, Phil Vane, would join Napalm in the 90s for a very short time.

After shows at The Mermaid, we used to go back to Jim Whitely's flat – the guy who ended up playing bass on the B-side of the *Scum* album. He'd have 20 or 30 people crammed in there, all in different states of inebriation. It was always a trek to get back to his place. Nobody had any money for cabs, so we'd have to walk, and it was miles away. That's being young for you. The funny thing about The Mermaid was that despite my initial fears that first time I went, I never had any grief from the punks. I was still rocking the metal look, with my cut-off denim over a leather jacket, with all the underground band name patches on the back. It was great to see people getting on with each other.

When I got to play The Mermaid with Napalm Death the crowd had changed a bit – it wasn't just punks, there were a few more metalheads in there, too. Things were starting to cross over. The punks loved metal bands like Celtic Frost because they heard bands like

Discharge in their music. And the tape-trading scene meant that metal kids were opening themselves up to punk and hardcore bands.

Napalm Death were right in the middle of all that. It was a massively exciting time. And it would get even more exciting for me, because I was about to join the band.

EYE WITNESS:
MARTIN NESBITT

Former Earache Records employee

Martin Nesbitt was living in America when Digby "Dig" Pearson called him at the end of 1988 to say he'd just released Napalm Death's second album, *From Enslavement To Obliteration*, on his label Earache and things were going crazy.

Earache's earliest releases, including Napalm Death's debut album *Scum*, had created a buzz in underground circles but *From Enslavement To Obliteration*, together with the patronage of John Peel and an appearance on the cover of the NME, had kicked things to the next level.

"Dig told me that the album was at Number One in the independent charts and everything had just gone nuts," says Nesbitt. "He said, 'If you come back, can you help me do Earache?'"

The label Nesbitt had moved to the US to work for had just gone bust, so he had nothing to lose. He booked a return flight to the UK and began working with Pearson at Earache, where he would watch the fortunes of both Napalm Death and the label itself rocket over the next few years.

The two men knew each other from Nottingham's underground music scene, and lived a few streets away from each other just outside the city centre. "I'd known Dig for a long time, you'd see him at gigs," says Nesbitt. "He was part of that scene. Bands would come over from America and stay at his house."

Before his six-month sojourn to the US in 1988, Nesbitt had been involved with Nottingham indie label Ron Johnson Records, worked in a local record store, and worked with a club called The

Garage that regularly put on indie bands who he says were, "Darlings of the *NME*. And in most cases, hardly anybody came to see them."

The small Nottingham scene meant that Nesbitt knew most of the local bands. It was via his friendship with one of those groups, Heresy, that he became aware of the crustpunk scene. Mixing the raw energy and attitude of hardcore punk with the political messaging of anarcho-punk godfathers Crass, crustpunk was a regional movement centred around second-tier British cities like Bristol, Bradford, Ipswich, and Nottingham, consisting of bands such as Chaos UK, Extreme Noise Terror, Concrete Sox and Napalm Death.

"You'd get people coming up from Bristol to check out the bands in Nottingham and vice versa," says Nesbitt. "I was blown away by the fact that this scene was totally unmanufactured, in complete contrast to whatever the *NME* would be losing their shit about in any given week. I started putting those kind of gigs on myself. Dig or the guys from Heresy would tell me about bands like DRI and Gang Green: 'This band is great, you've got to put them on.'"

Digby Pearson's involvement with the music industry – or at least its fringes – began in 1985 with the release of a five-track flexi-disc compilation titled 'Anglican Scrape Attic'. He launched Earache soon afterwards, partly as a way of claiming social security benefits without having to traipse to the unemployment office to sign on every fortnight. Napalm Death's *Scum* album, which came out in July 1987, would be the label's third release.

Three months later, on 1 October 1987, Martin Nesbitt booked hardcore trailblazers DRI to play a show at The Garage in Nottingham, supported by Heresy and Holy Terror. Opening the four-band bill were Napalm Death, with the recently recruited Shane Embury on bass.

"Shane's friend, Mitch Dickinson, had joined Heresy around that time," says Nesbitt. "Those two were so close. Shane came along with Mitch. 'Who's that bloke with Mitch? Oh, it's Shane. He's in a band too.'"

By the time Nesbitt had returned from America and was working with Pearson at Earache, Napalm Death had gone from being a fourth-on-the-bill curiosity to headliners in their own right. One of the first shows Nesbitt worked on was a prestigious gig at London's ULU venue, which was filmed for a BBC *Arena* documentary.

"Those gigs were chaotic," he says. "One thing that blew me away was that it was kind of innocent. It never seemed like they were deliberately thinking, 'We want to be the world's most extreme band.' They just fell into that extremity. It was a reflection of all the stuff they were listening to at the time being brought together in one place."

Pearson and Nesbitt initially worked out of the former's spare bedroom, before moving to an office in the centre of Nottingham. Nesbitt's exact role was undefined. "There were no official job titles, we were making it up as we went along," he says. "Dig wasn't very sociable, and I was more outgoing, so I ended up doing more of the stuff where I had to talk to people. I had a big record collection and Napalm would spend a lot of time around our house listening to music. They were getting into John Peel and starting to realize that there was a world of music out there beyond punk and metal."

That appetite for new music would be shared. Shane, Mitch Dickinson and Napalm Death drummer Mick Harris would constantly talk up the latest underground band they were getting excited by on the tape-trading circuit. Several of those bands would end up signing to Earache.

"Dig wouldn't have signed a lot of the bands they did if they hadn't been around," says Nesbitt. "It went from Shane and Mickey raving about Repulsion or Entombed to Dig checking them out and signing them."

The success of Napalm Death, as well as the likes of Morbid Angel and Carcass, helped raise Earache's profile, turning the label that had started in Digby Pearson's spare bedroom into an unlikely independent powerhouse. "The label was on fire," says Nesbitt. "The bands were getting loads of press and selling loads of records. Most of them would end up falling out with Dig, but it was great at the time."

Earache had become an unlikely brand in itself, even though no one at the time would have used that word. Inevitably, some of the label's bigger bands would jockey for position in the label hierarchy.

"The difference between Napalm Death and Carcass and some of the American bands was that the British lot were less careerist," says

Nesbitt. "Most of the British bands had no manager in their early days. There was all this buzz around them, but they were sleeping on people's floors after gigs."

In July 1989, Nesbitt accompanied Napalm Death on their first tour to Japan. "Shane and Mick Harris were close on that tour, even though Shane seemed to be the butt of a lot of Mick's jokes," he says. "Those two loved the attention but Lee and Bill didn't like it so much. There seemed to be a bit of friction there. Halfway through that tour, Bill and Lee told me they were leaving. I think they were fed up of how popular Napalm Death were getting. I remember during the last show on the Japanese tour, Lee said, 'Ever get the feeling you've been cheated?', which is what Johnny Rotten said at the last ever Sex Pistols gig."

Nesbitt would work at Earache until 1992. "Me and Dig had a big fallout and I got fired," he says. "To this day, I don't know why." He subsequently began managing Carcass, the band Bill Steer had left Napalm Death to focus on full time. A few years later, Shane approached Nesbitt with a question. "Shane asked me if I fancied managing Napalm Death after their first manager," says Nesbitt. "I said no. It sounded too chaotic."

The two men have remained friends long after their respective connections with Earache ended. "How has he changed?" wonders Nesbitt, "I don't think he has. He's a family man now, but he's still got that love of music he had when I first met him. That's something he'll never lose."

1987

 I was at home at my mom and dad's when the phone rang. It was Mick Harris. He said: "Do you want to join the band?"

It was the middle of 1987 and I wasn't really doing much. Mitch Dickinson had joined a band we liked named Heresy for a while, and I was hanging out with them. I went on tour with them for a few dates in Europe, crammed in the back of the van. It was my first time out of the UK, so that was a whole new experience.

Heresy had started to change from their punk beginnings into more of an American hardcore thing, and I'd dabbled in that a bit. I'd cut my hair off and was wearing a chequered shirt, which is what American hardcore bands did. I actually decided to go straight-edge – no alcohol, nothing harmful to your body. That lasted until I went on tour in Europe with Heresy. We ended up in a town in Germany called Geislingen, and this guy walked in with six or seven crates of German beer. That was when I thought, "Bollocks to this straight-edge thing, I'm having some of this." I'd lasted maybe two weeks.

When Mickey called, I was at a bit of a loose end. He'd been trying to get Napalm Death back on track for a few months. Justin Broadrick had left to join Head Of David not long after Napalm recorded the A-side of *Scum*, and Nik Bullen didn't stick around much longer. I don't think Mickey really knew what he was going to do, but he managed to put a new line-up together. He'd got Lee Dorrian, a guy from Coventry who I'd met before, in as singer, and Jim Whitely, whose flat we all used to crash in after gigs, on bass. Another local guy, Frank Healy, was on guitar.

I saw that line-up play a gig with Heresy and Concrete Sox at the Hand & Heart in Coventry early in 1987. Lee was sitting on the side of the stage with some lyrics, looking really nervous, and it just wasn't a great show generally. I remember Mickey being really upset afterwards. He said, "You should play drums, Shane." I just said, "Bollocks to that, you're the drummer in Napalm Death."

Things settled down a little bit after that. Frank Healy left and Bill Steer, who was in the Liverpool band Disattack and who I knew from the tape-trading circuit, came in on guitar. The line-up of Lee, Bill, Mickey and Jim recorded what would become the B-side of *Scum*, but then Jim decided to quit. I'm not sure why. I'm guessing Mickey's extreme sense of humour probably annoyed him.

That's when Mickey called me and asked if I wanted to join on bass. Funnily enough, Nik Bullen had asked if I would play guitar after Justin had left eight or nine months earlier. At that point, I really wasn't sure I could do it. I can play guitar reasonably well now, but it still stresses me out. Back then, there was no chance and I basically bottled it. It's one of my big regrets. But then I would have had to play lead guitar. Nah, I wanted to be a bass player.

When Mickey called and asked if I wanted to join, I was feeling a lot more confident. I'd already been writing songs on the guitar for Napalm Death since the previous year, even though I'd chickened out of joining the band – songs like 'Lucid Fairytale' and 'Practice What You Preach', which we'd later record.

"If you're going to do this, do it," Mickey told me down the phone. I didn't even have to think about it. "I'm not going to make the same mistake twice," I told him, and that was it. I was Napalm Death's new bass player.

Joining Napalm Death was a logical step for me. Back when I was going to see bands at the Birmingham Odeon, I was meeting all these different people from all over the place who were bonded by a love of heavy metal. It sounds like a cliché, but it's true – when you've got your arm around someone you've never met before, headbanging to Saxon, you feel part of something.

I got the same feeling from being around Napalm Death. It was this loud, crazy band who most people didn't understand. But the people who did get it had something in common. Part of the attraction was that it was our thing – you had to be into the extremity of it to get it. It was a real community.

I loved the A-side of the *Scum* album, but I think the band had lost it a bit on the B-side. It's obviously a completely different line-up, but the story I heard – and I'm not sure if it's true – was that a few people thought the A-side had been a bit too "metal", and that Mickey had made the songs shorter on the B-side in response. Mickey always says, "You don't like it cos you were just pissed off that you didn't join the band when Nik asked you." It's not that – I just really loved the A-side.

Either way, there wasn't much time to think about what I'd let myself in for. Napalm Death was making a stir, and Mickey wanted to push things forward as much as he could. When most people join a band, they have a few rehearsals then play a gig. For me, the first thing I did with Napalm Death was record a Peel Session.

John Peel's late-night show on Radio 1 was massively influential. He was this middle-aged guy with a really lugubrious voice who would play anything from extreme noise to Bhangra music. The more out there something was, the more Peel loved it, and he'd latched onto Napalm Death.

I'm not sure how the Peel Session happened. They might have called us, or Mickey might have pestered them. But I remember that we hired a van and drove down to the Maida Vale studios in London. We were late, which didn't go down well to start with, but once we got in there they were fine. Maida Vale was full of these long corridors, which really appealed to the *Doctor Who* fan in me. And we were totally vibing on the canteen because we had no money and it was so cheap.

The guy who engineered the sessions was Dale Griffin. He used to be the drummer in Mott The Hoople, one of the bands I saw on *Top Of The Pops* when I was a kid. He was used to extreme bands, but Napalm Death was something else. He gave us a sheet to fill out with the songs we were going to play. Most bands play four, but we put down 12 tracks. He looked at us and said, "How long is it going to be if you play all 12 tracks?" And we said, "Five minutes." He just started laughing.

Of course, Mickey Harris was his usual self during the sessions. He's a really hyperactive guy, and he used to click his tongue all the time. At one point, he did this one really loud click in Dale Griffin's ear, and of course he went ballistic: "You fucking twat, my ears are my life!" Mick being Mick, he just said, "Yeah, alright mate, calm down." For all that, Dale Griffin was asked years later who his favourite band to record was, and he said Napalm Death. We ended up doing three Peel Sessions over the years, and it was one of the best bass sounds I've ever had.

That first Peel Session was massively important to us. It was a real step up, but because we were part of that underground scene, you almost had to play down anything you'd achieved. You couldn't get too cocky, because other bands would let you know about it. For a scene that was supposed to be about unity and togetherness, there was a lot of jealousy and shit-talking, and when you're young you get wrapped up in all that.

We did the Peel Session in September 1987, and the very first actual gig I played with Napalm Death was on 1 October 1987, at the Garage in Nottingham. It was us, Heresy, Holy Terror and DRI headlining. I'd done the Peel Session, but this was different. I was so nervous. Jim, the guy who I'd replaced on bass, was in the front row. He wasn't there for any judgmental reasons, he was just a fan of the band. After we'd done, he said, "That sounds amazing", which meant a lot coming from him.

Pretty early on in my time in the band, we went to Europe for a couple of shows. Things were pretty flaky when it came to getting gigs back then. Napalm were supposed to be doing two shows opening for the German thrash band Kreator. They didn't transpire, so we thought, "We've got nothing better to do, let's go to Belgium instead." So we booked a show with a guy in a Belgian hardcore band via snail mail – this was way before the internet.

Bill was at college and he couldn't make it, which Mickey Harris was fuming about, so Mitch learned the set and came over to play guitar instead. We had Phil Vane from Extreme Noise Terror with us as well – plus any of our mates who could fit in the van. I remember we got bollocksed on the ferry going over. Lee was sick and I ended up throwing up on the side of the van. Mickey Harris and Phil Vane were just pissing themselves.

We played two shows in Belgium that weekend, only one of which was actually organized in advance. The first show was at a club in a place called Mol. It was this really narrow place that looked like a Belgian café. The second one was in Wakken. It hadn't been arranged – a friend of ours said, "There's a band playing, you can play too if you want. We'll give you a crate of beer." That second show was recorded and bootlegged – there was some very funny banter between Mickey Harris and Phil Vane on the soundboard, because Mickey would always talk down the mic between songs.

Like most things back then, we were doing it totally DIY. We didn't have a tour manager or anything like that. At one point, the van broke down because we'd run out of petrol. We ended up having to siphon some petrol from a car in an onion field so we could get to the nearest garage and get back home. I could see Mitch Dickinson thinking, "What the fuck have I signed on for here?" He liked to play music but he wasn't one for touring.

It was different for me. I was some kid from a small village in Shropshire, and now I was in this band playing gigs in Europe and having the time of my life. Bring it on!

1988

❝ A day or two before my birthday in November 1988, Napalm Death appeared on the cover of the *NME* with the words: "The fastest band in the world." The *NME* was the biggest weekly music paper in Britain at the time, and they covered everything from indie to dance music. The fact that we were staring out from the cover was just nuts.

We'd done a second session for John Peel in the spring of 1988, and people outside the underground scene were starting to take notice. A lot of people just didn't understand Napalm Death because of the speed we played at, but I think others were fascinated by it.

The speed thing came naturally to us. Mickey Harris was an amazing drummer, completely wild. For a while, Heresy and Napalm had this competition going on to see who could play faster, but Mickey was getting faster and faster. You'd think, "How fast is he going to be?" He was the grindcore Keith Moon.

We weren't analysing it that closely, but we were young and there'd be the odd cocky remark. Slayer's *Reign In Blood* was supposed to be the fastest album ever made, but I remember saying that Slayer would never be as fast as Napalm Death, which was a stupid thing to say and it came back to bite me on the arse. I heard that Slayer's guitarist Kerry King caught wind of it and wasn't happy. We never got a chance to tour with them until years later, and that's probably why.

Napalm were an interesting mix of people when I joined. You had Lee Dorrian, who was really shy and nothing like the outgoing frontman he'd become in later years. I was really happy when Lee started to come out of his shell. You had Bill Steer, who was an absolutely amazing guitarist, but also very quiet and didn't drink. Bill always seemed older and wiser than his years, even back then. Mickey was just Mickey – a lunatic!

Mickey and me were the main songwriters at that point, though Bill wrote a couple of tracks. Mickey had this two-string guitar that he'd sawed off so it was just a strip, and he'd come up with songs on that. He wrote 'Suffer The Children', which appeared on our third album, *Harmony Corruption*. We still play that song today – it's pretty amazing for a song written on a two-string guitar.

Writing songs for Napalm Death came pretty easily back then. The average track would be two or three riffs – we weren't doing prog rock epics. I don't even think I recorded the riffs, I just remembered them. There was one song called 'Musclehead' that we wrote completely on the spot with no planning or rehearsal and which ended up on a flexi-disc we gave away with the album when it was originally released.

I was finding my way as a musician. I was still influenced by the bands I was discovering through the tape-trading scene: "That's great, I like that riff, let's write a riff like it." The song 'Unchallenged Hate' was inspired by a couple of riffs by the death metal band Massacre. And a lot of the bands I was listening to, like Repulsion, had a really abrasive bass sound. I was just trying to emulate that distorted bass. Everything had to be on 11.

When I look back at the riffs I wrote for Napalm compared to Bill's, there's a purity to his stuff. I can see why it made sense for a certain riff to end where it did. Mine would have these strange notes in them, but that was just a lack of musical knowledge on my part.

I wrote a couple of pretty basic lyrics back then, but it was mostly Lee who took care of that side of things. If you listen back to the lyrics on the A-side of *Scum*, they're political but simple and direct. Jim Whitely, the guy who played bass before me, had written the lyrics on the B-side of *Scum*, and they were very different – very complex, almost poetry. That set a precedent for Napalm's lyrics right up to today.

I'm pretty sure Lee wrote most of the lyrics for our second album, *From Enslavement To Obliteration*, the day before we went into the studio. I remember reading them, thinking, "There's some pretty crazy stuff in here." He was coming from that anarcho-punk angle – a band like Crass were quite lyrical. That's the thing about Napalm, it was so extreme musically but it had this poetic, in some ways quite peaceful, side to it with the lyrics.

Scum had only cost £300 to record. *From Enslavement To Obliteration* cost about £600. We recorded it at Birdsong Studios in

Worcester, which was owned by Steve Bird. We rehearsed maybe four or five times for the record – 22 songs in total – but it all came together quickly. We recorded it over about four days, and slept in the studios in sleeping bags. We were all playing live in a really small room in the studio. I had headphones on to start with, but I took them off because it's easier to play that way – that probably hasn't done my hearing much good over the years. But I like the simplicity of how it was done – it was all of us together, which doesn't really happen anymore. The more you do something and get better at it, the more you start to analyse it. In some ways you can over-analyse things. Not everything has to be perfect. I'm at a point now where I like to have a quality recording, but I like to keep the mistakes as well. It feels more real.

From Enslavement To Obliteration came out in July 1988, and there was a real buzz around it. The NME used to print the indie charts and Napalm Death were Number One and Sonic Youth Number Two with *Daydream Nation*. Pixies, Dead Can Dance, Cocteau Twins – they were all in there. Even though I was into extreme music, these were all bands I loved. I was chuffed to be in amongst them.

Not everybody got what we were doing though, even other musicians. I remember David Vincent from the US death metal band Morbid Angel saying to me at the time, "Well, you're just making a noise." I said, "No David, we're not just making a noise... we're making an orchestrated noise." I get why people were baffled by the short songs and the extremity, but in my mind they were still songs, even if they lasted a second and a half.

We weren't touring constantly at that point, but we'd play gigs wherever we could get them. We still played at The Mermaid, but we'd go to places like The Frog & Toad in Bradford or The Caribbean Centre in Ipswich. We'd be on bills with bands who were our mates, like Extreme Noise Terror, Heresy and Cerebral Fix. Sometimes we'd get gigs in Germany or Sweden, so would pile into the van and pray that it didn't break down in the middle of nowhere.

Some of those gigs were pretty manic. The floor would be littered with broken pint glasses at the end. At one gig in Italy the promoter wanted Mickey to take down his drumkit. Mickey was giving it large: "I'm not taking my drumkit down for anybody." The promoter said, "You'd better take your drumkit down or we'll burn it down." I think even Mickey knew not to push it any further: "Oh, OK then, I'll take it down."

We didn't have the money to stay in flash hotels back then. Or any hotels. We did a couple of gigs in Germany where we played squats. We ended up sleeping in the van, because if we'd slept in the squats, we'd have been bitten to death by fleas. But there was a real community to it all – at a lot of places, people would put us up in their houses or let us crash on their floors. Some of those people would go on to form labels, and our paths would cross over the years.

Actually getting paid for gigs was hit and miss – you were lucky if you got money even half the time, especially in Europe. We did start to ask for a small guarantee when *From Enslavement To Obliteration* came out, which is where we'd at least get a little bit of money even if nobody showed up. That was frowned upon in certain circles, but we had to pay for our van so we could actually get there.

Of course, we got shit for "selling out" even back then. You'd get some drunk punk who'd point the finger at you because *From Enslavement To Obliteration* had come out on CD. I remember playing the Canterbury Arms in Brixton in South London, which was a really crusty punk venue, and we got a load of shit for that. I understood it from their point of view to a degree, but we just wanted to play music. We weren't in it for the money, which is just as well, because there wasn't any.

I'm not sure what those people thought about us appearing on the cover of the NME. We were all chuffed at the fact they wanted to put us on the cover, but we were worried they were going to stitch us up. Bill wasn't there when they shot us for the cover, so it was only Lee, Mick and me on the front. We did it at New Street Station in Birmingham, and the photographer was trying to get Lee to do a pose like the guy on the front of the *From Enslavement* cover, just screaming into the camera. Lee being Lee, he was really nervous and shy about doing it.

The interviewer was a guy named Steven Wells, who sadly passed away a few years ago. He was a tough cookie and we were shit-scared. I think he genuinely loved us, but he wanted to catch us out. I remember him saying that we were this really extreme band, but we were really timid. It was true – we wouldn't let anybody in. I'm not sure what I said in the interview. I don't think I said much, to be honest. I still hadn't come out of my shell.

That NME cover caused one problem. Someone at the dole office where I signed on had read it, and they called me in. I sat down with this guy and he said, "You're in this band Napalm Death. Are you making any income from it?" The thing is, we really weren't. We'd got paid a bit for the Peel Session, but we weren't making much money from our records. But there was a polite suggestion that I should sign off, so I got a three-day-a-week job renovating a house two minutes from where I lived. I was chuffed with that: get up, do a bit of work, nip home for some dinner, then go back to work for a few hours.

I got my first ever royalty cheque at the end of 1988, around Christmas – £2,000 for Napalm Death. I was gobsmacked. I didn't even have a bank account at the time, I had to go and open one just to cash the cheque. I went out and bought a stereo for £600, which was a fortune in those days. I've still got the amp. I keep it as some weird spiritual heirloom.

EYE WITNESS: PHIL ALEXANDER

Journalist/former editor of RAW and Kerrang! *magazines*

The British music press in the late 80s was a broad church encompassing everything from the sometimes snarky agenda-setting of the NME, *Sounds* and *Melody Maker* to the more grown-up deliberations of Q. And then there were the metal magazines *Kerrang!*, *Metal Hammer* and *RAW*, sitting balefully away from the more mainstream publications yet exerting their own influence within their respective sphere.

Phil Alexander was a young journalist working for *RAW* when Napalm Death released *From Enslavement To Obliteration* in September 1988. *RAW* had launched a few months earlier. Its bread and butter were popular rock bands such as Mötley Crüe, Bon Jovi and Poison, but Alexander had been brought in to cover the burgeoning underground metal and punk scene.

He was well placed to do that. As a teenager growing up in London in the 80s, Alexander had been in on the ground floor with everyone from US thrash pioneers Metallica and Slayer to homegrown punk and hardcore bands Concrete Sox, Heresy and The Stupids. He was also plugged into the independent anarcho and crustpunk scene too.

"That whole anarcho-punk scene had brought in these sensibilities that challenged people's values and preconceived ideas," says Alexander. "Anarcho-punk bands were telling you that multinational corporations were the scourge of the world, that sexism was a massive issue – stuff that regular metal bands weren't singing about. Napalm Death were weaned on that kind of thing, along with bands like Swans and early industrial music."

The regional UK crustpunk scene was thriving, with a host of labels springing up away from the mainstream music hub that was London. There was Atavistic in Bristol, Peaceville in Yorkshire, and Nottingham's Earache Records, which released Napalm Death's debut album, *Scum*, in July 1987.

"Earache, in my mind, already had a lineage and Napalm Death were part of it," says Alexander. "This was before John Peel had played them, but this scene was already starting to gestate."

Alexander bought Napalm Death's *Scum* the week it came out, from venerated West London independent record shop Rough Trade. "Music was getting heavier and faster, from the New Wave Of British Heavy Metal to Metallica and Slayer to early death metal bands like Death, and Napalm Death was a logical step on from that," says Alexander.

He saw the band play live for the first time at London's Clarendon Ballroom in December 1987, just a few months after their new bassist Shane Embury had joined.

"I turned up when they were soundchecking," he says. "It was a big stage and a big, empty room, and I'd imagine they probably felt a bit overawed. The set was full-on, but I don't know if it was their finest hour. It felt like they were still learning the ropes. It wasn't: 'Here is the future of music!' It was some blokes having trouble plugging in their pedals."

For Alexander, the release of *From Enslavement To Obliteration* the following year was a huge step up.

"*FETO* changed the equation completely," he says. "That opening track sounded like nothing that came before it – it's sparse, it's menacing, it felt like a shift. They were a different band, musically and as people too. They'd somehow crystallized something which would become massively important and influential without actually meaning to."

Alexander convinced *RAW*'s editors that they needed to cover Napalm Death. He and a photographer were despatched to Birmingham via train, where they met the band in a café.

"They didn't really know what they were doing when it came to interviews," says Alexander. "They were used to talking to somebody from a fanzine with an Instamatic camera. And they were probably a bit suspicious: 'Why is this bloke from a magazine that had Poison on the cover of their last issue talking to us?'"

"They weren't there to sell themselves: 'Let us tell you how great we are,'" he says. "Mick was loud, Lee probably said a couple of snidey things, but Shane was quite shy. He seemed to me to be a person who had something to say but wouldn't say it."

That interview was unlikely to convert many Poison fans to the Napalm Death cause, but interest in them was undeniably snowballing: *NME* covers, Peel sessions, a BBC documentary that gave the band more airtime than Ozzy Osbourne or Guns N' Roses.

"They were definitely on an upward trajectory," says Alexander. "What I didn't like about stuff like the documentary was that it made people laugh when it didn't seem to be a laughing matter to me. Were they the fastest band in the world? Probably. But they had something to say, and what they said really mattered. It still does. That sometimes gets overlooked – people just want to talk about the fact that they've got a one-second song and they once did a BBC documentary."

Alexander subsequently went on to edit *RAW* in the early 90s, before moving to *Kerrang!* and, eventually, *Mojo*. While his encounter with the band in that Birmingham café in 1988 remains the only time he interviewed Napalm Death, he continued to follow their career over subsequent years.

"The reason Napalm are important isn't just because they made two defining albums early on, it's because they've sustained that career and that love of music without compromise. They've been taken for granted at times, and I'm sure it's been difficult for them to carry on at certain points, but the belief system that was there in them in those early days is still there today even though the original members left."

"That's the same with Shane. It doesn't matter whether it's Napalm or Absolute Power or some mad electronic thing, he hasn't lost that joy of making music or the integrity that comes with it. There's something within him and Napalm that makes them keep pushing forward. They could be a parody of themselves by now. They could be utterly boring, but they've still got that belief in what they're doing and that sense of momentum."

1989

66 1989 was a rollercoaster year for Napalm Death. We appeared in a BBC documentary, we played live on a kids' TV show, we went to Japan for the first time… and then half of the band left.

When I joined Napalm Death, I never expected we'd end up on the BBC, but a director named Helen Gallagher was making a documentary on heavy metal for the BBC's *Arena* strand. *Arena* was this highbrow arts show, but she wanted to treat metal seriously for once. The idea behind the documentary was that she'd speak to lots of different musicians and bands – Ozzy Osbourne, Jimmy Page, Bruce Dickinson from Iron Maiden, Tom Araya of Slayer… and us.

There was a buzz around the band after *FETO* came out. Part of it was down to the fact that John Peel loved us, but people outside of that underground scene seemed to be fascinated by Napalm Death too – they couldn't work out what we were doing.

We were still trying to comprehend all the mad stuff that was happening around Napalm, and when the people who were doing the documentary got in touch, everyone else in the band was a bit suspicious – I think they thought it would be taking the piss. But I was up for it straight away. It seemed like good exposure for Napalm. Maybe the kid who'd grown up watching *Doctor Who* was a bit chuffed too: "I'm going to be on TV!"

As it turned out, the people who made the documentary seemed genuinely interested in us. They assured us that they wouldn't take the piss, and they didn't. I was living in Broseley at the time, and some of it was filmed in my bedroom. My mom and dad's house was tiny – there wasn't much room for the crew and their cameras. I remember my mom running around, making cups of tea for everyone.

They came down and filmed our show at the ULU in London too. That gig was manic. We still hadn't played that many gigs, so weren't exactly a well-oiled live machine. There was no choreography and no stage patter – Lee went for it when he screamed, but he was still nervous between songs. And then among all that, you've got all these nutcases stage diving.

A lot of the Napalm gigs back then were like that. Because of the Peel connection, we'd get all kinds of people coming to see us – Sonic Youth fans, Wedding Present fans. Some people didn't really know the etiquette of stage diving. They'd jump in feet first, which is going to hurt if you're on the receiving end of it in the crowd. There was a classic video of the band Minor Threat playing the 9:30 Club in Washington DC in the early 80s, which is pretty much the bible of stage diving. We were telling people, "You've got to watch that, that's how you do stage dives."

The people making the documentary kept filming and filming, but I still don't think we expected to feature quite so heavily in it in the end. We were still pretty underground, and when it was shown, I'm sure there were a lot of people going, "Who the fuck are Napalm Death?" Even regular metal fans didn't know what to make of us: "What is this shit?" But that documentary did us a lot of favours in terms of raising our profile even further. It made people curious about us – there might have been a bit of novelty for some people, but I'd like to think that others were really into what we were doing.

We got other TV stuff coming in too. We ended up on a kids' TV show called *What's That Noise?* It was presented by Craig Charles, who was in the TV show *Red Dwarf* and is a well-known DJ these days. We all piled down there in the van and stayed overnight at Helen Gallaghers house. We went to the pub briefly, but we didn't stay long. Mickey was bashing the inside of the van with a baseball bat. I never did know exactly what was going through his mind.

We met Craig Charles the next day. He'd been out on a session the night before, though you wouldn't have known – he was a total pro. They had a kids' orchestra on before us, which yet again made me think, "How did we end up doing this?" We were still a little nervous – "Are they going to take the piss?" – but Craig got it and was into the idea of Napalm Death. Lee and Bill did most of the talking, which is odd because they were quite shy usually. We ended up playing 'You Suffer' – all 1.3 seconds of it – and the track 'From Enslavement To Obliteration' itself. This went out at 5pm in the UK when kids were back from school, which was nuts.

Us being on TV was a big deal, especially when I was still living in Broseley. People would stop my mom and tell her they'd seen me on the telly. She was proud about it, but it would make her crack up. My dad was forever saying, "So-and-so's son loves your band, can you bring him a CD?" Later on, one of the guys I used to work with at the steel factory started doing something with the local council. One year he asked me, "Would you turn on the Christmas lights in Broseley?" I didn't do it. Kids TV is one thing, turning on some Christmas lights is another.

Coincidentally, around that time Napalm were lined up to appear on *Red Dwarf* with Craig Charles. They wanted a metal band to play in the background, and they asked us. But we couldn't do it for some reason – I think Mickey might have been away on tour with somebody. Bill's other band Carcass ended up doing it, which is ironic because by the time it aired at the end of 1989, Bill had left Napalm, and so had Lee.

In amid all the gigs and the TV stuff, we'd recorded a new six-song EP, *Mentally Murdered*. It was a transition from the *From Enslavement To Obliteration* album. Mickey was really getting into the death metal scene, and he was pushing more towards that vibe on the songs he was writing – they were longer and a bit more involved. That was where my head was at too. We'd joke about moving to the States and starting a death metal band. In hindsight, I guess Lee and Bill were feeling differently about the musical direction.

In the summer of 1989, between finishing the EP and releasing it, we went to Japan for the very first time. Japan has always been a special place to me. I loved stuff like *Godzilla* and some of the more extreme Manga, but I'd also discovered a load of killer bands through the tape-trading scene. One of them was S.O.B., who we established a really great friendship with, trading tapes and sev-en-inches and eventually releasing a split single with them in 1988. And years later, I met my future wife in Japan, which only strength-ened my connection to the country.

But in 1989, for some kid from Broseley to go to Japan was crazy. We got cheap flights, which meant going from London to Alaska, Alaska to Seoul in South Korea, then Seoul to Osaka. By the time we got there, we'd been flying for 24 hours, and we were totally fucked.

The guys who were looking after us out there wanted to put us up in those capsule hotels, which are basically like a tour bus bunk, except with a bunch of businessmen around you all watching porn. We said, "No, we're not going to do that", so we got ourselves a proper hotel.

The shows themselves were great. There were five or six in total, mainly with punk bands rather than metal bands. The divide between punk and metal out there was quite defined – there'd be a lot of fighting between the two sides. Some of the punks were linked to the Yakuza, the heavy-duty Japanese mob – you didn't get that at the Mermaid.

The crowds there had never seen anything like Napalm Death and they loved it, but their way of showing appreciation is completely different to audiences in the West. They'd start cheering and then it would suddenly stop and go dead quiet. It's a respect thing, which is very big in Japanese culture, but if you've never heard it before, it really throws you: "Why have they suddenly stopped clapping? Don't they like us?"

We all found being in Japan pretty mind-blowing, especially Tokyo. It's very space-age, with so many people around. Being Westerners, and unusual-looking ones at that, we had a lot of Japanese kids following us around. Bill especially had a lot of girls following him, probably because of his long blond hair. He's pretty shy and I think he was terrified. I've got to admit I took the piss a little bit: "Come on Bill, I'll protect you."

Mickey was walking around with his tatts on show and his shorts on, everybody was staring at him, but Mickey being Mickey, he grabbed a microphone off of someone selling stuff on the street and started singing.

I've got so many great memories of that first Japanese trip: picking up a bunch of *Godzilla* stuff, getting a ton of records that I couldn't get back home, buying early Nintendo machines (of course, Mickey ended up grilling his in an oven because he lost one of the games). But I look at the pictures of the four of us, and Lee and Bill aren't looking at the camera. I can see now that they'd already made up their minds to leave.

Mickey had overheard Bill and Lee talking in Japan, but he

didn't tell me about it. I don't think he was sure where they were going with the conversation. They didn't say anything at all to me about wanting to leave – they told Mick first, and he told me. I just went, "Wow". I couldn't understand why, because things were really starting to happen with Napalm.

I think part of the reason they left was because of the direction we were starting to head in musically, but also down to the fact that mine and Mick's relationship was quite manic, whereas Lee and Bill were more reserved. Bands can be tricky when you're young and immature. There's no guide book. Communication was hard back then – we didn't sit down and talk to each other about what we really thought, we just got on with it. Even today, after doing it for all this time, communication is still tough. If someone sends you a text, or you send someone a text, and it's ignored, people can get wound up – myself included. The best way is to talk about whatever's bugging you and argue it out if necessary, then you can usually simmer down and work out a compromise.

But those guys had their own things going on as well. Bill already had Carcass when he joined Napalm, and it was pretty much established by that point – their debut album, *Reek Of Putrefaction*, had come out on Earache, the same label as Napalm, in 1988. And Lee was getting more into doom metal. He was thinking about starting Cathedral, the band he was in for more than 20 years after leaving Napalm.

Today, I can see it from Bill and Lee's point of view. They were being honest – they weren't satisfied in Napalm and they wanted to do something else. But when they left, I was devastated. Probably as devastated as I was when the guys in my old band Warhammer told me they didn't want to do it anymore. We'd released a killer album in FETO, we'd been on the telly, I'd just been to Japan for the first time – Napalm Death was my life. Now I thought it might be the end of the band.

1990

66 Napalm Death looked very different at the start of 1990 to how they had a year before. Only Mick Harris and me were left from the line-up that had recorded *From Enslavement To Obliteration*. We had a new singer, Barney Greenway, and a couple of new American guitarists, Jesse Pintado and Mitch Harris.

I understand now why Lee and Bill wanted to leave, but they left us in a bit of a hole. We'd had our first proper UK tour booked for November 1989 and we had no singer and no guitarist. Getting a singer was fairly straightforward. Barney was a friend of ours before he joined. He was in a band from Birmingham called Benediction, and he used to come along to Napalm shows. He was actually in the audience when we recorded *What's That Noise?*, the kids' TV show with Craig Charles. Barney loved Napalm, so it made sense to see if he was up for replacing Lee Dorrian. He was very gung-ho about everything. The conversation was pretty easy:

"Do you want to join Napalm?"

"Yes."

That was easy.

The other question we were asking ourselves was, "Who the fuck do we get to play guitar?" Jesse Pintado was a guy from LA that I knew from tape trading. He was in a band called Terrorizer, who I really liked, and I was aware that he was a shit-hot guitarist. It seemed weird asking a guy from America to join Napalm Death, but there wasn't anyone else who could play the way we wanted to play.

It nearly ended before it had even started with Jesse, though. When he came over the very first time, he got turned back at customs. He'd brought these clippings from *Sounds* magazine: "Jesse Pintado joins Napalm Death." Except no one at our label Earache had actually sorted out a work visa for him. Me and Barney had gone to meet him at the airport, but they wouldn't let him through. They let us see him and he said, "Look, I don't know what's happened, but I've got to go home."

At that point Mickey called Mitch Harris. Mitch was a kid from Vegas and in a band called Righteous Pigs. They had a bad rap because of the stuff they were singing about: it was fun lyrics, like the Beastie Boys, but it was perceived as un-PC. "Oh, they're singing about all this sexist stuff, they must be sexist." No, they're not sexist, they're 18 years old, growing up in Vegas, playing backyard parties. They were just teenagers singing about teenage stuff.

Mick and Mitch had a project together called Defecation, just after Napalm did *From Enslavement To Obliteration*. In Mickey's head he was the perfect person, and Mitch was totally ready to leave Vegas and come to the UK. The only problem was that in classic Mickey Harris style, he hadn't told anyone else in the band. So when Mitch arrives, the rest of us go: "Right, OK, what's happening here?"

That's when things got confusing, in typical Napalm fashion. Jesse finally got his work visa just in time for the tour we had in November, but Mitch didn't, so he couldn't play with us until that was sorted. So when we finally went on the road, it was as a four-piece. Mitch was there but he was stuck on the bus. It must have been weird for him: he was over in the UK, but he couldn't play with this band he was supposed to be joining. He was in limbo for a little while.

That tour was called the Grindcrusher tour, and it was pretty ground-breaking. It was four bands: us, Morbid Angel from America, Carcass, and Bolt Thrower. It was the first proper tour any of us had done – seven days in the UK – and it was a big deal. That was the point where the kind of music we were playing really went from something fairly niche into something that got noticed by more people, especially in the metal world.

Not everybody was happy about that, though. Apparently someone from the band Chaos UK was throwing stuff at us when we played in Birmingham, because we were "sell outs". We'd heard it before, and we'd hear it again. Also, back in those pre-internet days, it wasn't common knowledge that Lee and Bill had left and this whole transition had happened. You'd get people saying, "It's not Napalm Death anymore without those two," which put my back up. Before you start whinging, you do know Lee wasn't the original singer? There were two before him. I dunno, I was taking it more seriously than I should have.

But that tour was a blast. There was a great spirit to it all. It's not like Napalm were Mötley Crüe, but we liked to drink and there were a few hangovers. That stuff helped bond us from the start. Me and Jesse and Mitch became pretty much inseparable.

Just after the Grindcrusher tour, we went over to America as a four-piece. Our very first show in the US was at CBGBS, the legendary punk club in New York. There was a buzz around Napalm – most people knew us from the tape-trading scene and the first two albums, but there were also people who knew us from the NME and John Peel. It was a pretty eclectic crowd.

CBGBS was a total dive, but I still couldn't believe we were there. We were on the bill with Prong and Blind Idiot God, who were this kind of hardcore/industrial jam band. We were meant to go on first, but they turned around and said, "You're now going to close the show at 2am." Prong played, and then Blind Idiot God started playing. They launched into this jam that went on forever. Eventually, Mickey turned to me and went, "Shane, I've had enough", and he gets up onstage and unplugs the guitarist. They were furious, but everybody else in there was thinking, "Thank god he did that."

After that first run of shows, Jesse was going to fly back to the US for Christmas. We asked him when he was coming back, and he said: "What do you mean?" He didn't realize he was joining the band full time. He thought it was just for that one tour. I think it was a tough move for him. He had a girlfriend back in LA, he came from a very close Mexican family. But we hit it off straight away. He was a lovely guy, very mellow and quiet.

Napalm Death had only ever had one guitarist before, so having two weirded some people out. I was fine with it. For me, Napalm had never stayed the same from album to album. The line-up changes coincided with the band starting to sound different, too. The *Mentally Murdered* EP, which we recorded with Lee Dorrian and Bill Steer, was moving away from the grindcore sound that we had on *FETO*. Mickey was really getting into death metal, along with the fast hardcore we listened to. That really came to the fore on our third album, *Harmony Corruption*. Mickey wrote most of the songs on that record. There were only a few tracks from me.

The biggest difference, though, was the fact that we recorded *Harmony Corruption* at Morrisound Studios in Tampa, Florida. Florida was where the whole death metal boom was coming from – bands like Death, Morbid Angel, Obituary, Massacre and Malevolent Creation. Morrisound was the epicentre of it all, and the producer, Scott Burns, had worked on all the big records.

I'm pretty sure it was Digby Pearson from Earache who suggested we record in Florida. We weren't going to argue: what, we get to go make a record in America, at this studio where all these bands we loved had worked?

Being in Florida was immense. I drove around in a rental car, blasting our NWA, Public Enemy and Skinny Puppy with Mitch and Jesse. We ended up sleeping on the sofa at Morbid Angel's house. Barney recorded all of his vocals in a day, stoned off his box. It was a brilliant experience, but maybe I should have paid more attention to the actual recording. I like the album, and I think the songs stand up, but it just doesn't sound abrasive enough for me these days. It's a bit too restrained.

People call *Harmony Corruption* Napalm's "death metal album". I suppose it is in some ways, but I don't think it's that different from what came before. If it had been recorded in the same way as the *Mentally Murdered* EP, people wouldn't have noticed, because a lot of the songs that Mickey wrote on his two-string guitar were the same kind of stuff he'd been writing before – they had the same structures. It was just tuned different, and because Scott Burns had produced it, it had a different sound.

It was around the time we were doing the *Harmony Corruption* album that we played in South America for the first time. We got the call that the Brazilian metal band Sepultura wanted to bring us down to their hometown of São Paulo for three shows. Sepultura were one of the first metal bands from South America to get noticed around the world, but they were getting flak themselves for being "sell-outs". Max Cavalera, their singer, said, "I'll show you how much of a sell-out we are – we'll bring Napalm Death down to play."

São Paulo was another of those places a kid from the West Midlands would never dream of visiting. All three shows were sold out, but weirdly Sepultura only headlined the third show – they opened the first two. We hadn't even finished mixing the *Harmony Corruption* record, but the kids there knew us from the first two albums – I think *From Enslavement To Obliteration* had just come out on vinyl. And the demo I'd made with my old band, Warhammer, had made it down there as well, which is weird when I think about the 50 quid we spent recording it in Shrewsbury.

That experience was crazy. The people who were looking after us said, "You need to go backstage before the crowd come in, cos they will not leave you alone." Napalm have always had a good connection with audiences in South America. There's the speed and intensity of the music – the A-side of *Scum* didn't sound that different from some of the crazy South American death metal bands that we heard through tape trading. But there was a lyrical connection too with songs like 'Siege Of Power' and 'Scum'. There's a rebellion to it that appeals to the people down there.

There seemed to be a buzz around Napalm in North America too, especially after *Harmony Corruption* came out in July 1990. Death metal was big there, and it turned a lot of people onto Napalm Death who might not have listened to us before. In America, *Harmony Corruption* is seen like *Scum* – this landmark album. By the same token, I suppose it turned a lot of our old-school fans off as well for the same reasons. To be honest, we've never really paid attention to what other people say, we've just done what we wanted to do.

Even when we were doing *Harmony Corruption*, I felt like we were in the shadow of what Napalm was before – or at least what people's perceptions of Napalm were. We were evolving in our own way – though maybe not as fast as some people in the band wanted us to.

EYE WITNESS:
SCOTT CARLSON

Repulsion bassist

Flint, Michigan sits in the shadow of its bigger neighbour Detroit, 60 miles east. Where the Motor City has a long and illustrious musical history, spanning Tamla Motown Records, proto-punks like The Stooges and the MC5 right up to hip-hop superstar Eminem, Flint's own legacy is sparse: its most famous exports were 60s garage-rock one-hit wonders ? And The Mysterians and 70s rock chooglers Grand Funk Railroad.

As a punk- and metal-loving teenager growing up in blue-collar Flint in the early 80s, Scott Carlson had no great expectations for a career in music. He and his buddy Matt Olivio had formed a band called Tempter, inspired by the nascent thrash metal scene emerging from San Francisco. The pair would rehearse and play parties and backyards whenever they could, with whatever musicians they could persuade to jam with them.

"There weren't enough people to make up a metal scene or a punk scene on their own, so all the weirdos migrated to the same places," says Carlson, who sang and played bass in Tempter. "It was punk kids, metal kids, underground theatre kids – this mix of different kids."

Carlson was a fan of British and European metal bands such as Venom, Bathory and Hellhammer, as well as third-wave aggropunks Discharge and GBH. He began immersing himself in the tape-trading scene, swapping the latest underground demos and rehearsal tapes with likeminded people from across America and Europe.

"It made you feel like you were in on something special," says Carlson. "You knew more than the average punter at a metal show. Those kids knew about Slayer and Metallica, but they didn't know about Sodom or Hellhammer. It made you feel like you were one up on them."

Carlson and Olivio's own musical career was fitful. After several line-up changes and a brief sojourn to Florida, they renamed themselves Genocide and then Repulsion. That's when they inadvertently hit on a sound that would prove to be hugely influential.

"Matt Olivio and I were having a hard time finding members to complete the line-up, especially drummers," says Carlson. "There was this one kid named Dave Hollingshead, who played drums in a skate-punk band. We wanted him to play like Slayer, but he'd never heard that stuff before. So we kind of moulded him by sitting in our garage day after day, pushing him to play faster and faster. That's how he developed the technique that would be dubbed 'the blast-beat'. It's basically a polka beat increased to machine-gun speed. If you have distorted bass and guitar with it, it sounds pretty intense."

That sound was perfected on 1986's *Slaughter Of The Innocent*, a demo album the band recorded in an attempt to get a record deal. The demo found its way via the tape-trading network into the hands of the young Shane Embury, living 5,000 miles away in Broseley, Shropshire.

"Shane wrote me a letter around 1986," remembers Carlson. "He told me about the band he had, Warhammer. I had their demo and I liked it. He said, 'I just got hold of your *Slaughter Of The Innocent* tape, we've trashed all of our songs and we've got a whole new set of songs that sound exactly like you.' He wasn't saying, 'You've been a big influence'. He was saying, 'We've written a bunch of songs that are exactly like yours.'"

Repulsion's own career barely made it past *Slaughter Of The Innocent*. "We sent it to every label and got no response, the wheels fell off and we put the whole thing on the shelf," says Carlson.

A year or so later, Carlson was working in a record shop in Flint when a box of vinyl imports from the UK landed on the counter. One of his record store colleagues pulled out a record called *Scum*, by a British band named Napalm Death. "It was a Friday night so we put it on," he says. "I just started laughing because it was so extreme and brilliant. Then we flipped it over and one of the songs started with a Repulsion riff."

Carlson didn't think anything of it, chalking it up to coincidence. Then the Napalm Death song shifted into a second part, which mimicked the same Repulsion song. "That's when I thought, 'Oh my god, they've heard us.' I was blown away."

Carlson checked the record's inner sleeve. He saw photos of home-made Repulsion T-shirts, and noticed that the band were namechecked in the album's "thanks" list. Weirder still, he spotted his own face in a collage of photos. The photograph had been snapped at a urinal at a local Megadeth show and had appeared in an underground fanzine that had evidently found its way back to Birmingham.

Other musicians might have taken a dim view of what Napalm Death were doing, but Carlson was honoured. "I never thought for a second that these guys were ripping us off. It wasn't thievery, they were laying it right out there."

The success of Napalm Death and Carcass prompted Scott Carlson and Matt Olivio to reactivate Repulsion in 1989. The same year, Earache officially released the shelved *Slaughter Of The Innocent* album under the title *Horrified*. Repulsion even received a postcard from John Peel, inviting them to come in and record a session if they were ever in the UK.

"Anything Napalm and those guys might have stolen from us, they returned tenfold," says Carlson. "Repulsion had been forgotten, and suddenly my music career was blossoming again."

Any remaining debt Napalm Death owed Repulsion was fully paid off when they covered the Michigan band's song 'Maggots In Your Coffin' on 1999's *Leaders Not Followers* mini-album. Repulsion would split and reform several times over the ensuing decades – a stop-start career that's the polar opposite to Napalm Death's unflagging endurance.

"I admire how hard Shane and Napalm work," says Carlson. "There were times when it looked like they might as well just give it up. I saw them play at the Whisky in LA in the mid-90s. They were opening up for some other band, and there was hardly anyone there. I remember thinking, 'How do they keep going?' But they stuck it out and turned it around.

"A lot of that is down to Shane's perseverance and longevity. He's been with Napalm Death since their second record and he's weathered pretty much everything. But he's also branched out and worked with all different kinds of people while staying true to his convictions. That's not easy to do for so long."

1991

❝ Napalm Death played our first proper US tour in the spring of 1991. It was the five of us crammed in a van, crashing on people's floors and grabbing showers whenever we could – some of us more often than others. It was about as unglamorous as touring gets, but it was beyond exciting. We met people I knew from the tape-trading scene, but I also met loads of new people, and I'm still in touch with a lot of them today.

There were some crazy gigs on that tour, and the craziest was our very first show in Los Angeles. It was at a place called the Country Club in Reseda, with us, Godflesh and the American death metal band Nocturnus on the bill. Jesse's dad was on the bus and Mitch's parents had come down from Vegas, so it was a pretty big night for them.

There were a lot of Mexican and Latin American kids in the crowd. Grindcore and death metal are big in that community – I guess they got off on the speed and aggression of it all because it lets people burn a lot of energy and frustration. We were trying to play, and there were a bunch of people literally lining up to stage dive. We had a bottle of fluid for the dry ice machine, and at one point this guy picked it up and started drinking it, then he just ran off and dived into the crowd. I remember Mickey standing up on the back of his drumkit, going, "This is a fucking doss" in his Birmingham accent while all this insanity was going on around us.

There was a serious edge to it as well. I'd heard rumours of how violent LA shows could be. The punk band Suicidal Tendencies were famous for gang violence at their gigs, but I never expected it at one of ours. At one point, this guy named Danny came up to us and said he was a friend of Jesse's. He told us, "You need to go backstage, somebody's going around with a knife, stabbing people." We found out later that there had been three stabbings, and one guy had died. It was gang related rather than anything to do with Napalm, but it was still pretty heavy. The guy who came up to us and warned us to go backstage was Danny Herrera – funnily enough, he'd end up joining Napalm a few months later.

That American tour marked the end of an era in a way. Not long after that, Mickey Harris quit Napalm Death.

Looking back, I think I'd seen it coming. Partly because he had just had a kid, but also because I could sense he was getting restless. Mickey liked hardcore and metal, but he loved mad experimental music too. Industrial bands like Ministry and Nine Inch Nails were in vogue at the time, and he wanted to do something like that. I was all for experimenting, but not every five seconds. Going from death metal straight into that would have been one turn too many, even though I was into that kind of music too.

It's funny, people sometimes think that because I'm a member of Napalm Death, I only listen to extreme music. That couldn't be further from the truth. I'd grown up listening to bands like Slade and Sweet, then graduated to Sabbath and Dio and eventually to more extreme metal and punk. But coming into Napalm's world really opened me up to a lot of stuff I'd never listened to before, and Mickey was a big part of that.

When I met Mickey, he said, "Have you listened to John Peel?" I knew who John Peel was – this DJ who played all this weird music – but he'd never really come onto my radar before. When you're a young metalhead growing up in the early 80s, you listened to Tommy Vance's *Friday Rock Show* on Radio 1. You might occasionally see Saxon or Judas Priest on *Top Of The Pops*, but the *Rock Show* was where you could hear 'Satan's Fall' by Mercyful Fate.

When I got know Napalm, I realized there was this whole world of music going on that I didn't know about. I started listening to Peel's late evening show on Radio 1, and because of that I got into bands like Swans and the Birthday Party, stuff I never would have heard a couple of years earlier.

Most DJs have a playlist they stick to rigidly, but Peel played whatever he wanted to play – you'd get Napalm Death or Extreme Noise Terror followed straight after by some mad African percussion music. Not everything was great: you might get a song where you'd think, "I love this", then it would be followed by something where you'd go, "This is utter bollocks", but maybe you'd slowly come to appreciate it. Peel once said that if he listened to something and didn't like it, he didn't think there was a problem with the music, he thought there was a problem with him, so he'd have to listen to it again.

I only met Peel a couple of times. The first time was at a show Napalm Death played with Extreme Noise Terror at the Caribbean Centre in Ipswich a few months after I joined the band. He came down with his son and his wife. He actually invited us round for Sunday lunch the next day. We should have gone – I don't know why we didn't. I kick myself when I think about it now.

There was a real division between metal/punk and indie music back then. If you listened to one, you weren't supposed to listen to the other. There were bands like 7 Seconds and Dag Nasty who had started as part of the US hardcore scene, but they had got into U2 and started doing this jangly guitar stuff. I remember me and Mitch Dickinson going into the Shades record shop in Soho to buy 7 Seconds' *The Crew* album and Dag Nasty's *Can I Say?*. The guy behind the counter said, "Are you sure you want to buy these albums, cos you look like heavy metal dudes?" That pissed me off. Of course we knew what they were.

We had the same thing in Napalm Death. What people didn't realize back in the early days was that we were grinding away onstage but we'd drive back from gigs in our van listening to My Bloody Valentine, Sonic Youth and the Cocteau Twins. I was a big fan of the Cocteaus. I got into them through Mickey. The swirling guitars, Liz Fraser's ethereal voice, the ambience of it all – there was something otherworldly about them. You'd go out drinking, and end up not getting the girl you wanted, so you'd come home and blast out *Victorialand* by the Cocteau Twins to console yourself. There was almost a communion going on with that record.

But the band I loved the most back then, and who are still a huge influence on me today, was Cardiacs. I remember seeing old flyers with them, Chumbawamba and Napalm Death on the same bill, but I'd never heard them. Then I was watching the TV show *The Tube* at some point in the 80s and they were on it playing their single 'Tarred And Feathered'. It was this weird, quirky kindergarten carousel music that I just did not understand: "What the fuck is this?"

But I'd videoed it, and I found myself watching it again and again. Ten minutes later, I realized it was the greatest thing I'd heard.

I became infatuated with everything about them – their music, the way they looked, the fact that no one else was doing what they were doing. They took elements of prog rock and mixed it with punk in a way that no one else did. Cardiacs are one of those bands that if you love them you really love them, and if you don't get them then you absolutely hate it. Mickey was always taking the piss out of me for liking them. He used to say they sounded like Madness. No Mickey, they don't…

I wore a Cardiacs T-shirt when Napalm Death were on the cover of the NME, and their manager, Mark Walmsley, got in touch with me, which eventually led to him becoming Napalm's manager a little while later. I'd go down to London from Birmingham to see Cardiacs play all the time. I got to know them pretty well, especially their singer, Tim Smith. We both liked things that kept us awake back then.

Me and Tim always talked about putting a band together, but we never got round to it. He had a serious heart attack in the late 2000s, and he sadly passed away in 2020. Napalm did a cover of the Cardiacs song 'To Go Off And Things' a couple of years before that, to help raise money for his medical care. That was one of the easier Cardiacs songs to play, but they've always been an influence on me in less obvious ways – they have very strange arrangements and time signatures, which I've tried to bring into Napalm Death at times. But there's no point copying Cardiacs. They were uncopiable.

It wasn't just Cardiacs who have influenced what I do. Bands like My Bloody Valentine and Sonic Youth have too, even if it doesn't always seem like it. With My Bloody Valentine, there's a dissonance in the guitar tones – it's a sound and a feeling that just seems to touch me. You'd listen to their records and think, "How the hell do they do that?" And you'd try to work it out. At first you're stumbling about, but you get better at it, and eventually you're mixing that stuff with a Discharge riff in a Napalm song.

I think that's one of the main reasons Mickey left in the end. He thought that Napalm was becoming too restrictive and that we were confined by what other people thought we should be. There was this perception that we were this straight-ahead grindcore or death metal band, even though we were listening to all this other music.

Mickey actually asked me to leave with him. I thought about it, but I was committed to Napalm. I could see that he had this vision for the band, and I had it too, but I didn't think it could happen overnight. I told him, "I'm pretty sure Napalm can get to where you want it to, just have a bit of patience." I properly reconnected with Mickey a couple of years ago. We never fell out, but we really became close again during the pandemic. We talk a lot about those times. It's funny, I think with Napalm we've got to where Mickey saw it going in his head back then. It just took longer than he would have wanted it to.

At the time, Mickey leaving was weird for me because he was the connection between "old" Napalm – the band I'd got into after seeing them at The Mermaid in Birmingham – and current Napalm. I'm sure a lot of people thought that it wasn't Napalm Death any more if Mick Harris wasn't in the band. They were probably the same people who thought that it wasn't Napalm Death if Lee Dorrian or Bill Steer weren't in the band, or Justin Broadrick or Nik Bullen a few years before that.

I don't agree, obviously. Not because I'm arrogant – I don't think I'm Napalm Death any more than Barney is Napalm Death, or anyone else who has been in the band for that matter. But it's the things that Napalm Death stand for that make it what it is: doing what you want to do and not paying attention to what other people expect you to be. That's something that's never changed in all the years I've been in the band.

In typical Napalm fashion, it wasn't too difficult to find somebody to replace Mickey. Danny Herrera, who had warned us that people were getting stabbed in the crowd at that first LA concert, was the perfect replacement. Not only did he know Jesse Pintado, but he was an amazing drummer who was up for playing as crazily as possible, and a good guy as well. Napalm Death had finally found a line-up that felt stable... at least for a few years.

1992

66 Napalm Death was always pretty full-on, but it got really full-on when four of us got a place together. Jesse and Mitch had already come over to Birmingham from the States, and now our new drummer Danny was here too. It made sense to all move into a house, though Barney wisely decided not to join us – I think the mess would have done his head in.

The first place we had was five minutes from The Mermaid. After that we moved into the infamous Napalm House in Sparkhill, a pretty rough suburb of Birmingham. It was like *The Young Ones* all day every day – a bunch of blokes in their early 20s living exactly like you'd expect a bunch of blokes in their early 20s to live. I'm pretty sure the first thing Danny saw when he moved over was me pissing up the side of a wall – inside the house. The next day he said, "Shane, man, do you realize what happened last night?"

"Oh fucking hell, what did I do?" I didn't have any memory of it at all.

I drank a little bit when I lived in Broseley, but not much. I never really liked the taste of beer. That obviously changed a few years later, especially when Jesse and Mitch came over. You go from not liking it to liking it a bit to really liking it. At times I've liked it too much, but getting smashed is part of being young.

We all partied, but Mitch, Jesse and me especially were like the Three Musketeers. One of our favourite haunts was Costermongers, a pub we used to hang out in. For quite a few years, my day would consist of going for a pint in Costermongers in the afternoon, picking up a couple of CDs from one of the local record shops, maybe going to see my mate Mole who worked in a skate shop. I'd come back home for a nap, then I'd head back out to Costermongers for another couple. Then it would either be off to one of the local gig venues to see whoever was playing or down to whatever rock or indie night was on at one of the clubs.

Whenever we got back from a tour, we'd drop our bags off, look at our watches and go straight out again. One time we ended up supporting Faith No More in Holland because their support band couldn't do it. We drove over thinking that people were going to throw shit at us, played the gig, then drove back. We walked straight into Costermongers to hear a Faith No More song playing through the speakers. That was a pretty cool moment. It seemed like each time we'd go into one particular place, we'd hear Thin Lizzy's 'The Boys Are Back In Town'. One day the guy who owned it said, "You've never noticed, have you?"

"What?"

"Every time you lot come down the stairs, we put on 'The Boys Are Back In Town'."

There was a real camaraderie between a lot of the other Birmingham bands. We were mates with the guys from Pop Will Eat Itself, who were more on the grebo/indie side of things. One night we were out with the Poppies, and their singer, Graham, jumped on my back. I fell over straight on top of him I heard this massive crack. I thought I'd killed the poor bastard. At one point, we had a T-shirt that said "Pop Will Eat Its Own Shit" on the front and "Real Hash-Smoking, Beer-Drinking, Satan-Worshipping Motherfuckers" on the back, which was taking the piss out of a Nirvana T-shirt. I'd love to find someone who still has one.

All the bands that I loved came through Birmingham and we'd hassle our agent to get us on the guest list: Jane's Addiction, Sonic Youth, The Smashing Pumpkins… We weren't just freeloading for the sake of it. We wanted to meet people we admired. I met Thurston Moore from Sonic Youth, The Smashing Pumpkins. When Nirvana played the Hummingbird, I got to meet them through a friend of mine who knew Kurt Cobain. They seemed very quiet, though I was probably speeding my head off and scaring them.

We really did immerse ourselves in the local scene. We liked to go out and drink, and we liked to make friends with everybody. Well, most people. There was a club called Edwards No.8, and for some reason one of the bouncers didn't like me. He wasn't happy that we'd get in for free: "It's only cos you guys are in Napalm Death." The woman who ran it, Sarah, told him, "I don't just let them in cos they're in Napalm Death, I let them in cos they're mad drinkers. Between them, they probably get through £150 a night."

It was a crazy few years. No wonder I had to stop drinking eventually.

Somewhere in all that craziness, we had to make a new album. *Harmony Corruption* had done really well, but Mickey had written a lot of it. With him not around, me, Mitch and Jesse pitched in with the songwriting for the follow-up, *Utopia Banished*. Back then, I could be pretty brutal with people: "That's not what I wanted." I wasn't being a diva, but with hindsight, that might have pissed people off. In fact, I know it did – sometimes Danny would have a couple of beers and bollock me about something I'd said to him. It wasn't meant out of malice, but you don't realize that what you see as honesty might be taken differently by other people.

But we had a great time doing that record. We recorded it in Wales with the producer Colin Richardson, who had engineered the *Mentally Murdered* EP back when Bill and Lee were still in the band. We were so chuffed with *Utopia Banished*. It sounded good, Barney wrote some killer lyrics, it got some great reviews, and people seemed really excited by it. But for some reason, *Kerrang!* magazine in the UK hated it. A journalist named Don Kaye gave it one out of five and slagged it off, which completely blindsided us.

I used to love it when bands got a kicking from magazines. I thought, "If they hate it that much, there must be something good about it." I remember Metallica's debut album, *Kill 'Em All*, getting crucified in *Sounds* when it came out in 1983. That made me want to go straight out and listen to it. And it didn't really do much damage to Metallica's career, either.

But it's different when it happens to you. These days I don't give a shit if people say they don't like Napalm. You're entitled to your opinion, I'm going to do what I want to do anyway. Back then, though, me, Mitch and Jesse were really pissed off with that review in *Kerrang!*: "What, this guy can't hear that there's some killer riffs on that record? Fuck him."

It wasn't the end of the world. By that point, Napalm Death were pretty well established, and even a bad review in a mag as big as *Kerrang!* wasn't going to have that much of an effect in the grand scheme of things. Even Barney said at the time, "You shouldn't pay attention to reviews." He was right, but it still bugged me.

Looking back, *Utopia Banished* is a really influential album, and not just with who you'd expect. When The Smashing Pumpkins played in Birmingham, I ended up talking to their bass player, D'Arcy, while she was having a cigarette outside. She said, "*Utopia Banished*, I like that album." I just said, "Are you serious?" That was such a big deal because I loved The Smashing Pumpkins.

That record was influential on the black metal scene that was happening in Norway and Sweden too, though neither scene would admit it back then. The whole black metal thing passed me by at the time. I loved Venom, Bathory and Mercyful Fate, who were the original black metal bands to me, but when it really started to kick off in the early 90s my head was somewhere else. Napalm toured with Obituary in 1992, and I remember seeing all these people in the crowd in corpse-paint, really stark white-and-black face-paint: "Oh, that's strange, something's going on here." But I was totally wrapped up in Napalm, and listening to bands like Helmet, Ministry and Skinny Puppy, so I didn't give it much thought.

Mickey Harris knew a lot of those bands. Back in the 80s, he was tape trading with a Norwegian guy named Metalion, who ran a metal fanzine called *Slayer*. In fact, when Napalm did our second Peel Session in 1989, Metalion came down to London in the back of the van with us along with the members of the band Mayhem.

Mayhem's guitarist Euronymous was central to everything that was happening in Norway. He ended up being murdered a few years later by a rival musician, Count Grishnackh, but back then he was a big Napalm Death fan. As that scene got more and more serious and Satanic and "evil", and they started burning down old wooden churches, it wasn't cool to admit to liking Napalm. I've spoken to some of the guys from the bands Dimmu Borgir and Emperor, who were part of it all, and they say there was a period where people would just be, "Fuck Napalm Death."

I get it. I used to headbang in the graveyard to Venom when I was a kid. I've carved a few inverted crosses. But there was a fair bit of front to the black metal bands as well. Years later, we did a few shows with a Swedish band called Marduk. One evening, I was sitting with Marduk's guitarist and he was talking in all seriousness about how much he loved *Emmerdale Farm*, this cheesy British soap opera. I just started cracking up.

It was a good time to be in Napalm Death around the time of *Utopia Banished*. We were young and having a blast. But that one bad review bugged me. It wasn't a big thing, but in a weird way it made me and Mitch rethink where the band was going. Which would bring a few problems of its own.

EYE WITNESS:
DAN LILKER

Bassist, Nuclear Assault / Brutal Truth / Venomous Concept

Dan Lilker met Shane Embury before he knew who he was. It was 1987, and Lilker and his band, New York thrashers Nuclear Assault, were in London to play a show at the Hammersmith Odeon. As he was walking through the venue's outer hall, he stopped to talk to a fan.

"This guy's name was David Charles," says Lilker. "I don't remember this, but apparently there was some other dude next to him. When I met Shane, he told me it was him: 'You were talking to a friend of mine, and I just stood there not saying anything.' I'm not even sure if he was in Napalm Death at the time."

The next time Lilker met his fellow bass player, he definitely knew who he was. This was November 1989, and the British band were playing their first US gig at CBGBs. Lilker had been in on the ground floor when it came to Napalm, introduced to them by someone who worked at Nuclear Assault's record label, Combat.

"A guy I knew ran in and said, 'Holy shit, you gotta hear this record, it's fucking manic,'" he says.

Lilker loved the record, and its follow-up *From Enslavement To Obliteration*. He began writing to drummer Mick Harris and guitarist Bill Steer. When Napalm turned up in the Big Apple for the CBGBs gig, Lilker made sure he was there. "They weren't widely known in the States," he said. "But people who knew about that stuff really knew them."

Their respective paths would cross numerous times over the next few years. When Nuclear Assault returned to London, Shane and his bandmates would go to their gigs and then end up at The Columbia, a notoriously debauched London hotel whose bar stayed open all night.

"Things got pretty messy at times, and you had to make sure nothing got wrecked too much," says Lilker. "We were all a bit more chaotic back then, drinking and smashing things. Mick Harris wasn't even a big drinker. He just liked smashing things up."

Lilker's subsequent grindcore band Brutal Truth toured the US with Napalm Death in 1992 under the banner of *The Campaign For Musical Destruction* tour, with Carcass and Cathedral also on the bill.

"They were a well-oiled machine by then," says Lilker of Napalm. "They were still intense, but it was a bit more refined – the way Danny Herrera played was different to the way Mick Harris played, which was basically like a human version of Animal from *The Muppets*. At that time, they had a magic combination of being raw and brutal but also having their shit together."

When Lilker was in the UK, he would frequently find himself hanging out at the Napalm House in Birmingham. That friendship with Shane would eventually result in him playing bass on Venomous Concept's second album, *Poisoned Apple*, with Shane switching to guitar.

"It was great fun," says Lilker of Venomous Concept. "Musically, it was so easy and low maintenance compared to all the other bands I played in. We were good at what we did, but it wasn't completely demanding or super-professional. It had that punk rock attitude."

Lilker's time in Venomous Concept came to an end when Shane decided to return to playing bass. "He was a bit nervous about telling me," says Lilker. "Technically, he was throwing me out of the band, but he really wasn't. He was just going back to bass and I happened to be obsolete. It happened around the time I was getting tired of touring. I just said, 'Don't worry about it, mate, take it away.'"

The pair's friendship came in useful at France's Hellfest festival in 2012. A combination of alcohol and the stress of playing sets with three different bands across the weekend meant Shane was unable to appear with Lock Up on the festival's final night. Luckily, Lilker's own band Brutal Truth were also on the bill.

"Shane was a bit under the weather – sometimes when he's been on tour, he might drink too much and not get enough sleep," says Lilker. "I'd filled in for him in Lock Up when he couldn't make a tour a couple of years earlier. We had this joke that if I was in the same place as Lock Up, he'd get me to play bass – we called it 'Lilker Proximity Syndrome'."

At Hellfest, Lilker Proximity Syndrome went from being a gag to reality. Ninety minutes before Lock Up's set, Lilker got the request: could he step in for the stricken Embury?

"I was, like, 'Dude, I haven't played these songs for two years'. So I sat there with my headphones and an iPod trying to remember them, and then went onstage with Lock Up. I think I pulled it off. Shane would take the shirt off his back for you, so I had to be there for my friend."

Lilker is quick to acknowledge the impact Napalm Death have had on heavy music. "By mixing super-fast hardcore with the heaviness and dirtiness of metal, they set so much stuff in motion and inspired so many people." Bass player to bass player, Lilker holds up his friend's influence. "He's cleaned up his tone a little bit from the old days, but he's still got a really mad style. In a musical sense, the whole term "grindcore" refers to the bass sound, and me and him have got that covered pretty well."

1993

66 1993 was a fairly quiet year for Napalm Death. We didn't play as many gigs as we had in the previous couple of years, but we were all busy with our own things. I released an album called *To Spite The Gland That Breeds* by a side project I had called Blood From The Soul, which really reflected the music I was listening to – Ministry, Skinny Puppy, Helmet. Mitch had his own band, Meathook Seed, which was him doing a similar kind of industrial-influenced thing.

But one thing Napalm did do in 1993 was release a cover of 'Nazi Punks Fuck Off' by the Dead Kennedys as a single. We were big Dead Kennedys fans – they were one of the most influential American punk bands of the early 80s, and their singer, Jello Biafra, is a legend. We've covered plenty of different songs over the years, but more than any of them that's the one that people have gravitated to.

Billy Gould, the bassist with Faith No More, was responsible for us covering it. One of the great things about doing what I do is that it's given me the chance to become friends with a lot of the musicians I really admire, and Billy is one of them. Faith No More have been one of my favourite bands since I heard them in the 80s through my friend Mitch Dickinson's brother.

I met Billy for the first time when they came over to play the UK in 1989 in support of their album *The Real Thing*. They were doing a signing in a record store in Nottingham and playing a show later that night. I was supposed to be going down to the studio where they were remixing the *Mentally Murdered* mini-album, but I wasn't going to miss the gig.

I'd already seen them play Birmingham, when they did a "Best T-shirt" competition. Some kid in a Napalm shirt was one of the winners, which gave me a real buzz. I'd heard Faith No More really did like us, so I thought I'd go along to the signing to see if I could meet them. I was just standing in the shop when Billy came up from behind and grabbed me, even though we'd never met. We started chatting and I ended up taking him and a couple of the other guys to the offices of our label Earache up the road. They got kitted out with hoodies and T-shirts – Carcass, Godflesh, Entombed. They loved it all.

I've become close friends with Billy over the years. Me and my friend Nick Barker stayed at his house in San Francisco once while I was over there. Billy had a dog called Sweet Pea who really didn't like big guys – me and Nick were terrified it was going to take a chunk out of us. When Billy went to bed, I stayed up watching these old Faith No More videos he had. That was quite a surreal moment – it was a connection with that kid listening to them for the first time at Mitch Dickinson's house. I've played with Billy at various times over the years, in the band Brujeria as well as in one of my recent projects, Tronos.

At the time, there was a compilation called *Virus 100* coming out to celebrate the 100th release on Alternative Tentacles, the Dead Kennedys' own label. A bunch of bands were covering their songs, and Jello Biafra asked Billy if we'd do one. Billy actually selected 'Nazi Punks' for us, I guess because it's a confrontational song and we were a confrontational band. The *Virus 100* compilation came out in 1992, but our version was released as a single in 1993.

We've had a few run-ins with Nazis and fascists at our gigs over the years. In 1991, we toured the US with Sepultura, Sick Of It All, Sacred Reich and Biohazard. For some reason, a bunch of these idiots turned up at our gig in Pennsylvania and it all started to kick off. Pete Koller, the guitarist from Sick Of It All, grabbed a bat and ran out and started fighting these skinheads.

A few years later we toured with a hardcore band called Sheer Terror. They're great guys but they get some dodgy people at their shows. Again, we were in Pennsylvania, playing this pretty packed club, when the local Nazi gang turned up. You could see these 400 or so metal kids in the crowd surrounded by this ring of Nazis. The older ones were shoving the young skinheads into the crowd to start fighting.

We were pissed off, so we came on and opened up with 'Nazi Punks Fuck Off'. And then we did it again straight after for good measure. That didn't go down well with the Nazis. We played another couple of songs and they rushed us. We had to run back-stage and barricade the door because they were trying to kick it down. It was getting properly hairy – I thought they were going to get through. The guys from Sheer Terror were laughing: "We told you not to do that you crazy bastards." I was just thinking, "Why did we do that?"

Sometimes it's not just the fans who give us aggro. We played Russia for the very first time in 1991, and one of the Russian bands we were with… well, I'm not sure they were Nazis, but they were saying some dodgy stuff. There was a bit of tension, but nothing really happened. A couple of years later we were playing a festival in Estonia and this Russian band were there too. I'm not entirely sure what went on, but I saw the singer saying something to Barney and then going for him. I'd been drinking Estonian beer all afternoon and I was up for a ruck, so I lunged out the dressing room window and jumped on this guy.

I'm not a fighter, but I started having a go at him – at which point their guitarist grabbed me around the neck. I'm not clear on what happened next but apparently I started going blue, so Mitch jumped on him and began battering him. For some reason the prog band Marillion were on the bill, and I remember their singer, Fish, laughing at me afterwards: "You mad Brummie bastard."

Obviously there's always been a political edge to Napalm. The A-side of *Scum* was very anti-war, ant-fascist, anti-corporate, and the band came out of the anarcho-punk scene. A lot of the gigs in the early days would be benefits, with the money going towards anti-racist/anti-fascist groups or local communities. Back when we played squat gigs, their vibe was to take some of the money and pump it back into the local area. We've played plenty of political benefits over the years. Napalm went to South Africa in 1993, after Apartheid had come to an end – Barney actually travelled there a few weeks before to do a lot of school workshops.

Politics is a weird one for me. It's not that I don't care, but I just don't know enough about it and I feel like I don't have the answers. People ask me about it in interviews. I sometimes feel I should say something, I don't always know what to say, so I keep quiet for fear of saying the wrong thing.

I was never completely comfortable with the politics in the scene when I got to know Napalm. There was always pressure to be "political". I've never been into the whole "fuck the government" thing – it's always been dogshit no matter who's in, you've just got to suffer it well. I remember vegetarianism and veganism were big back then, which were political statements. I was never a vegetarian, I liked burgers too much. Mickey would give me a hard time: "You only bought those fucking crisps because they've got cheese powder in them, and you know I can't eat them." "No, Mickey. You can eat them, you just don't want to eat them."

I found some of it pretty hypocritical too. There were people who were totally genuine and people I met who I thought weren't. Some people in that scene used to change their viewpoints very quickly – they'd be saying one thing one month and a completely different thing a couple of months later. I guess when you're that age – 16, 17, 18 – you're finding yourself, but I felt sometimes that people were following trends.

I've occasionally had grief over the years because of political stuff. There was a Coca-Cola logo on the cover of the *Scum* album, and I was in Germany one time when a punk looked at me drinking a can of Coke and said, "You can't drink that, Coca-Cola is a multi-national corporation." I just went, "I'm drinking a can of Coke, tough shit. Oh, and I see you're wearing Nike trainers."

Politics are very important to a lot of people, and I know some people see Napalm as this political entity but for me the band's relevance is in the music and lyrics and the extremity of it all. It's not that I think that what goes on in the world isn't important – it is. But it's not my focus. I don't want to talk about politics, I want to talk about which Mercyful Fate album is best – *Don't Break The Oath* or *Melissa*.

I didn't actually meet Jello Biafra face to face until the early 2000s. I'd started yet another band, Venomous Concept, and Buzz Osbourne from Melvins was up for playing guitar. I was in LA at the time, so I went over to meet Buzz at his house and Jello was there. Both of them are really smart guys, and very socially and politically conscious. I'm stuck in the middle of these two luminaries, "I really hope they don't get into a political conversation and ask me my opinion, cos I'll be a bit out of my depth."

Thankfully they didn't. We just ended up hanging out. Jello's a nice guy – he was telling me how he used to record all his mad ideas for Dead Kennedys songs into a dictaphone. We stay in contact from time to time. He sang on a Napalm Death track called 'The Great And The Good' from our album *The Code Is Red... Long Live The Code*, which came out in 2005. If we're ever in the same city as him, he'll always come down and get up onstage unannounced to sing 'Nazi Punks Fuck Off'.

With politics, I try to channel my energy into making music and being cool to the people I know. The world's a fucked-up place and things need to be discussed, but also what's going on with your own beating heart is important. If you can't fix that, you're not going to fix anything. Maybe that's what I've been trying to fix for a long, long time.

1994

"When I was younger, I used to go and buy records on the basis of a bad review. So I still don't know why that one crap review of *Utopia Banished* in *Kerrang!* pissed me off so much, but it did. And it definitely affected what came next with Napalm Death and our next album, *Fear, Emptiness, Despair*.

Looking back, that whole period around 1993–1994 was a weird time for Napalm. *Utopia Banished* had turned out well and we'd done some good tours, but things were changing around the band, and within the band too.

One of the biggest changes was out of our control. It involved Earache Records, Napalm's label since the band's first album, *Scum*. Earache had been founded in Nottingham in 1985 by Digby Pearson. Dig liked the same sort of punk and hardcore music that I liked. He saw an opportunity to start a label, so he did. The first two records to come out on Earache were *The Return Of Martha Splatterhead* by the Seattle punk band The Accused and a Concrete Sox/Heresy split album. *Scum* was Earache's third release, and it had the catalogue number MOSH003.

Dig and Earache were central to putting extreme music on the map, mainly because there were very few other labels who wanted to take a chance with bands like Napalm Death. Earache quickly became its own thing. It wasn't necessarily a sound, because Napalm or Carcass didn't sound like Morbid Angel or Godflesh. It was more of a standard – if a record came out on Earache, you knew what kind of thing you'd be getting. It was like a more extreme version of labels like 4AD, Creation or Sub Pop.

Dig did amazing stuff with Earache, but Napalm Death definitely played a part in its success. It wasn't just that we were selling a lot of records for them, we helped them out in other ways too. We'd go round to Dig's flat to help him do mailouts, spending hours putting records in cardboard envelopes ready to send off in the post. We'd talk about the latest stuff we'd heard through tape trading. Dig signed the Swedish band Entombed on Mickey Harris's recommendation, and they ended up becoming one of Earache's biggest bands.

There was a camaraderie between a lot of the Earache bands back then. I knew the guys from Carcass and Extreme Noise Terror before any of us signed to the label. But there was also a bit of competitiveness going on – nothing malicious, but we were definitely keeping an eye on each other musically.

Earache really did shape the landscape when it came to extreme music back then thanks to bands like Napalm, Morbid Angel, Carcass and Godflesh. As it became more successful, it was almost inevitable that major labels would start sniffing around, and in 1993 Digby signed a deal with Columbia Records to distribute Earache albums in the US.

I didn't have a huge problem with that. I thought it would help Napalm reach a much wider audience in America. It wasn't about the money, because we weren't making any. It was about being heard. But a lot of people weren't happy about it, and Barney was one of them. He saw the Columbia situation as selling out, and he was pretty vocal about it. I can see why he thought that, but I didn't agree. Napalm Death came out of the underground, and that was still part of who we were, but I'd always hoped we'd be able to step up to the next level. As long as we were staying true to ourselves, I didn't see it as a problem.

Me and Barney having different views of the Columbia deal was fine. We're both strong-minded people, we both have very strong opinions, and we can both be stubborn bastards when it comes to expressing them. But from my point of view, it seemed to reflect something that was happening in Napalm at a deeper level. It's not that we weren't getting on with each other, it just felt like we were starting to fracture a little.

Part of it was definitely musical. The negative review *Kerrang!* gave *Utopia Banished* shouldn't have scarred us, but it did. Me and Mitch in particular wanted to move the band in a different direction. We were listening to Helmet and Smashing Pumpkins and Jane's Addiction. We found some drumbeats more interesting than just blast beats, which was a shock to Danny. We didn't want to make Napalm less extreme, we just wanted to make it extreme in a different way.

There was another factor at play. Barney may have a completely different view of this, but I felt that a bit of distance was starting to open up between him and the rest of us. The four of us were still living together in the Napalm House, going out drinking and just hanging out. Barney had moved to London, he was reviewing games and albums for magazines, he had his social life down there.

That was fair enough, but there was less of a connection between us. When me and Mitch were in Birmingham watching Helmet tearing it up at a gig and going, "These beats are amazing, let's do something like that but with Napalm", he wasn't there with us, joining in. He might have said, "That's bollocks," but at least he'd have been there.

We recorded *Fear, Emptiness, Despair* with Colin Richardson in Parr Street Studios in Liverpool. Bill Steer came down and hung out. It was the first time I saw him drink, because he never touched alcohol when he was in Napalm. The band went out together while we were there, but it wasn't quite like it had been before. Part of it was because Danny's mom had just passed away, so it was difficult for him. But partly because there was all this other stuff hanging in the background.

Utopia Banished had been a really easy record to make, but *Fear, Emptiness, Despair* was more difficult. There might have been some subconscious pressure because of the Columbia deal, even though we were determined we wouldn't let it change what we were doing. But the process of recording it just wasn't as smooth as *Utopia Banished* had been.

I can see it today from Barney's perspective. He'd been completely happy with *Utopia Banished*, and he had a clear view in his mind of what Napalm should be. But because he was down in London, he didn't know what was going on in our heads when it came to the music side of things. It didn't help that I was a bit of a twat towards Barney at times as well. I started to take the lead with vocal patterns, telling him what to sing where and generally treading on his toes. I understand now that kind of stuff doesn't help, but it summed up where we both were at that point.

We weren't trying to completely reinvent Napalm from the ground up, but me and Mitch were pushing for something different.

We were definitely on separate pages when it came to the direction of the band at that point, even down to the *Fear, Emptiness, Despair* artwork. I got one of the guys from 4AD to do the cover and I remember Barney scoffing at it: "Pfft."

Interestingly, there's a different mix of that album to the one that actually came out, done by a guy named Pete Coleman. I'd got some sample pads and I was trying to put all these noisy samples throughout the album to try and make it more industrial sounding in a way. Dig didn't like that at all – he insisted we get it completely remixed by Colin Richardson. Was he right? I don't know. It would have been interesting to put it out to see what the reaction was, but that might have just been too much.

Barney made it clear that he didn't like the album to the point where he didn't want to go out and do press for it, so I ended up doing it. That really rubbed me up the wrong way. If you don't like something, fine, but don't go around telling people. With a few very rare exceptions, there are egos in bands and Napalm are no exception. Noses get put out of joint and egos inflate. There are still egos now, me included, but we're better than we were back then. Things still come to the surface occasionally and there are clashes, but we mostly know to step back and let things cool down. Back then we were kids – we didn't know how to communicate properly.

The album came out in June 1994, and we toured with Entombed in Europe and Obituary in the US. We had a bus driver in the States called James Brown – not the funk guy, obviously. He loved honky-tonk music, and he'd be vacuuming the tour bus at 2 o'clock in the afternoon with his honky-tonk blaring out at full volume while I was laying in the bunk with a hangover. It used to drive me mad.

The opening band on the US tour was Machine Head, and there was a massive buzz around them. I could see why people were getting excited about it – all the elements in what they were doing were what people wanted to hear, it was totally fresh. We actually extended our tour by two weeks, just us and Machine Head, and we had a great time. There were some crazy shows. When we played LA, our friend Brujo from the band Brujeria – who I'd started playing with a year earlier – was at the gig, being generous with certain things. That was a mad show.

There were a few other weird things going on too. We'd heard that Slayer were going to be touring, and we were keen to open for them. One of our friends said, "Play the new Slayer album between sets, it might be seen as a good thing." And in the end, Machine Head got the Slayer tour. That was when me and Mitch looked at each other and went, "Shit, something weird is going on here, what is it?"

I think it might have had something to do with the fact that years before, I'd proudly said that Napalm Death would never slow down to Slayer speed. It was the kind of dumb shit you say when you're young that you live to regret. But I also think it might have been down to the fact that Napalm were generally going through a bit of a strange time.

As I've pointed out already, people have accused Napalm Death of "selling out" ever since I've been in the band, but we really started to get it a lot around the time of *Fear, Emptiness, Despair*. That's bullshit. "Selling out" would have been making *Utopia Banished II*. We could have easily done that. Maybe we shouldn't have been so immature and got pissed off with one review. But we were following our hearts, something which Napalm have always done.

We got criticism for changing the tempos in the songs: "They're not doing blast beats as much anymore, they've sold out." And people were pissed off that the records were coming out on a major label in the US, but that wasn't our choice, it was Earache's. I'm not sure what we actually gained from the Columbia deal. It certainly wasn't money. I think most of that went to Earache.

I sometimes wonder if me and Mitch were trying to forcibly change something that didn't need to be changed. For some people, it was just too much of a shift of direction. On the other hand, people talk to me and say it's one of their favourite Napalm albums. It was an album I felt we had to make at the time, but the fracture in the band only seemed to be getting wider.

EYE WITNESS: JIM WELCH

Former Earache Records US label manager

Jim Welch bonded with Shane Embury over food at St Mark's Pizza, just up the street from punk mecca CBGBs in New York. It was November 1989, and Napalm Death were in the Big Apple to play their first ever US gig at the iconic venue, a show co-organized by Welch. The band needed to kill time before they played, so he took them to what he proudly describes as the best pizza restaurant in New York.

"Shane's a passionate person for music, and back then he was a passionate person for fantastic pizza too," says Welch. "And it didn't come any more fantastic than St Mark's Pizza."

The CBGBs show would be pivotal for both Napalm Death and Jim Welch. It marked the point where this underground band got a proper foothold in America, and it sparked off a fruitful working relationship that lasted until the mid-90s and a friendship that endures to this day.

Welch was an early adopter when it came to Napalm Death. He'd read about the crustpunk and grindcore scene happening across the Atlantic in the pages of influential American punk fanzine *Maximum Rocknroll*. When he walked into his local record store in Hartsdale, New York and saw a copy of *Scum* hanging on the wall, he immediately bought it.

"I was a fan of extreme music, but this was something else," says Welch. "I thought it was the craziest record I'd ever heard."

Welch was plugged into the US underground scene, booking punk and metal gigs while he was still at university. His first job after finishing his education was at independent label Combat/Relativity Records, where he worked with bands such as San Francisco hardcore band Attitude Adjustment and death metal pioneers Death.

It was Welch, together with music journalist and future Brutal Truth/Venomous Concept singer Kevin Sharp, who engineered Napalm Death's show at CBGBs. That show, on 17 November 1989, was America's first taste of these grindcore standard-bearers in the flesh.

"CBGBS was packed to the walls, nobody could get in," says Welch. "The crowd was a mix of people from the punk/hardcore scene and cooler indie kids who might have read about them in the CMJ magazine. There were a few early death metal fans there, but it wasn't a dominant part of the crowd."

The CBGBS gig was more than just a success on the night. It ultimately secured Earache a deal in the US with Relativity's distributors, meaning the UK label's albums would get proper Stateside releases. The first record to come out as part of the deal was Napalm Death's *Harmony Corruption* in 1990 – an album that gave the band a foothold in the US.

"We had to strike a balance when it came to marketing the band," says Welch. "We made sure that people knew about Napalm Death's roots in punk and hardcore, and that they were the leaders of the grind-core scene. It wasn't just, 'Napalm Death have gone death metal.'"

Welch and Combat put their money where their mouth was. Between February and September 1991, Napalm Death played more than 90 shows in the US. By the time they reached Los Angeles, they were headlining the 4,000-capacity Hollywood Palladium. Jim Welch was along for a lot of the shows.

"That's when I really noticed that Shane was always making music, working on four-track music," he says. "He was into lots of different kinds of sounds, and some of the stuff he was doing was really experimental. Over the years, he'd send me what he was working on just for me to listen to. There was this tireless creativity that's still there today."

Welch was laid off by Relativity in July 1991, a product of the record company's decision to move away from rock and metal towards hip-hop. Earache boss Digby Pearson immediately offered him the job of running a new American office. Working from the kitchen of his apartment, he helped turn this subterranean label into an unlikely success story. "In 1992, we were probably the second-biggest-selling independent label in America after Sub Pop," he says.

Inevitably, the mainstream record industry was starting to take notice. Bigger labels were starting to sniff around Earache's bands, and Welch himself. He ended up taking a job with Columbia Records, a subsidiary of global powerhouse Sony. At the same time, Columbia signed a deal with Earache to release its key records in the US. It was a controversial decision, not least with some of the bands who were part of the package.

"We knew it would be complicated, but also we knew it would take things to another level for these bands," says Welch. "Napalm Death didn't have to release a record on Columbia, Carcass didn't have to. When the options were put in front of them to make that decision, some of the musicians felt one way, some felt another way. But at the end of the day, they all decided to do it."

Welch says Napalm Death's new paymasters were realistic about the band's commercial potential. "They weren't deluded – they didn't think Napalm Death was ever going to write a hit single," he says. "But they thought Napalm could double their sales and sell 100,000 records in the US for sure. And Columbia wanted to treat them well and make sure they were respected for what they had created."

In the end, Napalm Death released just one album via the Columbia deal, 1994's *Fear, Emptiness, Despair*. Despite the controversy, Welch viewed it as a success. "Napalm sold more records than they had before," he says. "It wasn't a 'hit', but then it was never supposed to be."

Welch left Columbia in 1996, around the same time the label's deal with Earache ended. He went to work for Atlantic Records, but stayed in contact with Shane. "We'd still meet up for pizza at St Mark's Pizza whenever he was in New York."

St Mark's Pizza went out of business years ago, but Napalm Death have endured. "All the personalities in the band have had their roles over the years, but if it wasn't for Shane, I don't think the band would be here today. That integrity he had when he started out is still there, and it's untainted. He's the glue that holds it all together."

1995–1996

66 Every band goes through a sticky patch. It's the nature of bands, they're complicated things. Napalm Death have been through several sticky patches over the years, though the period in the mid-90s was probably the stickiest of all.

Looking back, we've tried to make every Napalm album different to the one before. Grindcore is great, but just playing that and nothing else can become repetitive. It's sometimes difficult to get everyone to lock into the same vision of staying true to who you are as a band while also trying to bring in other elements.

We'd released *Fear, Emptiness, Despair* in 1994, which we were proud of but some people didn't like it because they thought it didn't sound like Napalm Death. Those people probably wanted us to make *Scum* over and over again, but that would have been impossible. Aside from the fact that none of the people who played that record had been in the band for years, that's not where our heads were at back then. Or at least not where mine and Mitch's heads were at. We wanted to constantly move forwards, which is not a bad thing at all.

I'm pretty sure Barney saw things differently. He's always had a clear view of what he thought Napalm Death should be. He's not resistant to change, but he didn't want to lose what he saw as making the band what it was. Neither did I, it's just that what he saw as making Napalm what it was, and what I saw as making Napalm what it was, weren't exactly the same.

There was kind of a stalemate between us. Me and Barney were getting along, but there was so little communication about what we wanted from Napalm. A lot of that was because of the distance between us – Barney was down in London, the rest of us were in the Napalm House in Birmingham.

Barney always said he couldn't have handled living with us. It was pretty chaotic and messy. I've always felt that as much as Barney is massively geared towards Napalm, he always wanted to keep a grip on reality whereas the rest of us were happy living in our own little world, going to the pub, playing video games and listening to music. I've grown up in a lot of respects over the last 30 years, but I'm still that person who gets up in the morning, eats something and then grabs a guitar.

Even if we'd been living together, things might not have been any different. There's quite a lot of diplomacy involved in being in a band. If you have an opinion on something, whether it's the way you think a song should sound or a bigger decision that affects the band as a whole, you have to be courteous and say, "This is what I want to do," and then be prepared for the four-hour conversation that will follow.

I'm much better at it now, but I didn't always have that kind of diplomacy. Sometimes I can be really blunt when I'm telling people what I think we should be doing. I see it as being truthful, but other people think it's controlling. When you're in a band, you sometimes forget to communicate and you end up hurting people's feelings. I look back and think, "I was having a go at somebody about something, but maybe that was me projecting my own problems onto the situation." You have to be conscious of these things, because that's the only way you can change how you want to be.

Me and Barney are both very passionate about Napalm. He has his vision of what it should be and I have mine. I'm always questioning myself and what we should be doing – I wanted better for Napalm, but I wasn't really expressing it the right way. With Barney, especially around the time of *Fear, Emptiness, Despair* and *Diatribes*, it felt more like, "If it isn't broke, let's not fix it." And he's as right in that view as I am in mine. But back then, my approach wasn't to sit down and talk things through, it was more: "I want this."

Making albums is a strange experience. You're so wrapped up in it that you don't always realize how different it might be from the one that came out before. It's only when you come to do the next album that you can hear what's different about it. And sometimes I think fans don't allow the bands they like to change. I remember getting an advance tape of Metallica's *Black Album* before it came out. It wasn't as fast and thrashy as their 80s records, and they were working with a producer who had done stuff with Bon Jovi, so people instantly said, "They've sold out." It still sounded like Metallica to me, except they were making the next logical move.

That's what we were trying to do with *Diatribes*. It wasn't our *Black Album* – though I wouldn't say no to some of Metallica's sales – but we weren't remaking *Scum* or *From Enslavement To Obliteration* or *Harmony Corruption* again either. Bands can fall into a formula, which is something we never wanted to do, and still don't. Around the time of *Diatribes*, me, Mitch and Jesse were left to our own devices. Jesse's songs were a bit more old school, but me and Mitch were pushing the boundaries of what Napalm could be.

We put the *Greed Killing* mini-album out at the end of 1995, a couple of months before *Diatribes*. The song 'Greed Killing' itself threw a lot of people because it's pretty accessible by Napalm Death standards. I get why they were freaking out – listen to a song like 'Scum' and listen to 'Greed Killing' and they're poles apart. It was very clean-sounding, which I'm sure horrified a lot of Napalm fans. But then I meet people who got into the band around that time and who love the song. The Swedish grindcore band Nasum, who gave us a real kick up the arse when I heard them a few years later, always told me they loved 'Greed Killing'.

Diatribes came out in early January 1995. It starts with 'Greed Killing', but in hindsight we should have probably started it with a song called 'Antibody' which was on the mini-album, just because it's more frantic. Sometimes things like that colour people's perceptions of an album: "Oh, the first song sounds more commercial than anything they've done before, the rest of the album must be shit." *Diatribes* isn't exactly a commercial album, but if it had started with a blaster then perhaps people would have thought about it differently. Or if we'd put a couple of the other faster songs from the mini-album on it, it might have helped.

By the same token, I'm really proud of the fact that we did something different. There's a track on there called 'Cursed To Crawl', which was sparse and industrial sounding. It was influenced by a band we loved called SLAB!, who I'd heard on the Peel show. 'Cursed To Crawl' didn't come out quite like I wanted it to, but I loved the fact that some people just couldn't get their heads around it. We had friends in Germany who had loved the band for years, they'd always turn up to gigs, and they'd say, "But why did you make a song like that?"

Diatribes isn't our best album, but it's far from a bad one. It got some decent reviews when it came out, but it seemed like there was less excitement surrounding it than there had been around previous Napalm records. And of course a contingent of people hated it just because it didn't sound like what they thought Napalm should sound like.

We did a really long tour in support of the album. We played in the US with Sheer Terror, which is where we had that run-in with the racists in Philadelphia, then we came back and toured Europe with Crowbar and then At The Gates, and then we went back to the States... it was probably eight months in total.

I look back and I can see that Barney probably wasn't 100 per cent happy. Credit to him, he hung in there, which I really respect. We played a show in Wolverhampton, all our families were there. My dad said to Barney, "You're not going to leave this band, are you?" And Barney said, "No." But we felt he wasn't into it, or he was just tired. Either way, it seemed like the connection was gone.

We decided to ask Barney to leave. Danny was the one who had his back. He wanted us to try and work things out, but we'd made up our minds. It was one of the hardest things I'd done. Me and Barney have our differences at times, but we are close. When *Harmony Corruption* came out and Mickey Harris was first starting to wobble about whether or not he wanted to be in the band, Barney was worried. At one point, he even came up and hugged me and said, "What will I do, Shane?", though I think he might have been on the Pernod and black. I just said, "Calm down Barney, it'll be fine."

Now here we were a few years later, and we were asking him to leave. We all went down to see him to tell him. I can't remember exactly what was said, but I know it knocked Barney for six. Even though he didn't seem happy in the band, I think it completely blindsided him. The way it was presented to the press afterwards was that Barney had left of his own choice, but that wasn't the case.

I spoke to him about it afterwards, and he felt we treated him very unfairly. I can see that now, but it seemed like the right thing to do for the band at the times. In hindsight, I would have done it differently – we wouldn't have asked him to leave for a start, we'd have tried to work through the problems. But what was done was done. And the way things turned out, I was the one who had to ask him to come back a few months later.

1997

"We didn't have any specific replacement in mind when we asked Barney to leave, but we had an idea of who could be a good fit: Phil Vane from Extreme Noise Terror. We'd known Phil for years. Extreme Noise Terror came from the same scene as Napalm, and I remember seeing them at The Mermaid in Birmingham in the 80s – they'd turn up with these crazy hairstyles, mohicans and spikes all over the place. Napalm did shows with ENT, and I'd been on tour with them years before, just hanging out in their van for a laugh.

ENT were still active around that time, but they weren't gigging a lot. So I contacted Phil to see if he'd be up for joining Napalm, and he was. There was no audition, it was just a case of: "Fancy joining the band?" "Yeah."

Phil was a lovely guy. We liked similar music and he had some interesting ideas. We felt he understood where we came from and where we were going. We rehearsed with him during the day and he spent a lot of time at the Napalm House. At the time I was single, so we'd have a few beers and get on the Playstation. He'd sit there watching me play Tomb Raider.

I'd written a couple of songs for one of my side projects, Blood From The Soul, but I thought they'd work better with Napalm Death. In a way, Barney not being there gave us a bit more freedom to make the music we wanted to make, though with hindsight that wasn't necessarily for the best.

We started recording the new album at Framework Studios in Birmingham with Colin Richardson, but it became evident when we were recording that it wasn't working with Phil. What we hadn't really taken into account was that Extreme Noise Terror had two singers, so he was part of a duo. Barney's got such a powerful voice, and Phil just didn't have the same power. It had seemed fine in rehearsal, but when we got in the studio with him, his tone versus the tone we were imagining in our heads was completely different. Colin Richardson, our producer, felt the same: "I don't know if this is right."

Phil had been in the band maybe three months at that point and it put us in a difficult position. Things hadn't worked out with Barney, so we'd asked him to leave. Now things weren't going as well as we wanted with the guy we'd got into replace him. We could have persevered and hoped it would come together, but we all knew that wasn't going to happen. That's when we made the decision to let him go.

That was the second hard conversation I'd had in just a few months. I had to tell him: "I'm sorry to say this to you, but it's just not working." He was pretty upset about it, as I would have been. I tried to be as honest as possible as to why and not fob him off with some bullshit. I think he was OK by the time we finished talking. We hugged and he got in the car and drove back to Ipswich.

It's a shame it didn't work out with Phil. Looking back, maybe we should have auditioned singers rather than appointing some-body just because we knew them, but there was a lot of spontaneous decision-making going on back then. Despite what had happened with Napalm, Phil and I stayed friends. Years later, he sang a song on the second album by another of my bands, Venomous Concept. He had that English punk/hardcore style, but you could always hear a tinge of his Ipswich accent.

Sadly, Phil passed away suddenly in 2011. He was only 46, which is way too young to go. Compared to some people I know around our age who are still pretty manic, Phil had toned down a lot of the madness of his younger years. He'd just had a young son, which makes me think about my own life now I have kids of my own. But I've got great memories of going on tours with Extreme Noise Terror, and Phil coming out to a couple of Napalm shows in Europe when Mitch Dickinson stood in for Bill Steer many years ago.

After I'd told Phil that I didn't think it was working out, he asked me, "Who are you going to get?" I said, "I don't know. But I'm thinking of asking Barney back."

The idea of Barney returning to Napalm Death might seem like a weird one. His leaving in the first place was a big deal because he was such an important part of the band, and it had devastated him. We asked him to leave because it didn't seem like he was into what we wanted to do with the band and there was always the risk that those problems would resurface if he came back. And the thing is that Barney had sung on an Extreme Noise Terror album in the few months he was out of Napalm – kind of a job-swap with Phil. That was strange. I've always wondered if he did that as a fuck you to us: "I'll show them."

But the simple fact was that there wasn't anybody who could do the job of singing for Napalm Death better than Barney. Years before, when he first joined, there was no audition. It was purely based on me and Mickey Harris wanting him in the band: "He loves Napalm, he'll be perfect." Me and him butted heads plenty of times, but that's just because we were two stubborn people. Even when things weren't great around the time of *Fear, Emptiness, Despair* and *Diatribes*, we never actually fell out – we just weren't communicating properly.

It was down to me to speak to Barney because nobody else wanted to do it. I can't remember exactly when I did it, but it was pretty much as soon as Phil left – it might have even been the same day. I took a deep breath and called him. I can't remember what my exact words were, but it was something along the lines of: "It didn't work out with Phil, he just didn't have the power you have. Maybe we shouldn't have done what we did, but we thought it was the way forward, but it turned out not to be. So I'm asking you if you'd consider coming back."

Barney's initial reaction was pretty much: "Huh." I can understand that. He told us later that he felt he'd been treated really unfairly, and that it had really knocked his self-esteem. But he heard me out, and we talked about stuff.

One thing he did say was that he wanted to listen to the songs we'd written, so I sent them to him and he went, "Oh, this is really heavy." Of course it was heavy – what else was it going to be? We weren't going to cop out.

We'd recorded a couple of songs with Phil, but they never got to the point where they were mixed. With Barney singing on them, it made us realize just how integral he was to Napalm Death. It felt like his attitude had changed when he came back in, which isn't surprising. He was a lot more vocal about what he liked and what he didn't like.

We called the album, *Inside The Torn Apart*. It's a strange title. It referred to the fact that we'd been in this strange, claustrophobic, torn-apart place where people weren't as close as they'd once been. That's reflected in a lot of the lyrics. It's not as socially conscious as some other Napalm Death albums. It's more about the stresses of not just being in a band, but of being human, and how we change as people and how our interactions with other people change. The couple of years leading up to the album had really brought that home.

I like *Inside The Torn Apart* as an album. It's faster and heavier than *Diatribes*, but it wasn't a step back to earlier Napalm. I'm not sure Barney was completely into all of the songs back then, but he really threw himself into it.

Looking back, everything that happened with Barney leaving the band was petty bullshit, though it didn't seem like it at the time – certainly not to him. I've told him since that we shouldn't have parted ways with him at that point. Of course, the communication issues we had weren't completely ironed out when he came back but they were better. They still aren't perfect, to be honest. Me and Barney are friends, but it's sometimes hard for us to talk to each other.

Like most bands, Napalm are a strange bunch of people – we don't always see eye to eye, but in a weird way that makes us stronger. The tension makes for better records, even if it sometimes means other things are difficult. But then being a member of Napalm Death, you're used to life being difficult.

EYE WITNESS: BARNEY GREENWAY

Napalm Death singer

Barney Greenway was so surprised to be offered the job of singer in Napalm Death that he crashed his bike. It was 1989, and the 19-year-old had cycled down to a phone box near the place he was living in Birmingham to call his friend Mick Harris. The drummer and his bandmates had just got back from their first ever Japanese tour, and he had some news.

"He said, 'Lee and Bill have left. Do you fancy joining?'" recalls Greenway. "I thought about it for half a second then I said, 'Yeah, I'll do it.' I was so excited I came off my BMX on the way back. I was thinking. 'Is this the stupidest thing I'm ever going to do?'"

Greenway was a fixture on Birmingham's underground music scene in the late 80s and Napalm Death were on his radar even before they released *Scum*. He was a regular attendee at their gigs, and an avid proselytiser when it came to their boundary-pushing brilliance.

"I'd go around to people saying, 'This is the best thing ever,'" he says. "And they'd go, 'It's shit.' Even some of the punks who had grown up on GBH and Subhumans and Crass – these free-thinking anarchist-type punks – thought it was unintelligible."

For Greenway, the band's anarcho-punk-inspired political agenda was on equal footing with their musical extremity. "For me, the two things have always been very easy bedfellows in Napalm, and that continues to be the case," he says. "I wouldn't even say politics is necessarily what Napalm sing about. It's about basic humanity. If the idea is to improve the situation and the world and people and other sentient beings, politics can often get in the way of that."

Greenway's memories of those early gigs are hazy, a product of The Mermaid pub's scrumpy and other, stronger substances. But he quickly got to know the various members that passed through the band between 1986 and 1988, Mick Harris and Shane Embury in particular.

"Shane was quite shy when I first met him," says Greenway. "He didn't really express himself until you put a tape that somebody had sent through the post in front of him, and then his whole thing just flipped. He was utterly consumed by music back then and still is. When he wants to know about something, he'll slice away every layer. He wants to know about every detail, not just what's coming out of the speakers. And that really helped me discover stuff through being exposed to what he listened to, bands like the Cocteau Twins."

Greenway watched Embury go from being a fan of Napalm Death to being a member of the band, a journey he would take himself a couple of years later.

"He didn't have to be like Lee Dorrian onstage, jumping up in the air every 20 seconds," says Greenway of his future bandmate's early shows. "Shane's bass sound did the talking. That is a bass sound that has been very rarely equalled, in terms of the sheer concrete-mixer character of it. It's one of the best, alongside Lemmy, alongside Rainy from Discharge. When Shane plays, it looks effortless, but you try and get other people to do what he's doing, and they'll fall on their arses."

Greenway, who at the time sang in another Birmingham band, Benediction, occasionally worked as Napalm Death's unofficial roadie prior to joining. It was a job that involved "drinking copious amounts of alcohol and pretending to lift stuff for them".

Despite the split with Lee Dorrian and Bill Steer, he stepped into the band in good spirits. Embury and Harris were upbeat about Napalm Death's future. "They were just happy they were able to carry on," says Greenway, who had to learn 25 songs in two weeks ahead of the upcoming Grindcrusher tour.

"It was mad – I'm 19 years old, I'm going out and playing to a thousand people a night," he says of the tour, which kicked grindcore and extreme music to a new level in the UK. "You feel indestructible."

As the band's new singer, Greenway got to see the internal dynamics of Napalm Death up close. Mick Harris wrote a lot of the songs for the band's third album, the death metal-influenced *Harmony Corruption*, on his two-string guitar, but Shane was bringing plenty of musical ideas to the table. "Me and Shane were writing lyrics, most separately but together on a few songs," he says. "That definitely wouldn't happen now. I need to isolate myself, pull the phone out of the wall, close the blind and lock myself away."

Harmony Corruption, recorded in Florida, would be Mick Harris's last Napalm Death album, with Danny Herrera replacing him on follow-up *Utopia Banished*.

"It was worrying losing Mickey and his spontaneity, but then in the natural order of things, Shane became the biggest voice," says Greenway. "Being from the scene we're from, we'd always say, 'There is no hierarchy.' But the mere fact that people are pushing for ideas is going to form a hierarchy, and Shane was very powerful in that respect. Personally, I felt strongly about stuff, but I wasn't sure about bringing it up. I felt a bit overwhelmed."

Greenway says that he wanted to bring in new elements while preserving Napalm's original ethos. But in his view, the *Fear, Emptiness, Despair* and *Diatribes* albums found the band drifting too far from their core values, and he made his opinions clear.

"The fast, chaotic stuff took a back seat around the time of *Fear, Emptiness, Despair*," says Greenway, who was living in London when Embury and guitarist Mitch Harris began writing that album. "I didn't like it and I said so in rehearsals. Shane has always said that I was disappointed because I wasn't there when they were listening to all this new music and writing these songs, but that wasn't the case at all. I could still have come in and had my input. With hindsight I like a lot of stuff on those albums now, but it was shock to turn up and hear those songs: 'Where's it gone?'"

The tension between Greenway on the one hand and Embury and Harris on the other eventually reached breaking point before the band's next album, *Inside The Torn Apart*.

"I made my feelings known a bit too much," he says. "Shane and Mitch must have just thought, 'This is too problematic for what we're trying to do and we should just let him go.' I was ejected."

The unexpected dismissal hit him hard. "I felt betrayed. It was a mixture of being really pissed off and just really sad at the same time."

When Greenway returned to Napalm Death he, "Made it known that I wanted my input to be more than it had been," he says. "I'd started to feel like my opinion had been pushed to one side, and that I wasn't valued as much as I should have been. And Shane, to his credit, said, 'This is what we've done with Phil, you can change stuff if you want to.'"

That rekindled sense of unity helped see the band through some tough times in the late 90s, when they split from their manager and their label, Earache, and endured some severe financial hardship. Similarly, the *Enemy Of The Music Business* album, released in 2000, represented a realignment of their musical views. "Before that album, I phoned Shane and said, 'We need to do an album that fucking rips people's guts out,'" says Greenway. "And he went, 'Yeah,

I agree.' I was, like, 'Oh, you do?' That rejuvenated us. Collectively, it gave us a profound sense of freedom."

It wasn't a completely easy ride in the years following, though. The death of former Napalm guitarist Jesse Pintado from alcohol-related illness in 2006, despite his bandmates' attempts to help him, was a blow. Mitch Harris left the band in 2020, although he made an appearance on 2020's *Throes Of Joy In The Jaws Of Defeatism* album.

"Danny's a very laidback guy, he takes a backseat, which means me and Shane are the two main decision makers," says Greenway. "Shane can be stubborn, which is something I've struggled with down the years, because it makes me stubborn. I dig my heels in, which can create problems sometimes."

As with many partnerships, the relationship between the two men is defined by their differences as much as their similarities.

"There are things that come up that I think we should not do for ethical reasons," says Greenway. "Say if a sports shoe company with issues around the treatment of workers in their supply chain was to approach us, there's no way we should be getting involved with that. There have been many, many occasions where I've had an argument with Shane about that stuff. He does understand the reasons, it might just take a little longer for him to grasp certain things when it comes to that stuff."

Similarly, Greenway takes the opposite view of the extra-curricular musical activities to his bandmate. Not because he thinks Shane should focus all his time on Napalm Death, but because of the stresses the extra workload can bring.

"I've had a conversation with him about how much he's doing," says Greenway. "He got really defensive about that. I had to leave it alone – if you're on a tour bus, you have to live with that person for the next few weeks."

Yet for all the differences, and the occasional flashpoints that still happen, theirs is a long-standing friendship built on mutual respect and an artistic vision that is closer now than it's ever been before.

"We agree on the fact that the point of Napalm Death is to carry forward the extremity and not to conform to musical norms. I always want to move it forwards, keeping it abrasive, extremely confrontational. I had a sense at points that we were losing the edge. I don't ever want to feel that again.

"And after everything we've been through, the ups and downs we might have had, Shane is the most loyal person I know. When it comes to the people around him, he's always very mindful of making sure they're taken care of and they're OK. I owe everything to him and Mickey Harris and people like Nik Bullen who founded Napalm Death, because I wouldn't be here without them."

Shane with baby sister Sarah. Broseley, 1974

L-R. Mike Clarke, Shane, Wayne Aston, Mitch Dickinson – Shane's first band, Warhammer. Broseley, 1984

L-R. Shane, Mike Davidson, Ken Owen, Bill Steer, Mitch Dickinson, unknown. The Mermaid, Sparkhill, Birmingham, summer 1986

L-R. Shane, Mitch Dickinson, Pete Giles – Unseen Terror. Broseley, early 1988

L-R. Mick Harris, Shane, Bill Steer, Lee Dorian. Photo shoot for the Napalm Death 'Mentally Murdered' E.P., Vienna, 1989

L- R. Mick Harris, Mark "Barney" Greenway, Mitch Harris, Jesse Pintado, Shane; the Napalm Death *Harmony Corruption* line-up. Tampa, Florida, April 1990

L-R. Simon Coles, Mitch Harris and Shane.
Oktoberfest, Munich, 1990

Shane with mom Ann Embury. Broseley, 1991

With Sepultura's Andreas Kisser. USA, 1991

L-R. Dan Lilker, Shane, Barney. Milwaukee Metal Fest, 1991

L-R. Jim Plotkin, Jim Welch, Karl Angel, Shane.
At the Knitting Factory, New York, 1991

L-R. Justin Broadrick, Kevin Sharp, Shane. 1991

L-R. Mark Walmsley, Jesse Pintado, Shane, Mitch Harris.
Ferry to France, probably 1991

L-R. Mitch Harris, Shane, Dan Lilker. Milwaukee Metal Fest, 1991

L-R. Mitch, Shane, Danny, Jesse, Barney.
Napalm Death circa 1991

With Carl Stokes. The White
Hart, Ironbridge, Shropshire,
1991

Shane being a goofball. Edwards No. 8, Birmingham, 1992

With Jesse Pintado. USA, 1992

With Scott Carlson. Whisky a Go Go, Los Angeles, 2003

Barney, Shane, Mitch and Danny. Napalm Death
Smear Campaign line-up. Leipzig, Germany,
2006

Shane at home with sister Sarah and dad Tom.
Broseley, 2006

With Simon Efemey (left) and Ronnie James Dio.
Birmingham NEC, 2007

L-R. Danny, Barney, Shane, Mitch. Napalm Death *Time Waits For No Slave* line-up. 2009

Shane with his wife Madoka and baby Izumi. Asakusa, near the Sensō-ji temple, Japan

Shane with his children Izumi Embury and Hiroumi Embury. Birmingham, 2018

Shane, John Cooke and Danny Herrera. Hobbiton, New Zealand, 2015

With Simon Efemey, Australia, 2017/18

Shane and daughter Izumi Embury.
Camp Bestival, East Lulworth, July 2019

With Russ Russell, Tronos recording session.
Parlour Studios, Kettering, December 2020

L-R. Igor Cavalera, Jaz Coleman, Russ Russell, Shane.
Parlour Studios, Kettering, February 2022

With Mick Harris, Scorn recording session. Birmingham, 2022

Shane with a framed photo of little Shane. Birmingham, 2022

With Nicholas Bullen, co-founder of Napalm Death. Birmingham, 2023

1998

"The end of the 90s was tough for Napalm Death. Barney was back in the band, and he was more fired up than he'd been before he left, which made me more fired up as well. But everything else seemed to be hard going.

The last few albums we'd made had been good, but they hadn't gone down as well as some of our earlier ones. That was partly because we'd changed musically, but also because the scene around us was changing. Nu metal was the big thing at the time, and we had no connection at all to that, even though some of those musicians loved Napalm.

There were other things happening around the band, which was out of our control to a degree. Our relationship with our manager, Mark Walmsley, was starting to fall apart. I got to know Mark in the late 80s through Cardiacs, who he managed, and I liked him. Napalm pretty much managed ourselves early on, but after Mickey Harris left, I felt we needed something a bit more organized, so I asked Mark. He became our first proper manager. He was good for Napalm for a long time, but then things started to go wrong.

Mark had some stuff going on his personal life and his eye wasn't on the ball. We were having problems and at some point, Mark pretty much vanished, leaving us to sort things out ourselves. We weren't the first band to have problems with their manager, and we won't be the last. But it was something else to deal with when we could have done without it.

At the same time, our relationship with Earache was coming to an end, and we'd grown together. In the early days, we were all really close. Through Napalm, Earache got bands like Carcass, Morbid Angel, Terrorizer – we'd hear them through tape trading and recommend them. But credit to Digby Pearson, who founded and ran Earache. He was the one who actually released their records when few other labels would have taken a chance on them.

Every band in history has their ups and downs with their label at various points, and Napalm were no exception. We butted heads with Earache lots of times over the years. Sometimes it was their fault, but sometimes it was ours. A record comes out, you get a bit full of yourself, you think you're more important than you are. You can behave like a twat sometimes when you're young. You can behave like a twat when you're older as well, to be honest.

Earache and Dig have got a bad rap over the years from some bands that have been on the label at various points, but I can see it from the other point of view. I tried doing a small label myself a few years later and it was tough. You're trying to balance putting out music by bands you love with all these different personalities and problems you don't foresee. It didn't help that there seemed to be some tension going on between our manager and Earache behind our backs. I never found out what it was, but that might have even forced us to do a new album, *Words From The Exit Wound*, and get it out as quickly as we did.

We had a good time making *Words From The Exit Wound*. At one point, our producer Colin Richardson went to bed and left us recording. The next morning the guitar track had disappeared. I'm still not sure what had happened – either a ghost came in or Mitch Harris accidentally deleted it.

The album came out just a year after *Inside The Torn Apart*, in June 1998. The music on that record was OK, but we were tired. We'd been doing this for a decade without a break, and things were getting tougher.

Words From The Exit Wound would be our last album for Earache. We'd signed a seven-album deal with them around the time of *Harmony Corruption*, which even our manager said was a crazy thing for us to do. To be honest, we would probably have been off the label a lot earlier if we hadn't done. By that point, the relationship between Napalm and Earache had run its course. They were probably getting as tired of us as we were of them.

Because we were coming to the end of the deal with Earache, there was very little budget to support the album. We did a small tour of our own in the UK, but it was only a few dates. Luckily, we got a tour opening for Cradle Of Filth at the end of the year, or the album wouldn't have got any support at all in Europe. We stopped off at our manager's office and basically raided it for all the CDs, vinyl and T-shirts we could get our hands on to sell on tour. That was the only money we were bringing in. We got back just before Christmas and after everything was paid off, we'd made about £400.

When you're on tour you're displaced from reality, but it hits you when you come home. I went to stay at my mom's for two weeks over Christmas. I was in my early 30s, I had no money. You don't want to be a millionaire, but you're behind on the mortgage and the bills, thinking, "What am I going to do?" I was starting to have massive anxiety attacks because of it all. It was doom and gloom.

I suppose I could have looked for a real job, but no one would employ me, and even if they did I wouldn't have lasted. The only proper job I'd had was in the steelworks back in the late 80s, and I'd ended up walking out of that to go and see a gig in London. So I was stuck with Napalm Death, except that didn't seem to be going so well.

How did I get through it? With a lot of beer and a lot of heavy metal. Friends would come over and stay at the Napalm House, we'd get drunk and play Saxon's *Wheels Of Steel* at full volume. Or we'd scrape together what money we had and go out on the piss. It was just a case of trying to get through it.

They were dark times being in Napalm Death at that point. We had no label, no manager, no direction and it felt like things were teetering right on the edge.

1999

"When you first join a band, you don't think ahead. You don't think you're going to be doing it for 10 or 12 years. Or maybe you do, but you certainly don't know what being in a band for 10 or 12 years actually involves – all the highs and lows, the fallings out, the times when you've got no money, the general stresses of it all. By the end of the 90s, I'd pretty much experienced it all.

I look back on the mid to late 90s as a weird time in Napalm Death's history – our "wandering years". We were trying to push things forward with the way the band sounded, and the albums we made during that time – *Fear, Emptiness, Despair*, *Diatribes*, *Inside The Torn Apart* and *Words From The Exit Wound* – have some really good songs on them, but there was increasingly little interest around them. It felt like people were taking us for granted a little bit. Maybe we were taking ourselves for granted. Maybe we hadn't pushed ourselves enough, or maybe we'd pushed ourselves too far away from what we were in the early days.

But a few things happened that changed things for Napalm. One key turning point was that we got a new manager, Rudy Reed. My friend Mitch Dickinson had met Rudy and liked him a lot, and Mitch suggested we meet him. We were all feeling quite lost at the time, so we didn't have anything to lose. We all piled into Barney's little car and drove down to meet Rudy. We hit it off straight away – he was a nice guy, we liked him and he seemed to like us. After a few more conversations, he agreed to manage us.

A few people had said to Rudy, "You're taking on a minefield with Napalm Death", but I think he liked the challenge. He fired us up and gave us a bit of confidence. Some managers have a way of segregating individual band members, telling one person one thing and another person something else, but that's no good – you're supposed to be a team. Rudy wasn't like that. He spoke to everyone equally. He also helped get us a new record deal with a new label called Dreamcatcher, which had been founded by a guy named

Martin Hooker. Martin used to run the label Music For Nations, which put out a load of thrash metal albums I liked in the 80s, so it made sense.

Things were starting to come around full circle musically for me too. Around the time Napalm were making *Words From The Exit Wound*, I reconnected with my friend Nick Barker. Me and Nick are like brothers. We'll have a right old ding-dong and fall out for six months, but then we'll make up and it'll be exactly like it was before. He's like me – his passion for music is insane, he's a superfan. And his love for Napalm is unparalleled.

I first met Nick when he was working as a drum tech for my mates' band Cancer in 1991. There were more than a few drunken nights back then and we got on really well. He always moans that I never asked him to join when Mickey Harris left: "Why didn't you fucking ask me?"

We lost touch a little bit after that, but a few years later I started hearing about a British black metal band called Cradle Of Filth, who had a bit of a buzz around them. I saw a photo of them and thought, "Oh, that's my mate Nick." When we were doing *Words…*, Cradle were in Birmingham recording their album *Cruelty And The Beast*, so we ended up crossing paths.

I hadn't seen Nick for a few years at that point, but it didn't take us long to properly bond again. We'd have mad drinking sessions and come back to the Napalm House and listen to music and talk about all the old thrash and grindcore albums we loved. All that coincided with a yearning I had to do something faster and crazier than Napalm Death. On the last couple of records, we were spending two or three days on a cymbal track. I missed the old-school way of doing it.

That's how Lock Up was born. Lock Up was a band Nick and I put together with Jesse Pintado, Napalm's guitarist. Me and Jesse wrote most of the songs that would appear on the first Lock Up album in the Napalm House – I had my little four-track in my bedroom. We never even bothered rehearsing. It was really spontaneous and crazy. We were just pissing around with it really.

Lee Dorrian was going to be involved in Lock Up at the start. I asked Lee if he wanted to sing, but then I somehow forgot about it.

That's the thing with Lee – sometimes you'll hear from him regularly, sometimes you won't hear from him for months. Especially back then, when there weren't really mobile phones or email. He told me that he'd written a bunch of lyrics for Lock Up: "I was ready to sing, I had lyrics, but you never let me know!" It's a shame, because it would have been great. I don't think Lee's ever forgiven me.

We ended up getting Peter Tägtgren, who had been in the Swedish death metal band Hypocrisy, to sing on the first Lock Up album, *Pleasures Pave Sewers*. I didn't know Peter very well, but Nick was a mate of his because Peter had produced a lot of the newer black metal bands. It cost £1,000 to make. It was quick and easy and fun – it was done in the spirit of the old Napalm records. It's funny, so many bands say the same thing. You start out doing things quickly and cheaply, and they sound exciting. Then the bigger budgets come in and everything starts to get a bit bogged down.

That first Lock Up album was more brutal than the Napalm albums we'd been making over the past few years. Lyrically, it was embracing the imagery of metal – demons and Satan and the occult. People thought we were trying to be some Satanic black metal band, but we were using all that imagery as metaphors for stuff that was more personal to us. I was always a huge fan of Ronnie James Dio. He was a classic lyricist – he would sing about rainbows and dragons, but there was always a deeper, more true-to-life meaning behind them. You'd try and decipher what he was really singing about on a song like 'Heaven And Hell'. You couldn't do that sort of thing in Napalm Death, so being able to do it in Lock Up was kind of satisfying.

Lock Up is something that we've kept going on and off over the years, although the line-up has changed. We did a second album, *Hate Breeds Suffering*, in 2002, with Tomas Lindberg from At The Gates replacing Peter as singer. That one cost us about £5,000 to make, but it was just as filthy sounding.

Lock Up's *The Dregs Of Hades* came out in 2021. It was recorded during lockdown, and it was really driven by the guitarist, Anton Reisenegger. Anton's a total riff monster, and he had all this stuff for a new album. Nick didn't really want to do it anymore, and I thought, "Is it really worth the effort?" But Anton was keen, so I went for it. We did it via Zoom, but it turned out really well. And it was pretty spontaneous, which was weird given the circumstances.

I've got to be honest, back in 1998/1999, Lock Up was more exciting to me than Napalm was. That was partly because my own tastes were changing. Me and Mitch Harris had spent a lot of the 90s being really excited by stuff on the more alternative side of things, and the idea of blast beats just wasn't exciting for us. Everybody was doing it, to the point where it was getting boring.

But towards the end of the decade, I started rediscovering my love of extreme music. A lot of this was down to a Swedish grindcore band called Nasum. It was Mitch Dickinson who introduced me to them. I heard them and thought, "Fucking hell, this is amazing." Even now, I'm pretty selective about what grindcore I like – if you play me a bunch of grind bands, there'll only usually be one or two at most that I like. But Nasum had something different. They were obviously fans of old-school grind and Napalm in particular, but there was a real ferocity to it that I hadn't heard in a long time. I remember Mitch Harris saying, "What do you like about this band so much?" I couldn't really break it down. It just sounded so fucking exciting.

Hearing Nasum gave me the kick I needed. Between that and Lock Up, it made me think that Napalm needed to step up. Mitch was a bit strange about it: "Why are you suddenly back into this stuff?" I wasn't suddenly back into it, it's just that certain things were vibing me up that hadn't done for years. There's lots of music that I love and that I've loved for years, but I always like to keep searching out new things to keep things interesting. You might not like everything you hear, but sometimes just a little bit of something can inspire you and lead you down a completely different path. Buzz Osborne from Melvins calls me a "musical anthropologist". That's a good description.

Coincidentally, Rudy was doing some work with a producer named Simon Efemey. I knew Simon from going to gigs at the Birmingham Odeon in the early 80s – Saxon, AC/DC, Tygers Of Pan Tang. Simon had gone on to work with bands like the Wonder Stuff, who I was a big fan of, but we'd lost touch over the years. So it was really great to reconnect with him after all that time.

The first thing we recorded with Simon and his engineer, Russ Russell, was the *Leaders Not Followers* EP. It was our manager Rudy's suggestion to record a covers EP, but we were up for the idea – it was a chance to pay tribute to some of our influences. We did 'Maggots In Your Coffin' by the US band Repulsion, which was an obvious one because they'd been a huge influence on Napalm in the early days – they were one of the very first grindcore bands, even though they never actually got to release a proper album until after they'd split up.

I'd always wanted to cover a Canadian band called Slaughter – we did a song called 'Incinerated', purely because we knew Mitch's guitar would sound heavy as fuck on it, and it did. The other bands we covered were Raw Power, Possessed and Death – all had influenced us when we were younger. That's the thing about Napalm – we never hide what or who our influences are. If we rip off a riff from some other band, we'll always admit to it.

No disrespect to Colin Richardson, who had produced the last five or six Napalm albums and was a great guy, but Simon and Russ brought a different energy to the session for *Leaders Not Followers*. We'd be in there, drinking and rocking out to 'Neon Knights' by Black Sabbath. We hadn't done that for a while, and it felt good. It wasn't about getting hammered, it was about having a vibe, and Simon was really good at bringing that out. Mainly because he's nuts, in a good way.

The *Leaders Not Followers* EP came out in October 1999 and it went down well. People saw it as Napalm Death reconnecting with their roots, which is really what it was. The first Lock Up album had come out a few months earlier and that did pretty well, and I was about to record another album with the band Brujeria. After the doom and gloom of the past few years, it felt like things were starting to turn around.

EYE WITNESS: BILLY GOULD

Bassist, Faith No More / Brujeria

Billy Gould had never heard anything like Napalm Death when a friend popped one of their cassettes on in his car as they were driving around San Francisco. It was the late 80s, and Gould was the bass player with acclaimed US band Faith No More, whose catholic sound spanned everything from funk to post-punk.

"My friend and all his buddies were into the whole Earache thing, which was completely unknown to me," says Gould. "So it was a whole new area of music that I got exposed to all at once." Part of the attraction for Gould was how far Napalm Death pushed things without ever descending into noise for its own sake. "There was definitely an aesthetic approach to what they were doing," he says. "It wasn't about virtuosity – they were using music as a kind of lever to get something accomplished with it. Metallica had been a departure from traditional metal in that it was more aggressive than what had come before, but Napalm Death were taking things to a much greater extreme. To me it was really interesting."

What Gould didn't know was that the admiration extended both ways. Five thousand miles away in Birmingham, Faith No More were a major influence on Shane Embury – not necessarily in the way he played within the confines of Napalm Death, but certainly in terms of opening up his mind to the possibilities of what could be done within the parameters of rock music.

These two like-minded musicians met in the flesh in late 1989, when Faith No More played Nottingham's Rock City club. Shane made his way over from Birmingham earlier in the day to attend an in-store signing by the American band.

"We met properly at the signing and we got a tour of the Earache offices," says Gould. "It surprised me that Shane liked Faith No More, because I felt like we were a pop band next to Napalm Death. But what really struck me was how easy they were to talk to. When I had a conversation with them for the first time, it was no different to talking to the people I knew back home."

A friendship quickly blossomed. Gould and his bandmates

would go to rock clubs with Napalm Death whenever they had a night off in Birmingham. The members of Faith No More would attend Napalm shows in their native San Francisco, where the British band had a small but dedicated following. "There was a core of people, a very specific group, who knew about them," says Gould. "Weirdly, it never really penetrated the Bay Area metal scene, which was really vibrant at the time. Napalm Death's crowd was very much their own crowd."

It was via his friendship with Gould that Shane ended up in Brujeria. "I went to school with a guy named Juan Brujo. Brujo and his crowd of people lived in East LA, where there was a huge connection between the Latin community and grindcore."

Gould and Brujo founded Brujeria at the end of the 80s, garnering notoriety on the grindcore scene for their deliberately offensive, Spanish-language lyrics.

"It was fun – it wasn't supposed to be like a regular rock band with all the politics and problems," says Gould. "We could have rotating members. Anybody could be a member of Brujeria at any given time."

One of those people was Shane, who took part in the drunken recording sessions for Brujeria's first album, *Matando Güeros*. "It was a complete party atmosphere," says Gould. "Somebody would be playing guitar and somebody else would play bass while everybody sat around drinking beer and eating burritos. Then somebody in the control room would say, 'Hey, I want to do something', and they'd hop on the guitar."

The pair's musical collaboration didn't end when Gould left Brujeria in 1999. The Faith No More bassist was one of several musicians Shane enlisted to play on the debut album by Tronos, the band he put together with Napalm producer Russ Russell.

"I like Shane's musical sensibility," says Gould. "He's got a strong inner voice and a real personality in what he does. It's good for me because he doesn't follow clichés – the chords he uses and what he does all comes from him."

Similarly, Gould's admiration for Napalm Death remains undimmed more than 30 years after he first met them.

"I've seen them play so many times over the years, and I've never seen a bad show," he says. "They completely stand out from any other band they play with, in a measurable way. There are times when I've thought, 'I'm a little tired tonight, I don't know if I should go see them'. Then I end up going and every time it reminds me how great they are."

"I've seen them touring in tough conditions, I've seen them crashing out in one room. But they're still into doing the shows and putting everything into it. And that's admirable."

2000

"Even if you're wrapped up in your own band, you're aware of scenes changing around you. Napalm Death had seen grindcore, death metal and nu metal all come along. We'd always stuck to what we wanted to do, for better or for worse. But hearing Nasum and being involved with Lock Up had made me think, "Napalm needs to step up."

Barney was thinking along the same lines. The *Leaders Not Followers* covers EP was a bit of a reset for us, and he was as vibed up about going back towards a more extreme sound as I was. In fairness, there had been a little bit of that on our last album, *Words From The Exit Wounds*. There were tracks like 'The Infiltraitor', which had a bit of old-school blasting in it. But looking back, I can tell our hearts weren't fully into it at that point.

Me and Barney had a conversation about where we'd go next, and the idea of Napalm doing something faster and more extreme. He said, "Let's go for it. But if we're going to do it, let's do it properly." We'd been talking about doing a split album with Nasum, and I'd written some tracks for it and demoed them on a four-track. I played them for Barney, and he went, "Fucking hell, yes."

Nasum had definitely renewed my interest in grindcore, but that wasn't the only thing I was listening to. I was hanging out with Nick Barker and his mates in the Napalm House, having these mad sessions, and they'd be listening to black metal. That stuff had pretty much passed me by when it was all kicking off, partly because they were really sniffy about Napalm at the time, but I was listening to Emperor and thinking, "I like some of these riffs, I can incorporate some of this stuff into what we're doing and make it ours."

Mitch was slower in wanting to return to doing more of a grind album than me and Barney, even though I think the songs we were writing were more than just grindcore. It wasn't that we wanted to remake *Scum* or *From Enslavement To Obliteration*, but we wanted it to have the same impact as those records did, but 12 or 13 years later.

The experience of recording the new album was different to the previous few albums. We were down in Parkgate with Simon Efemey and Russ Russell, a residential studio near Hastings. It was nice to lock ourselves away from everything else, there was a lot of camaraderie to it all. We'd go into Battle and hang out and talk about what we wanted to achieve with it. We were all on the same page. We were getting to know Russ Russell – him and Simon are pretty much brothers to us these days, but we didn't really know him that well back then. Russ would become really important to Napalm later on.

When I look back, we'd had a lot hanging over us while recording some of those late 90s albums, sometimes to the point where it had distracted us. And Colin Richardson had always got a great production, but in Napalm we were constantly treading a fine line between wanting stuff to sound good and wanting things to be full-on. Barney always says that we're an unapologetic noise band. I'm not sure I completely agree with that. We make a good racket, but there are structures in our songs.

But this time things felt different. We still had a few money problems, but musically it was a great record to me. Simon was pushing us to go a little bit further, just to give it a go. When the other guys had gone to bed, me and Simon would stay up late and rock out to AC/DC's *Powerage*. AC/DC had an edge to them: the guitar was really in your face. That's what we wanted.

Somebody once told me that Napalm Death were "enemies of the music business", and I loved that phrase. It was the perfect title for the album. I'm not one of those people who hates record labels. I've had bad experiences a few times, but I've had more good ones. But Napalm still felt like outsiders in the wider music industry, even though I was starting to see bands like Slipknot come through who said they'd been influenced by us. So we called the album *Enemy Of The Music Business* – it fitted the music perfectly.

With the last few records we did on Earache, I got a sense that they were wavering about the band: "Another Napalm album?" To be fair, they were probably as fed up of us as we were of them. But this time people seemed to be paying more attention than they had in a while. The album got some great reviews, and we did the main stage at Wacken, the massive German festival. That was a crazy show, and we ended up doing a load of press around it, which showed that people really were into it. It was nice to realize that somebody actually gave a shit after doing it for that many years.

Just before *Enemy Of The Music Business* came out, *Kerrang!* gave us their Spirit Of Independence Award at their annual awards ceremony. I'm normally pretty sceptical about that kind of thing, but they got John Peel to present us with that award. He'd supported us so much in the early days and genuinely loved the band, so that felt really special.

That was only the second time I'd ever met him. There's only a couple of people I've ever been awestruck to meet, and he was one of them. John died in 2004. He was only in his mid-60s, far too young. He was still interested in stuff other people weren't into even at that age. In a weird way, we've tried to emulate him on some of the later Napalm Death albums by having a classic Napalm song followed by something that's really out there.

I finally got to go around to his house a few years after he died. The family have a website called The John Peel Archives, and they get people from different bands to pick tracks from his record collection. They wanted someone from Napalm to get involved, and I jumped at the chance to do it. I went to his house where his records are still kept. His collection is massive – literally thousands and thousands of albums and singles, all numbered and indexed. It starts at the top of the house and goes all the way down – part of the floor is cut out to get it all in. We'd done a split flexi-disc with the Japanese band S.O.B. – it was totally rare, but he had 10 copies of it. I ended up picking stuff by Slade, Sweet, Crass, Repulsion, Metallica – it was a journey through my childhood.

Peel wasn't the only person I got to meet at that awards ceremony. For some reason, they'd invited Green Day to pick up an award and asked Wattie from The Exploited to give it to them. I remember seeing The Exploited playing their single on *Top Of The Pops* – these mad, obnoxious punks with massive mohicans. My mom said, "Look at the state of their hair." I said, "Mom, this is amazing."

When Wattie presented Green Day with this award he absolutely laid into them onstage: "Fucking fake punk band, fuck them."

It was absolute comedy, though I'm not sure Green Day found it so funny. I met Wattie afterwards and we got on straight away. Drinks were drunk and various substances were consumed in the toilet. He has a really strong Scottish accent – but the drunker I got, the more I seemed to be able to understand him.

A few years later, we played in Scotland and Wattie was there. After the show, he said to me, "You oughta come and have a fucking beer in ma local." So me and Simon Efemey, who was doing our sound, get in his car and he drives off. He's driving through all these red lights: "Ah, nobody round here's going to stop me." We end up in this pub and just carry on drinking and doing various other things. I'm thinking, "I was watching this guy play 'Dead Cities' on *Top Of The Pops* when I was 13 years old." I was hungover as hell the next day. But it was Wattie; it was worth it.

Napalm Death and The Exploited did a festival in France years ago, and some magazine took a photo of me and Wattie, which they used as a big poster. On one side of the poster you've got a couple of female metal singers, and you flip it over and you've got these two big, ugly blokes absolutely wired off our tits. I want to find that picture and get it framed.

We got to go on tour with Nasum in Europe at the end of 2000. More than anyone, they were the band that had given me a kick up the arse around the time we were leaving Earache, so it was nice to get the chance to play with them. We got to know those guys well on that tour, and the whole experience was pretty eventful. For some reason Mitch Harris decided to jump off a roof on the first or second date of the tour and broke his foot. Most people would have decided to go home at that point, but not Mitch. He carried on, playing with his foot in a cast, which was pretty heroic.

A couple of days later, our tour bus broke down so we ended up touring in two separate vans. Barney and our guitar tech Stevie were driving one, our tour manager Jez Hale was driving the other. Mitch was in one van with his foot up, smoking hash. Jesse Pintado was in the same van, traumatizing everybody by quoting lines from TV's *The Fast Show* non-stop: "You ain't seen me, right?" Well, it was traumatizing certain people.

At the same time, Russ Russell was in the back making all this crazy techno music, and Jez was playing All Saints non-stop just because he loved them, and all these heavy metal musicians were singing along to it. Nasum were in the other van. Their bassist, Jesper, had a drink of somebody's Pepsi, except it had something a lot stronger than caffeine in it. The poor bastard couldn't sleep for three days.

The whole thing was totally delirious. At one point we stayed in this apartment and I had a dream that I was in the movie *Tron*. The whole place seemed to be made of wires, but I also saw blackness and stars and heard an angelic chorus. I thought, "If this is dying, it's not that bad." Then I threw up all over Mitch's shoes and went back to sleep.

That was the point where I thought, "I need to take a break, this is too much." Of course, that was never going to happen.

2001

In April 2001, we played Malaysia for the first time. I was well aware of the scene there because I was tape trading with people there years before. They liked their grindcore and their metal as much as anyone in the UK and the US. It sounds cheesy to say it, but this kind of music really does cross boundaries.

We played a show in the Malaysian capital, Kuala Lumpur. It was absolutely nuts. The place was rammed and sweaty, and kids were leaping off the stage. It was the kind of gig that reminded me of being 18 and going crazy. We probably didn't make a lot of money going to Malaysia, but that wasn't the point. It was a chance to play to people who had never seen Napalm Death before. To go to a place where they've not experienced this kind of music live is such a great feeling. It really makes you realize why you do this.

But there was more to it for me than just playing a gig. I love going somewhere different and experiencing something I've never experienced before. You meet people from different cultures, you get to eat food you'd never eat anywhere else, you see things you never even thought about seeing.

I come from a small village in Shropshire where everybody knew everybody else's business. You'd see other countries on the TV, but you never dreamed of ending up in any of them. Broseley was my comfort zone when I was young, but Napalm Death opened up the world to me.

I've lost count of all the countries and cities we've been to over the years. We've always tried to play as many different places as we can, just for the experience of it. The first time you go somewhere new, it's always memorable. We went to Russia for the first time in 1991. It was just as Communism was collapsing, and you could see the separation. McDonalds and Pizza Hut had just opened, and people were desperate to try this new Western food, but they didn't have enough rubles so they'd literally offer to trade you their coats for pounds or dollars.

We were playing two arena shows in Russia, 7,000 people a night, and we were headlining. They were the biggest shows we'd done. The people in the crowd hadn't experienced anything like us before, so they were swinging their hair and coats around. Security just didn't know what to do, and they were getting really heavy-handed, shoving people and dragging them out.

Napalm have been back to Russia quite a few times over the years, and because of that we've ended up playing shows in some of the neighbouring countries too. We've been to Belarus, Albania, Georgia, even Kazakhstan. In Georgia, they took us out to eat and there were about 900 plates on the table – so hospitable and generous. They treated us like kings, even though they might not have had a lot of money. You're lucky to get a three-day-old sandwich at some of the places we've played in the UK.

The world is a lot more connected now, but back in the 90s it wasn't. Albania and Kazakhstan were really under the radar in terms of touring – bands just didn't go there. But every gig we played was amazing, and the people were just so knowledgeable. There was one fan who turned up with a ton of Napalm Death stuff, 99 per cent of which was legitimate. He had stuff that I never even knew existed: "Where the hell did you get this from?" I spent about three hours with him signing his records. The last time we toured Russia, he ended up promoting a show for us.

We've been to South America quite a few times over the years, and it's always crazy down there. We played Brazil around the time of the *Harmony Corruption* record in 1990, but we didn't go back there until 1997. That second time, we had some shows lined up with the Brazilian band Krisiun opening for us. It was probably the first proper South American tour a band of our ilk had done.

We'd been brought over by a Dutch guy who lived out there named Eric de Haas. The first show was supposed to be in Cascavel, but it didn't happen. Eric said he'd go and see what was going on. He said to us, "Guys, stay right here, do not leave until you I come back." So we waited and he eventually came back. The first thing he said, "You need to get on the bus right now, we have to go."

It turns out the guy had said to Eric: "The band needs to play." Eric has this crazy laugh and he laughed in the promoter's face. Then the guy gets heavy, which is when Eric decided we need to get out of there. I remember hurtling down the road in the bus in the middle of this crazy thunderstorm while being chased by someone or other. It was scary, but we were young and stupid – we were pissing ourselves laughing.

South America can be quite hairy. Some places we weren't allowed to leave the hotel without security and once I went off to the shops on my own once and got an absolute bollocking when I got back – I could have been mugged or worse. There's been a couple of times where the McDonald's next door to where we stay has got 24-hour security and a sniper on the roof. We played a gig once where the stage was built on scaffolding that was so rickety it seemed like it could break at any moment.

But the atmosphere and energy at South American shows is always insane. In Santiago, Chile, there is always a contingent of fans who don't want to pay to get in so they rush the door just before the show. That was one of the best gigs I've ever played. There were something like 5,000 people there, and when they got into it, this football chant went up: "Oh-ay, oh-ay, oh-ay, Napalm! Napalm!" I was standing there and I flashed back to my eight-year-old self, living in Broseley and listening to Slade. At one point during the show, my bass stopped working. The tech was trying to fix it while 5,000 people were throwing shit at the poor guy.

Columbia was eventful too. We were playing this bullfighting ring in the city of Medellín. It was election week and politicians were getting shot, so there was already craziness in the air. We got there to find out that somebody from the local authorities had decided they didn't want the show to happen. The military police looked very scary and we weren't about to argue with them, so we left.

The only problem was that a bunch of people had turned up expecting to see us play, and the gig had been cancelled. Not surprisingly, they weren't happy and they kicked off. There was a 100-year-old statue of a bullfighter that got pushed into the river. Then they set fire to the big wooden door to the venue. It was chaos, but we couldn't do anything about it.

We were playing in Bogotá the next day, so people thought, "OK, we'll just go see them there." All these fans came down from

Medellín, except the Bogotá show was sold out and they couldn't get in. There was a total riot before the gig even started. The military police were there, tanks, tear gas. We didn't know what to do – it wasn't like Napalm Death had caused a riot before.

The local promoter said, "Please, you have to play this show." So we said we'd play the gig. We walked into the venue and everything was smashed up, there was broken glass everywhere, but the weirdest thing was that the gig itself was really mellow.

We've had some weird exchanges in South America. In Argentina, they interviewed our guitarist Jesse, and they made it seem like he was living in some huge mansion in England and that we were some raging capitalists raking in loads of money. They should have come and stayed at the Napalm House for a couple of nights. They'd have realized how far from the truth that was.

Napalm have always been popular in South America when other places have lost interest. We played there when the whole nu metal thing was blowing up. I've got a video of us in Chile, and there's a massive turnout at the show. Then we got back to Europe and we're playing to a couple of hundred people in the small room at the Markthalle in Hamburg. The fans in South America have never been governed by MTV or any of that stuff. They're into what they're into, which is really admirable.

I've thought quite a lot about why Napalm Death are popular in certain countries, especially in places like South America and Asia. It's down to the music for sure – that means a lot to people. I'm not a political person, but Napalm have always stood with the oppressed, whether it's down to race or sexual preference or just being beaten up by the authorities. That's reflected in the lyrics, and it's something people grab on to. They fight for this music, they fight to hear it.

We played a show in Zagreb in Croatia in 1996 with At The Gates. The war had only ended a few months before, and we were one of the first bands to go over there. You could still see the effects of it. We have a song called 'Contemptuous'. The lyrics are: "Sadness, despair/Sometimes the things I cherish are all I've got." This young girl came up to me, and she'd had it tattooed on her arm. That's when you realize something you've done has had a real impact on someone's life. At that same gig, me and Tomas, the singer from At

The Gates, had a few cases of Coca-Cola. We started giving it out to these kids and they just lost it because it was probably the first Coke they'd been able to get their hands on in a long time.

We've been to a lot of places where people have come up to me and said, "I started my band because of you." It makes me proud, but it's also a weird feeling. When you're writing a song, you never think it might impact people thousands and thousands of miles away years later. That still happens even now.

I think of all the places I've been with Napalm, and it's incredible. Being in Israel and sitting inside a van that's literally being shaken from side to side by fans who are so happy that you're there. Or travelling through Russia at night and getting to where you're going at 3 o'clock in the morning and being greeted by two girls who are waiting with shots of vodka. Or visiting the Aztec temples near Mexico City then going through this heavy metal market called El Chopo, checking out all the bootleg shirts. I couldn't have afforded those experiences if it weren't for the band.

It's funny, when I was a kid I think I was afraid to leave Broseley. The world looked like a big place. But I've been to a lot of places and met a lot of people, and I've realized it's not so big after all.

EYE WITNESS: DAN TOBIN

Former Earache Records press officer

Like many people in the late 80s, Dan Tobin discovered Napalm Death through John Peel's radio show. "I was in my girlfriend's kitchen and this racket came out of the radio," he says. "I was thinking, 'What the hell is that?' I was into heavy stuff, but I'd never heard anything like it."

The next day he went into his local record shop. "I said to the guy who was working there, 'I heard this thing on the radio last night, it sounds like a massive noise.' And he just said: 'Napalm Death'."

Tobin walked out of the shop with the band's second album, *From Enslavement To Obliteration*, under his arm. While the support of John Peel and a subsequent *NME* cover had put paid to the idea of Napalm Death being a truly underground phenomenon, they were still beyond the pale for most listeners.

"A lot of people, even metal fans, thought Napalm Death were a joke because they were so extreme," says Tobin. "The Radio 1 DJ Steve Wright had a quiz on his afternoon show, and the punishment for getting a question wrong was being blasted with Napalm Death. Idiotic, but that's how they were viewed."

Tobin saw the band play live several times, but didn't meet them until he started working at their label, Earache, as a press officer in 1994. "I was a bit in awe of Napalm, but Shane especially was really friendly," he says. "Shane was good friends with Mitch Dickinson, who was working at Earache at that time. We'd all end up at Mitch's, nerding out on records and listening to the two of them talking about seeing bands at the Mermaid in Birmingham.

"With Shane, though, you could talk about bands that you wouldn't talk to other people in metal circles about – This Mortal Coil, Dead Can Dance, the Cocteau Twins. Stupidly, I thought the members of Napalm Death would just listen to grindcore, which of course they didn't."

Tobin joined Earache around the time Napalm Death released *Fear, Emptiness, Despair*, which saw them dialling down the extremity of their earlier releases a notch.

"There was some tension in the band," says Tobin of that period. "They thought, 'Do we stick with what we know for the rest of our lives and become the AC/DC of extreme metal, or do we do something different?' Of course, with Shane and Mitch Harris being interested in so many different kinds of music, there was no way they were going to stay the same."

The metal scene itself was changing. American bands such as Fear Factory, Sepultura and Machine Head were pushing the boundaries of the genre forward, retooling it sonically and aesthetically for the modern era. Napalm Death were taking the same approach with *Fear, Emptiness, Despair* and follow-up *Diatribes*, though they struggled to have the same commercial impact as their US counterparts.

"Rock City in Nottingham was probably the biggest rock club in the country at that point," says Tobin. "We badgered the DJs to play 'Greed Killing', which was a song we felt was a good modern representation of Napalm Death. It was the first time anybody would have heard it. They put 'Greed Killing' on and the floor just emptied. Then they put Fear Factory on and it filled up again."

That reaction was disappointing, but not disastrous. Napalm still had the support of Earache, even if tensions sometimes arose between band and label owner Digby Pearson.

"Napalm's success was a mutual effort – as brilliant as they were, it was Dig who put out those early records and he undoubtedly hyped them up to the BBC for the *Arena* documentary," says Tobin. "Things inevitably change, and people go from being mates having a laugh together to it being a business with more staff being hired and more outgoings. Egos start coming into it, on both sides."

Despite that, Tobin says that Earache still wanted the best for Napalm Death. Label and band pushed to make the band seem relevant in the changing musical climate, but the band's profile in the music press had tailed off. Matters weren't helped by Barney Greenway's sudden departure in 1996 and equally sudden return months later.

"That was chaotic," says Tobin. "Earache were spending money on Napalm Death, and all they were getting out of it was musical chairs between bands."

Things got even more chaotic a few years later. Napalm Death's original manager, Mark Walmsley, seemingly vanished, breaking off contact with the band and leaving them with serious financial worries. At the same time, their contract with Earache was almost up. *Words From The Exit Wound*, released in 1998, would be their last album on the label.

"There were many reasons that relationship ended," says Tobin. "Napalm were in a bit of turmoil around that time, but Earache had changed too. The label had gone from being reliant on extreme bands like Napalm Death, Morbid Angel and Carcass and were signing newer and more contemporary bands. When anything new and shiny comes along, some people are going to be excited by it and some people are going to have their noses put out of joint. Plus Napalm got a new manager, Rudy Reed. Almost overnight it went from a few grumbles into what was pretty much a war, with lawyers involved. It was a combination of factors."

Despite the fractious end of Napalm Death's time with Earache, Tobin remained in contact with the band. Inspired by a chance meeting with Michael Eavis at the 2016 Glastonbury festival, he persuaded the festival's organizers to let Napalm Death play the following year.

"They'd only had about three heavy bands ever play Glastonbury, which is ridiculous," he says. "I just badgered them until they caved in. Even then they said, 'OK, you can have one band, that's it.' It had to be Napalm – it was a no-brainer. Glastonbury is a political festival, you couldn't put Mötley Crüe on because that would be playing into their idea of what metal was."

Napalm were booked to play the Shangri-La area, which held around 4,000 people. Half an hour before the band were due onstage, the field was empty. By the time they came on, it was packed.

"There were a few Napalm Death shirts and some people had come because they thought it would be a bit of a novelty, for sure," says Tobin. "But most people were curious. What they got was Barney doing some brilliant between-song banter about slum land-lords and women's rights. The guy who ran the area turned to me and said, 'They're speaking the language of Shangri-La', which is the most Glastonbury thing he could have said."

For Tobin, who left Earache in 2020 after more than 25 years at the label, that Glastonbury appearance embodied Shane Embury's willingness to push against expectations of what the band should and shouldn't be, irrespective of what other people thought about it.

"Years ago, I remember being in a bar in Nottingham with them," says Tobin. "We were having a few drinks and there were these punks in the other corner who were giving him grief: 'You're a sell-out.' Shane just said, 'Selling out what? Who am I selling out to?' They wouldn't stop, so in the end, he dropped his trousers, bent over and showed them his arse. What else can you do?"

2002

“ Sometimes with Napalm Death it feels like we take one step forward and then one step back. The *Enemy Of The Music Business* album had re-energized the band. Thanks to the influence bands like Nasum were having on us, we'd reconnected with our extreme roots and people suddenly seemed to be interested in us again.

Napalm's new album, *Order Of The Leech*, came out in October 2002 and it seemed to carry on the momentum. Musically, it's a good album – it loses a bit on the drum sound compared to *Enemy*, but it's still pretty fired up. But as always with Napalm there was stuff going on in the background that was distracting us.

One those things was money. We'd had problems a few years earlier with a VAT bill . We'd worked hard to get ourselves out of that hole, touring whenever we could, but there were still financial issues hanging over us. I don't think me and Barney were properly addressing what was happening on that front – I certainly wasn't. These days, Barney especially is all over the financial side of things, but back then we didn't really have a clue. We were musicians, not accountants. Musicians want to play, and that's when they get taken advantage of in the music business.

It also felt like me and Barney were starting to drift apart again a little bit. When we made *Enemy Of The Music Business*, we were all there in the studio together. With *Order Of The Leech*, Barney came down to the studio, did his vocals and left. I understand why now – we're in our early 30s, we all have our lives to lead. But I didn't really understand it back then.

Things were also starting to get a bit weird with Jesse Pintado. He was the loveliest guy, but he had a lot going on around that time. Jesse had a long-term relationship that fell apart, and that hit him hard. He was drinking a lot more too, which was having an effect on his life.

I was no saint when it came to drinking, especially on the road. When you go on tour, it's so easy to pick up a can of beer and spend the day drinking, unless you're really disciplined. That's all good and fun, but then you come home and you can't spend your days like that. I was lucky, I knew when to turn it off. I'd find ways of occupying my time – watching horror movies or reading books or collecting stuff. Jesse didn't have that off switch. He'd come back off tour and carry on drinking. The booze began to fill up his time more and more, and it was changing him as a person.

Jesse started to become a little flaky around the time of *Order Of The Leech*. Right before we were due to start it, he said that he was going off to do a project with someone or other. I said, "We're going in the studio in four days." He said, "Don't worry, fool. I'll be back in a few days." But he wasn't, so we had to do it without him. He ended up not playing on *Order Of The Leech*.

As I've said, I was no model of sobriety. I had lots of mad times when I was drinking. One memorable occasion was when we played a festival called Mind Over Matter in Austria in 1999. The plan was to drive out on the tour bus, play a festival in Switzerland one day and the Mind Over festival the next, then come home. It was basically a weekend away. I said to a few mates, "There's room on the bus, does anybody want to come to these shows with us." So a few people piled in – Nick Barker was there, Frank Healy from the band Benediction, and a couple of other people.

We were leathered before we even left Dover. We stopped off in the French city of Metz, which is where things began to get ridiculous. We all hit a few bars, and got even more tanked up. Our producer, Simon Efemey, was doing our live sound. For some reason, Simon enjoys getting naked when he's drunk. On the way back to the bus from the bar, we went past a fountain. Simon decided that he wanted to strip off and run around naked in this fountain, and I decided to join him. There was a policeman there, so Simon went up to him and said, "Do you mind if we take off our clothes and get in the fountain." The policeman looked at him suspiciously and then went, "OK, yes. We'll give you five minutes, then you've got to get back on your bus." So we spent the next five minutes splashing around in this fountain, absolutely pissed and stark-bollock naked.

As it turned out, the first show in Switzerland had been cancelled, so we turned up at the Mind Over Matter festival still drunk.

At this point, Nick Barker proceeded to buy three bottles of Tequila to keep the party going. We polished them off between us, and then me, Nick, Simon and Frank Healy stripped off again and spent most of the day running around this festival naked. I can't even begin to imagine what that looked like – four large, crazy, drunken, naked Englishmen terrorizing people. Thank fuck camera phones hadn't been invented back then, or I'd never be able to live it down.

Our poor tour manager, Jez, was trying to round us all up. As soon as he got us on the bus, one of us would run off. It was like trying to herd cats. Really pissed-up cats. Eventually, we all ended up in the back lounge of the bus, headbanging to Judas Priest and Saxon – still naked, of course. Barney, Mitch and Danny were looking at us, like, "What the fuck are you doing?" Funnily enough, we all put our clothes back on before we went to bed.

I've drunk a lot over the years and woken up with my fair share of hangovers, but I wouldn't say that I've ever been an alcoholic because I always knew when to stop. I was a binge-drinker – I wouldn't drink for a while, then you go on tour or play festivals and you go mad. It's partly a self-destructive thing – this is how you're supposed to behave when you're in a band. I think it might partly be a shyness thing too. If you're not the most naturally out-going person, it helps break down those barriers. And of course sometimes you just want to be an idiot. But eventually, you start thinking, "Why do I want to be an idiot? What do I gain from that?"

I had a wake-up call when it came to drinking in 2002. I'd been getting really bloated on tour, and it was intensely painful. I thought it was an extreme form of IBS, but our tour manager Jez thought it was something else. I ended up in hospital in Germany, where they told me I had acute pancreatitis. With pancreatitis, what happens is that the enzymes that are supposed to digest your food are eating into the flesh of your stomach, which can be linked to the alcohol you're drinking. It's intensely painful – you can't go to the toilet, you feel so bloated. I ended up missing a gig on that tour because of it, which I was absolutely gutted about.

It did have the effect of stopping me drinking for a few years, but bit by bit the drinking started to seep back in. It was partly just boredom – I'd get drunk, put some heavy metal on and have a session on it. And then in 2010, I started to get ill again.

We were on the road in the US, and I was feeling the same as I had in 2002. I knew the signs, so I went to a local clinic in Atlanta. They wanted to put me straight in the hospital, but that would have costed me an arm and a leg. I thought, "I know the score – don't eat much, take sips of water." I took some painkillers and lay in the back of the bus for a month. It wasn't as severe that time, but I knew it could develop that way. The painkillers were nice and I lost a bit of weight, so it wasn't all bad.

Poor old Jesse wasn't as lucky. Around the time of *Order Of The Leech*, his drinking was becoming quite serious. I was really close to him, and it was tough to see. We ended up telling him to go home to Los Angeles to spend some time with his family and try to get himself sorted. Of course, you can tell someone they need to get help, but they've got to want it themselves. Unfortunately, that wasn't where Jesse was at.

The period around *Order Of The Leech* felt weird and disjointed, and not just because of what was happening with Jesse. We'd made a good record, but things had slowed down again with Napalm. We played a few UK shows at the end of the year just after the album came out, and we did a three-week US tour at the start of the following year, but it was nothing like some of the tours we'd done there in the past. The last two albums hadn't been properly distributed in the States, so our profile had dropped a little bit across there too. And then there was this sense that we were all drifting apart again. One step forward, one step back.

2003

66 When I played live with Brujeria for the first time in 2003, there was one rule: don't die on tour.

Brujeria are a band I've been involved with on and off since the early 90s. It's the brainchild of a guy named Brujo, who is one of the craziest people I know. At that point in 2003, Napalm had gone a bit quiet. We'd done a few shows at the start of the year, but that was it aside from one or two festival gigs in the summer. Me, Barney and our manager Rudy were trying to address those overdue VAT issues, which was fairly exhausting. I figured I'd go to the States and hide away from reality a bit. So when Brujo asked if I wanted to play a few shows with Brujeria, I thought, "Why not?"

Billy Gould had told me about this mad Mexican guy he'd gone to high school with back in LA. This guy, Brujo, was the lead singer in a band called Brujeria, which means "Witchcraft" in Spanish. Brujo and a mate of his called Junior had come over to Reading to hang out with Billy and Faith No More.

We got talking and just hit it off. I told them I was planning to come over to the States to stay at Mitch's house in Vegas and then head across to Los Angeles to see Jane's Addiction. Brujo said we should hang out when I got to LA, and we ended up spending a bit of time together. He drives this old black police car, which was pretty funny – he's one of those people who knows everybody and everybody knows him.

Brujo doesn't come from a musical background, but he and his friends loved Terrorizer, the band Jesse was in before Napalm Death. Latin American kids loved grindcore generally, and Brujo thought, "Let's do a band that speaks for them." Their music and lyrics were totally OTT, but in a way that American death metal bands weren't. Their songs were all about drug lords and gruesome killings and the occult, but it was done in a way that was absolutely hilarious. I don't speak much Spanish but Jesse's father used to laugh all the time whenever we listened to Brujeria, and Brujo would be there laughing because Jesse's dad was cracking up. It's not as on-point lyrically as Napalm, but Brujeria really speaks to its audience, and there's a lot of humour involved.

Billy has played bass on all the Brujeria albums because he went way back with Brujo, and Dino Cazares from the band Fear Factory was in there too, but they never revealed their identities. They built up a myth that they were Mexican drug lords. They had some crazy launch party for one of their early seven-inch singles in San Francisco where every seven-inch supposedly came with a gramme of cocaine. I wasn't at that one, but knowing Brujo I can imagine how nuts it was.

I happened to be staying at Jesse's place in LA when Brujeria were recording their debut album. Brujo said, "I want you to play on the record, this is the studio, be there." I was going to see Alice In Chains that night, so I put my bass in the trunk of the car I was using, went to the gig, then drove over to the studio in Glendale with Jesse.

We got to the studio and just started recording these riffs. I was absolutely shitfaced. Jesse, who didn't really drink at that time, was so pissed he couldn't even play a riff. Junior, who was there as well, said, "You can't be that drunk Shane, I can still understand you", but I have very little memory of that session. I know I was there, because I've seen footage of it, but beyond that, it's a blur. I remember getting the finished album and listening to one of the songs and thinking: "That sounds really like Napalm Death." When I watched the video back, and it was me playing on it. I didn't have a clue.

The album, *Matando Güeros*, came out in 1993. "Güeros" was slang for white Americans, and "Matando" meant kill, so it pretty much meant "Kill Whitey". The cover was very controversial – it was a photo of somebody holding up a severed head. Not surprisingly, it was banned in quite a few countries. I'd love to tell you which songs I was on from that album, but I honestly can't remember. Although, one is called "Granudos Locos", which is "Crazy Longhairs" – that's definitely one of mine. But beyond that, I have no idea.

There are some great characters in and around the band. Brujo's cousin, Pinché Peach, is like the Bez of Brujeria – he's quite straight offstage, but once he gets up there and goes off, he's a lunatic. At one point, there were three vocalists onstage – Brujo, Peach and Fantasma. Fantasma was a guy named Pat Hoed, who used to call himself Adam Bomb and did a radio show where he'd interview bands like Slayer. Pat was also in a punk band called Down By Law – he's beyond knowledgeable about that scene. Then you'd get Dino and his crew hanging around. It was total chaos.

We all had our nicknames in Brujeria. Billy was Güero Sin Fe, Dino was Asesino, and I was Hongo. What I like about Brujeria is that no one takes it too seriously. There's a rotating cast of characters involved and sessions happen when they happen. There was a seven-inch called 'El Patron' at one point, which was dedicated to the late drug kingpin Pablo Escobar. It was Dino on bass, me on guitar and Billy making this Godflesh-esque noise on bass. Random stuff like that would happen with Brujeria all the time.

There have been four Brujeria albums to date, and I've been involved in all of them in some way or other. Dino played guitar on the first three albums, and he'd have some riffs. I might have a couple of songs. Jesse would have a song or two when he was around. Everyone pitched in whenever they felt like it. It was pure chaos.

It surprised me when Brujo told me that he wanted to do some shows, because it was never meant to be a live band. But Dino's group Fear Factory had just imploded, and I think they both felt it would be a good time to do it. Brujo hadn't done it before, so he wasn't sure how well it would go, but even practising for the tour was wild.

The very first show we played was in Chicago in October 2003. It was in this massive place, and Brujeria were playing with a bunch of Latino bands. The show was OK, though it was nothing special. But the second show was in Monterey in Mexico, and that was absolutely nuts. Brujeria are huge down there, and Brujo's like a rock star to those kids – if he walks down the street, he'll get mobbed. We turned up in the van and Dino pulled the window down. Once people saw it was us, they started rocking the car. Of course, Brujo loved the attention.

The place we played in Monterey officially held a thousand people, but there must have been 1,700 in there. It was a totally Mexican audience – no Americans. These kids just couldn't believe they were actually seeing Brujeria. It reminded me of the early Napalm shows, just in terms of craziness.

At some point, Dino quit, so Brujo asked me to play guitar because he wanted to do some more shows. That made me really nervous. I'm fine playing guitar offstage, but doing it in front of thousands of people at a gig in Chile is another matter. I got Jeff Walker from Carcass involved to play bass, which helped my nerves. Later on, my friend Anton Reisenegger from the Chilean band Criminal got involved too, as did Nick Barker, who called himself Hongo Jr. in my honour.

That rule about not dying on tour with Brujeria was funny, but also accurate. The whole party ethos is what it's all about, and Brujo knows what a mad bastard I used to be. Luckily, I wasn't drinking when we did those first dates, which is probably a good thing. But even then, touring with them is like touring with no other band. At gigs you'd get people coming up to you and saying, "This is your cut, Shane", and handing me this chunk of money.

Brujo is crazy, but he's good crazy. He always says I'm more Mexican than I am English. When you're writing songs for Brujeria, you really fall into that mythos he's created. Usually when I tell him a song makes me laugh, he loves that. That's the whole vibe of that band. He's very punk rock. He likes to go against the grain, and he enjoys the chaos of things. You'll be driving with him from Monterey to Guadalajara through some pretty dodgy area, thinking, "Someone is going to stop us and decapitate us in a minute." And those guys are just laughing about it. The minute you show any fear, he'll be on you. Sometimes with him you have to let go and enjoy the ride.

Brujeria's a strange entity, and I'm not sure how someone from Shropshire ended up being part of this insane Mexican-American band. But I love the fact that the band has become more and more popular. Because of Napalm's schedule, I haven't always been able to tour with them, but if I'm free I'll always do it.

Things have calmed a little bit on the partying front with Brujeria, but it's still full-on. A few years ago, Napalm were booked to do a tour but one of the bands pulled out so I suggested Brujeria – I was ready to play two sets. We needed one more band, and it just so happened that Lock Up's fourth album was about to come out, so I said, "Put Lock Up on the bill as well, I'll do three sets." By the end of every night, my ears were fucked. The last few dates were tough, but I'm prone to being a lazy bastard and just sitting around on tour and I figured it would liven things up.

Brujeria continued to be busy as a band. I played with them whenever I could, but it was not always possible. At the end of 2022, I did another tour where I played with Napalm and Brujeria. The hardest thing isn't remembering the songs, it's going out and doing these epic tours then coming back when it's done and trying to have a normal life with your family. One day I might get used to it, but not yet.

EYE WITNESS: RUDY REED

Former Napalm Death manager

In the middle of 1998, Rudy Reed got a phone call from Shane Embury. Reed was a music industry veteran of more than a decade's standing, helping launch the UK office of influential Dutch punk/ metal record label Roadrunner in the 80s and managing a string of bands throughout the 90s. He was aware of Napalm Death's history and significance, and now they wanted his help.

"Shane basically said the band were in trouble," says Reed. "They were having problems with their label, their previous manager had disappeared and Shane said, 'Do you mind if we come and see you?'"

Soon after that conversation, the two parties were sitting opposite each other and talking about the mess Napalm Death were in. "They told me their woes and I said, 'Well, I think you're pretty fucked,'" recalls Reed. "I think it was the first time somebody had cut through the bullshit and told them how it was."

He identified their current predicament as the product of a failing relationship with their long-time record label Earache, apathy on the part of the public and a lack of self-confidence within the band.

"They had lost their mojo, they weren't getting as many gigs as they should have," he says. "I think they were devalued." Reed was up for the challenge of taking on the band and their problems and he agreed to take over managing them. "There was still something anarchic about them," he says. "They reminded me of Motörhead, with the same kind of no-compromise, fuck-you attitude."

His most urgent task was to resolve the issues between band and label. When attempts to renegotiate the band's deal with Earache went nowhere, Reed approached industry veteran Martin Hooker, the man who had released Metallica's first three records in the UK via his original label Music For Nations. Hooker had founded a new record company, Dreamcatcher, and Napalm Death were the perfect flagship band for it.

Reed also suggested the band record an EP of cover versions of songs that had influenced them when they were younger, correctly guessing it would revitalize them musically. That EP, 1999's ferocious *Leaders Not Followers*, marked the first step in Napalm Death's creative resurgence.

"I wanted to reacquaint them with their early days, give them a sense of where they came from, in the hope that the next album would have the same attitude as their first few albums did," he says. "And also give them a sense of fun after a fairly draining few years." *Leaders Not Followers* was produced by Simon Efemey and engineered by Russ Russell.

"The band needed people around them at that point who related to them and cared about their music and them as people, and that's what Simon and Russ brought," says Rudy. "Shane and Simon had gone to the same gigs in Birmingham in the early 80s, so there was that extra bond between them."

As Reed guessed, the flush of confidence and enthusiasm the EP gave Napalm fed into their next album, *Enemy Of The Music Business*, released in September 2000. It was a return to Napalm Death's core principles of uncompromising extremity without being a mere re-tread of past glories.

It also succeeded in galvanizing interest in the band at a time when the music press were more interested in the hugely successful nu metal scene. Reed secured them the cover of *Kerrang!*, which had recently overtaken the once-mighty NME to become the UK's biggest-selling music magazine. The same publication enlisted John

Peel, who had so influenced the young Shane Embury's musical taste, to present Napalm Death with a prestigious Spirit Of Independence trophy at the magazine's annual award ceremony.

It wasn't just the metal heartland that was suddenly paying attention once more. Reed engineered a string of unlikely TV appearances, including a performance on the massively popular British early evening music show *TFI Friday* and, more absurdly, a stunt on youth-orientated show *The Priory* where they recreated a famous clip from a 70s kids' TV show which involved attempting to drink milkshake on a rollercoaster.

"We got offered tons of TV around that time, and most of it was ridiculous," recalls Reed. "Shane was up for pretty much all of it. Barney was more cautious." That approach to how the band was perceived highlighted the dynamic between the bassist and the singer. The divisions of the mid-90s that had resulted in Barney's temporary departure had eased, but Reed says the two men were still prone to the occasional flare-up.

"They bicker like brothers," says Reed. "You love that person but sometimes you don't like them. Barney's more interested in the political aspect of what the band means to people, Shane's far more of a musician and sometimes that results in a clash. But it's the tension between those two approaches that makes Napalm what it is. It's a constructive, small-'d' dysfunction."

Of course, *Enemy Of The Music Business* was successful in reinvigorating Napalm Death's career. They sold out a show at the 2,000-capacity Astoria theatre in London, their biggest UK headlining show in years. Their success in Britain had a knock-on effect in Europe and America when it came to touring.

"Some musicians find being on the road difficult, but not Shane," says Reed. "If you give him the option of playing a hundred gigs or 500 gigs, he'll always take 500."

But the band's touring schedule meant that Reed also got to see first-hand the booze-fuelled chaos of Shane's life at that time.

"Watching Shane and Simon sitting at the back of the tour bus, drunkenly headbanging while naked to Judas Priest at 5 o'clock in the morning was joyous," says Reed. "But at that point, he didn't know how to put the brakes on, on tour. I had to pull him out of hospital at least once. Music can indulge that kind of extreme behaviour. I've worked with a few of those characters. Sometimes the only time the brakes come on is when they hit a brick wall. And Shane hit that brick wall."

Reed admits that his focus on Napalm Death was drawn away by another band he looked after, Britrock hellraisers The Wildhearts, before stepping away from management completely in 2004 for health reasons. He says the period when he was involved with Napalm "gave them back a sense of authority and importance that probably helped them survive".

He stayed in contact with members of the band today, not least Shane. "There's a side to Shane that people don't get to see," says Reed. "He's funny, he's sweet, but he sometimes finds life a little bit difficult to navigate. He's as mixed up and messed up as we all are. But he's the soul of that band. If you cut him, he bleeds Napalm Death."

2004

" A friend of mine, Kevin Sharp, watched a documentary on Frank Zappa and said he saw a lot of similarities between Zappa and me. He didn't mean musically, more because of this need to constantly keep busy and jump from project to project.

I briefly met Kevin in 1989 when Napalm Death did the Grindcrusher tour. He was writing for a magazine in New York called CMJ and working for Relativity Records, and he'd come over to check out the tour. But I got to know him properly when Napalm went to the US to play CBGBs for the first time, and we became instant friends.

Kevin was in a grindcore band of his own in the 90s called Brutal Truth. When they went on hiatus, he went back to his hometown of Atlanta and we lost touch for a while. In 2003, Napalm toured the US with Nile, Strapping Young Lad, Dark Tranquillity and The Berzerker. It was a great tour, total fun, though the bus we were on was far from luxurious.

A week or two before the end of the tour, something happened with the bus driver – he must have got ill. Lo and behold, the guy they sent out to replace him was Kevin. He was nothing like the guy I knew from before – he'd moved to Chicago, he had this cowboy hat on, he liked his bourbon.

After the tour finished, I decided to go back to Chicago with Kevin. So we drove all the way from Tampa to Chicago in this rickety old shuttle bus, and chatted about music all the way. We'd always talked about doing something together, but never got round to it. At one point, one of us said, "Why haven't we done anything together yet?" I had some Discharge-influenced punk tracks, so we decided to do something with them.

We wanted to call the band Venomous Concept. It was a play on the legendary US hardcore band Poison Idea, who we both loved. But it was also a tribute to Japanese hardcore bands, who would just stick together random words to come up with a brilliant name: Chicken Bowels or Howling Furies.

I originally asked Mickey Harris if he wanted to be part of Venomous Concept. I'm not sure if it was lack of confidence or something else, but he wasn't up for it, so Danny Herrera did it instead.

Kevin knew Buzz Osborne from Melvins pretty well, so he asked him to play guitar. I'd met Buzz once before, when he was with Jello Biafra, but our friendship really started properly with Venomous Concept.

Buzz is like me times 500 when it comes to making music – he's always got a ton of different things on the go at any one time. He loves all different kinds of music. I did think, "Is he going to be able to play fast, Discharge-style hardcore stuff?" And of course he could.

I love Melvins anyway, but I really admire Buzz as a person. He's very quickfire when it comes to humour – he's ultra-fast, and sarcastic, which I like. And he's been doing Melvins since the 80s, so he's seen everything. He started out on the underground scene, he was in a band with Kurt Cobain, he's been on independent labels and major labels, he's seen all these different musicians come and go, but he's got the same worldview he's always had.

Buzz has a great attitude towards the business side of music. Most labels give you contracts that are the size of the Bible and expect you to understand it all. Buzz's way of thinking is, "If I've got to hire a lawyer to explain this contract to me before I sign it, fuck that – I'm not gonna sign it." Venomous Concept's debut album, *Retroactive Abortion*, came out on Ipecac Records, the label belonging to Mike Patton of Faith No More. Their contracts are a single page – they say what they're going to do and they do what they're going to say. If only more labels were like that.

We recorded the Venomous Concept album in Glendale, where the Brujeria albums were made. It cost about $3,000 in total. Buzz and his wife have all these dogs. At one point, me and him were walking down the street with his dogs. We've got mad hair, so all these people were looking out the window, going, "Who are these two guys with Sideshow Bob haircuts and all these dogs?"

Even now, Buzz is someone I look up to. Melvins did a tour recently that was 45-dates long, and I know they'll have done it in a van – they don't use tour buses. That's the epitome of punk rock to me.

Napalm Death shows can be pretty intense, but Venomous Concept shows are a chance to have a bit of fun. We only ever did one show with Buzz, because of everyone's schedules. He said, "You don't mind if I rip the piss out of you onstage, do you?" I just went, "Nah, that's fine." So that's what he did throughout the show.

A few years later, when I was still drinking, Venomous played this small club in San Francisco. Billy Gould from Faith No More had come down to see us. I was on guitar at the time, and I broke a string 20 minutes into the set. I thought, "I could either change the string or have a beer with Billy at the bar." So I got offstage and went and stood and had a drink. That was quite surreal, watching the band I was supposed to be onstage with from the crowd. Kevin was getting seriously pissed off: "Are you gonna change your string?" "Nah…"

Buzz left after the first album because I don't think it was what he thought it would be, but Venomous Concept is an ongoing thing. We've done five albums in total. The first four are all hardcore punk, but I felt it had the potential to be something different. Our fifth record, *The Good Ship Lollipop*, came out at the start of 2023 and we started to veer away from that.

We recorded it in a different way because of the pandemic. Kevin Sharp came over to the UK when the travel restrictions lifted, and we had a blast doing it. Everyone in the band likes different kinds of music, so we thought we'd just have fun with it. There's more of an AC/DC groove to some of the songs.

People might wonder why we did an album like that, because it's pretty different to the ones that came before. But there's never been a plan behind Venomous Concept. It started off as an excuse to play music I like with people I like, which is my reason for doing any project.

2005

66 The second-to-last track on Napalm Death's 2005 album *The Code Is Red... Long Live The Code* is called 'Morale'. It didn't sound like a typical Napalm song at that point. It's solemn and sad, and we put all kinds of strange things on it musically – it sounds like a funeral march. It's my attempt to write something that Swans would have done in the 80s. It goes into a short, atonal instrumental called 'Our Pain Is Their Power', which fades out to nothing.

That was deliberate. In my head, 'Morale' was meant to sound like an end point for Napalm Death. Something heavy and intense. If we never did another album, that's what we would have finished on.

It sounds dramatic but before we recorded *The Code Is Red...*, I wasn't sure if Napalm Death had a future. Our then manager Rudy had taken on another band, The Wildhearts, and he was preoccupied with looking after them for various reasons. There weren't many shows happening, there were a lot of differences of opinion, lots of personality clashes and money was an ongoing worry. I was still doing Lock Up and Brujeria, Mitch was making crazy techno music, Barney was living in Rudy's house and doing his own thing. It felt like the band was starting to shatter. There wasn't a positive feeling about things from any of us.

I was still living in the Napalm House and we were behind on the mortgage. Jesse was back in the States trying to get himself sorted out and Mitch had recently got married and understandably wanted to move into a house with his wife, so we had to do all this signing-off stuff on the house. The whole period was stressful. Friends were coming down all the time and we were getting wankered at the weekends, which was fun at the time but probably wasn't so helpful. Maybe if it hadn't all been so messy, my mind would have been clearer, but I don't think any of us really knew what the hell was going on. There was just too much chaos.

There were a couple of bright spots for me, though. I'd met someone when Napalm toured Japan in 2004. Her name is Madoka, and we started a relationship. Brujeria were starting to do small tours of the US, which gave me the chance to hop over to Japan and see her more often. I think I was pretty much escaping life back home as well.

A new record label, Century Media, was interested in signing us. They were one of the biggest independent labels in Europe. Our last two albums, *Enemy Of The Music Business* and *Order Of The Leech*, had been overlooked in the US because they were never properly distributed over there. When we'd recorded a second *Leaders Not Followers* covers album in 2002 or 2003, it ended up just sitting there, unreleased.

The Century Media deal was on the table, but it hadn't been signed. To be truthful, I was already semi-finished with Napalm in my head. I was spending time with Madoka in Japan, meeting lots of interesting characters out there who played different styles of music. Or I'd be in LA, hanging out with various friends who were doing things like soundtrack composing. I felt like I had a lot of other things to do, and the possibilities seemed to be opening up way more than they would have done if I'd just stayed in Birmingham. Then out of the blue, Barney told us: "I've been thinking about it, let's give it one more shot."

That took me by surprise. A big part of me really felt that Napalm were coming to the end of the road. I didn't want to believe it, but I was starting to focus on other things I'd got going on. I thought Mitch and Barney felt the same way, so Barney's email was unexpected. That probably was the thing that kept Napalm going. We decided to sign the deal with Century Media. They finally released the *Leaders Not Followers: Part 2* album in August 2004 and then we went into the studio to make a new album.

We recorded *The Code Is Red... Long Live The Code* at Foel Studios in Wales. Foel was owned by a guy named Dave Anderson, who used to play bass with Hawkwind in the 70s. Dave was great. He'd tell us bits and pieces about when he was in the band, which Russ Russell really loved because he was a massive Hawkwind fan.

We didn't have decent internet, so I would call Madoka on the phone. She was working in Tokyo, and I'd phone her at 5 o'clock in the morning because of the time difference. The signal in the studio was rubbish, so I had to walk up the hill in the pitch black, getting stared at by goats, just to get some bars on my phone. But we were in that stage of our relationship where romance is banging on your door and you want to talk to each other every chance you get.

One of those early morning calls did land me in trouble with Dave Anderson, the guy who owned the studio. There were cows in the next field, and he said, "Whatever you do, close the gate after you when you go out or come back or the cows will get in." I'd stumbled back from one of my 4am phone calls in the dark and I must have forgotten to close the gate. I opened the window the next morning and there were 20 cows in the garden in a semi-circle. They'd got in and shat all over Dave's lawn. He wasn't impressed.

The Code Is Red... was the first Napalm album that Russ had done without Simon Efemey – Russ had started producing the second *Leaders Not Followers* album, but Simon had finished it off. There was no drama behind it – Simon had started a family and he wanted to take a break from producing, though he carried on doing our live sound. The two of them always worked really well together, so it made sense to get Russ to do the record.

I first met Russ when Napalm played a venue in London called the Barfly in the late 90s. We clicked straight away – it turned out he'd been at a lot of the same shows in Birmingham as I had in the late 80s and early 90s, like Jane's Addiction at the Hummingbird.

Having someone like Russ involved when you're at the stage we were is massively helpful. We've still got the obvious grind influences, but there's so many other little things flying around and Russ gets that. He knows the best and the worst of our abilities. Russ has produced every Napalm Death record since *The Code Is Red...* and I've worked with him on other stuff too. Simon Efemey still does Napalm's live sound, and one of my ambitions is to get Russ and Simon to produce a Napalm album together soon – that would be incredible.

Despite everything that had been going on in the band, *The Code Is Red...* was a really enjoyable album to make. I had some songs that were fast but a little bit more leftfield. Some of them had been written for other projects I was working on, but they felt right for Napalm at that point. Creatively, it was great – we'd rehearsed beforehand, but some of the stuff we were doing was coming together spontaneously. Russ was up for trying anything and everything – that enthusiasm he had rubbed off on us.

Barney did an amazing job on *The Code Is Red…*, especially on 'Morale'. Back in the 90s, after *Utopia Banished*, Barney was the one who didn't want to change, which of course was one of the reasons he left after *Diatribes*. But after he rejoined, he seemed more geared towards trying different things. Fast-forward to 'Morale', and he was totally into the idea. When he did the clean vocal tone on that song, I got goosebumps – it was that good.

Ever since 'Morale' we've had at least one similar song on every Napalm album. Not one that sounds exactly the same as that, but something that challenges people's perceptions of what Napalm Death should be. When Mickey Harris was in the band, he wanted Napalm Death to try different things. So did I, but I didn't want to change everything overnight. I always used to tell Mickey to have patience, we'd get there eventually. With a song like 'Morale' and some of the things we've done since, it feels like we've got there.

We got a few guests on *The Code Is Red…* too. I'd got to know Jello Biafra quite well, and he came in and sang on the track 'The Great And The Good'. Our old friend Jeff Walker from Carcass was on 'Pledge Yourself To You', and we got Jamey Jasta from the hardcore band Hatebreed to sing on a couple of tracks. We'd known Jamey for years – he'd put on a Napalm show in Connecticut on the *Diatribes* tour, when Hatebreed were just starting out. They were just finishing off a UK tour when we were recording *The Code Is Red…*, so Barney picked him up and drove him over to this strange studio in the middle of South Wales. He must have thought, "Where the fuck am I going?"

I'd met Corey Taylor from Slipknot too. We were hanging out at the back of the tour bus. I tried to get him to come down and sing on the album, but it didn't happen – I'm not sure if it was his choice because Slipknot were so busy or if there were some politics involved with his label, Roadrunner.

We finished recording and mixing *The Code Is Red… Long Live The Code* in October 2004 and then we went straight on tour with Cannibal Corpse in the US for four or five weeks. We weren't exactly touring in luxury. We were travelling in an old airport shuttle bus. It had no toilet so you had to piss in a Gatorade bottle, and it broke down more than once. But we carried on. They were weird, uncertain times – it wasn't exactly starting over from scratch, but it did feel like an uphill struggle.

Although we had a new record deal and a new album, the stress hadn't completely gone away. I remember doing a photo session not long after we finished the record, and I felt this immense pressure in my head. I just had to get away, so I went to see Madoka in Japan. As soon as I got there, the stress lifted. Everything seemed OK.

The Code Is Red… Long Live The Code was released in April 2005. I was chuffed with it, especially given the mood in the band a year or two before. It's still a surprise that we managed to get it together to do that record. Things were starting to change behind the scenes too. Rudy Reed had stepped back for personal reasons, so we started co-managing ourselves, along with an agency in Germany called MAD, who we still work with today. And Barney began looking after the band's finances and trying to get them sorted. It's a job he's really good at, which is why he still does it today.

We played almost a hundred shows in 2005, which was more than we'd done in the past couple of years. We went over to Japan, which was great because it meant I got to spend time with Madoka. Jesse came back for a little while – it was great to see him, even though it was pretty clear that he wasn't doing so well.

Towards the end of the 2005, we went back to South America for five or six shows. A couple of them got cancelled. That's when those thoughts start creeping in again: "What the hell am I doing here? Maybe it's time to do something else." But you cling on and hang in there. After everything that had happened over the last few years, it felt like things were finally starting to turn.

EYE WITNESS:
SIMON EFEMEY

Napalm Death producer / sound engineer / long-time friend

The Birmingham Odeon was a Mecca for young heavy metal fans in the early 80s. Simon Efemey was a regular attendee, heading to this grand old 2,500-capacity theatre whenever the bands he loved passed through town. It was at the Odeon that the teenage Efemey met Shane Embury for the first time.

"He was one of those kids you'd see all the time at shows," says Efemey. "He stood out with his mad hair and constant headbanging. He was a little bit shy back then, but once he had a drink in him, he loosened up."

There was a bond between people who loved metal back then, a sense that everyone was in it together. That was certainly the case with Efemey and Embury. "We'd all end up back at New Street Station in Birmingham after seeing Saxon or Tygers Of Pan Tang or a band like that, waiting for the last train and talking about the stuff we liked. He was so passionate about music, he really loved it. You knew he was one of those kids who would never get a 'proper' job. He was following the music."

Birmingham Odeon closed down in the mid-80s and the pair lost touch. Efemey embarked on a career as a producer, eventually working with West Midlands indie bands such as The Sandkings and Ned's Atomic Dustbin. But he began seeing pictures of a band called Napalm Death. He instantly recognized their bass player. "I thought, 'Fucking hell, there's Shane,'" he says.

Their paths crossed again at a gig in the early 90s. "I was working with the Wonder Stuff, so it could have been one of their gigs, or it might have been something gothy. But it definitely wasn't a metal gig. That's the thing about Shane – even though he's in Napalm Death, he embraced everything."

Efemey started working with the band at the end of the 90s after his friend Rudy Reed had just taken over managing Napalm Death.

"Rudy had talked the band into getting it going again: 'Let's make a cracking record, let's reboot it, get the press interested,'" says Efemey, who produced 1999's *Leaders Not Followers* covers E.P.,

2000's fearsome *Enemy Of The Music Business* and 2002's *Order Of The Leech*.

"It was interesting watching how Napalm worked in the studio. Shane and Mitch Harris, their guitarist, were the ones focusing on the music." Shane's got a really good ear for detail, and he's mad for drums – he started out as a drummer. If there were mistakes, he'd pick up on them. He was really anal about it, in a good way. He knows when he wants something right, and he'll go on about it until it is right. It's no good trying to bullshit him. He knows what he wants doing, and usually it's correct."

Efemey stepped away from producing the band after *Order Of The Leech*, but he continued to handle their live sound. It meant he was in the thick of the carnage that surrounded the band – and especially Shane – in the early 2000s. He was there on the memorable occasion when the bassist invited several friends to join the band at a couple of festivals Napalm Death were playing in France and Austria.

"The tour bus was basically a massive piss-up," says Efemey. "The first gig got cancelled, so we had to park the bus up in some French city for the day – Lille or Metz, maybe. We'd had a few drinks in some bar and we all decided to strip off and jump in this fountain, which set the tone for the rest of the weekend."

When the entourage turned up to play at the Austrian festival the next day, Embury and his buddies were still drunk. "Napalm played their set, which I can't even remember, cos I was so drunk," says Efemey. "Then afterwards, somebody said, 'Let's all get naked.' So me, Shane, Nick Barker who had been in Cradle Of Filth and Frank Healy from Cerebral Fix stripped off and started wandering around the site, stark-bollock naked. People were going, 'What the fuck's happening?'

At one point, Shane – still naked – went up to Lemmy and put his arm around him. Lemmy turned around and went, 'What the fuck are you doing? Fuck off!'"

The alcohol-fuelled misbehaviour didn't stop at harassing members of Motörhead.

"We used to play proper old-school heavy metal in the back of the tour bus – Dio, Judas Priest, stuff like that," says Efemey. "A Swedish band called HammerFall were playing the festival, and Shane said,

'I'm going to red card them, they're false metal.' So we made some red cards like the ones football referees use, and Shane walked on their bus and stood there brandishing this red card, saying, 'Death to false metal!' Stark-bollock naked, of course."

That love of metal was what sparked Embury and Efemey's Absolute Power project. Their self-titled 2011 album was a love letter to the bands they'd grown up watching at the Birmingham Odeon three decades earlier. "We wanted a proper metal band of our own that we could sing along to," says the producer. "That's what Absolute Power was about. It was old-school riffs and melodies and some cheesy words. We had a lot of fun doing it.

"But then Shane is a really prolific musician, and not just in the metal world. He's got Lock Up, his Dark Sky Burial project, all these other things on the go. He's always writing, and I think it's because he still cares. He's not complacent in any way. He wants whatever he does to be great, and the older he gets, the better he wants things to be. Me and him are the same: we're never going to stop."

2006

66 After *The Code Is Red... Long Live The Code*, things felt more stable in Napalm Death than they had since the early 2000s. We were touring more than we had been in the previous couple of years, and people seemed to be into what we were doing again.

I don't know whether we were thinking we should strike while the iron was hot or were just on a creative roll, but we didn't waste any time going into the studio to record our 12th album, *Smear Campaign*. We returned to Foel Studios in Wales in the summer of 2006 with Russ Russell. Me accidentally letting a herd of cows shit all over the owner's garden hadn't put him off having us back.

Smear Campaign was an enjoyable record to make. I'd written a few songs for another project I was considering starting, but I thought, "Do I really need to jump into another band at this point? I've got plenty on the go with Napalm at the moment." Mitch seemed more motivated for this album too. Maybe he felt some of the songs we had were closer to how we used to sound, or maybe he was just happy that people seemed to be warming to us again.

I don't see *Smear Campaign* as us taking a step back. There was plenty of extremity on the record, but we did a couple of slower, more experimental tracks again, based on how well 'Morale' from the last album had gone down. People seemed to have less of a problem with us doing something a little bit different than they had in the 90s. It's funny how opinions change – I get a lot of people coming up to me and telling me how much they like *Diatribes* or *Fear, Emptiness, Despair* these days.

Lyrically, *Smear Campaign* was an interesting album. Barney had a theme in his lyrics, which was religion – the morality of it, how it governs people, how it interferes with people making choices for themselves. It's very personal in that respect. Barney has always said that he doesn't see Napalm as a political band – it's more of a humanitarian thing for him. For me, religion is like politics. I'm not religious, but it's too easy to say: "Fuck religion". There are plenty of people who have taken what it says in the Bible or any other holy book and warped it, but I also know people who find great comfort in their faith without being judgmental of other people. There's a balance to be struck.

The cover of *Smear Campaign* was done by Mick Kenney, who did the art for *The Code Is Red...* as well. I've known Mick for years. I met him when he was a kid with dreadlocks and a Mayhem T-shirt. He was an aspiring drummer, and I taught him the "cheat beat" I'd accidentally invented back in the Warhammer days. A few years later, I started hearing about this crazy grindcore band called Anaal Nathrakh. Someone told me, "Oh, it's that guy Mick with the dreadlocks." Things have a way of coming back round. Mick ended up moving out to Los Angeles to live and work. I encouraged him to go: "If it doesn't work out, you can always come back." He's a really talented guy, and super-positive. Every time I was down, I'd speak to him and he'd cheer me up.

Smear Campaign came out in September 2006, less than 18 months after *The Code Is Red...*, and in typical Napalm fashion we ended up doing a long tour of the States with Hatebreed and Exodus. The first time I saw Exodus was supporting Venom at Birmingham Odeon in 1985, back when I was in Warhammer. I didn't see them again until we got a chance to play with them in the late 90s. I was hanging out with their guitarist Gary Holt and their singer, Paul Baloff, who was a complete madman. The 17-year-old in me was thinking, "These guys were our heroes back then, and now we're playing with them."

We did that tour with Hatebreed and Exodus in an RV. People told us at the time that it wasn't the smartest idea to do it in a vehicle that didn't even have any proper bunks for people to sleep in. Danny was up above the driver, Barney and Mitch shared a double bed, I was on the coach and our sound guy AK slept on the floor. Not surprisingly, several weeks of living like that made people pretty cranky. There were various points where arguments erupted and fights ensued, though in fairness that's happened at several points in Napalm's history. Danny is an easy-going guy, but the rest of us are pretty feisty. There's never much actual violence but there are a lot of raised voices. We aren't capable of sitting down and talking through things.

There was one dark cloud on the horizon at that time. A few weeks before *Smear Campaign* came out, Jesse Pintado died.

Jesse's problems with alcohol had got pretty bad over the last few years. He never drank when he joined the band, and even later on he wasn't a manic drinker. But alcohol is always around when you're in a band. You're on the road, there's always booze to hand, then you come home and it's hard to adjust. I always threw myself into books or movies, but it was hard for Jesse to come home and put his energy into something else. Things just got worse for him – he just couldn't turn it off.

The last thing Jesse played on was *Enemy Of The Music Business*, although he's credited on *Order Of The Leech* and *Leaders Not Followers: Part 2*. It definitely wasn't a case of us saying, "You're not in the band anymore." We said, "You've got to go home and be with your family and get help." There were a lot of questions from fans and journalists about where he was. We were always careful what we said. I understand why people wanted to know, but it was ours and Jesse's business, and no one else's.

Jesse came back for a little bit after *The Code Is Red...*, but the problems he had were still there. You try and help people as much as you can, but they've got to want to help themselves. It's a cliché, but like a lot of clichés, it's true. He went to Spain for a bit, then he moved to Italy for a while – a friend of mine who lived down there bumped into him a couple of times and said that he wasn't doing too well.

Jesse ended up moving back to the US. The last time I saw him was at a gig on the US tour we did with Cannibal Corpse at the end of 2005. It was good to catch up, even though he seemed to be a little nervous. I had a conversation with him after that on the phone. He told me he was getting Terrorizer back together, and I told him I was glad he was doing it and wished him all the best with it. That was the last time we spoke.

It sounds horrible to say, but when I got the news that he'd died, I wasn't completely surprised. We'd tried to be there for him, but it did feel like he was on a downward spiral. People deal with death in different ways. For me, I think I shut off the reality of what had happened and I just cut the feelings off. People would call me up and say, "I'm sorry to hear the news, are you OK?" and I'd say, "Yes,

I'm fine." Not because I wasn't sad about Jesse – I was heartbroken. I just didn't know how to properly express my emotions at the time.

Weirdly, his death affects me more now than it did then. I'll sit and think about him sometimes. Just little memories, like me sitting on a wall in front of the Napalm House with a bag of fish and chips and him pushing me off because we were both pissed up. He was a laidback guy, but he could lose his rag occasionally. When we did *Diatribes* and we were trying to move forwards, some of the songs Jesse wrote had more of an old-school spirit. I remember arguing with him about whether they should be on the album. He came in one night and gave me an absolute bollocking: "Just cos you think this, it doesn't mean you're right. This is a good track." I look back and go, "Yeah Jesse, you were right, it was a good track, I was just being a dick."

I think back to when Jesse and Mitch moved over to the UK in the late 80s. They were both kids. Jesse joined the band in 1989 – he stayed at my mom's house in Broseley to start with. Mitch was 19 and Jesse was only a year or two older. You can't drink until you're 21 in California, so they loved it here. I almost felt like a guardian to Jesse and Mitch, and later Danny, like it was my responsibility for them being over here, even though they'd all made the choice to do it themselves.

I stayed in touch with Jesse's sister. She came out to see us whenever we were in town. I think it's harder for his dad because it's obviously upsetting for him to have lost his son. But Jesse's dad always was an amazing guy. He used to have this big strip with the name of Jesse's original band Terrorizer on the back of his suv, and he was so proud of what Jesse had done.

It's inevitable that as you get older you lose people that you know. Phil Vane died in 2011. He was only a few months older than me. That was a big loss, because he was one of the first people I got to know when I was starting out with Napalm. Our friend Mieszko Talarczyk from the band Nasum, who had really inspired us back in the late 90s, died in the tsunami in 2004.

A couple of years ago, LG Petrov from the band Entombed passed away from cancer. They were on Earache at the same time as Napalm, and we knew those guys really well. Another friend of ours, Trevor Strnad from the Black Dahlia Murder, died suddenly in 2022, which came completely out of the blue. We'd toured with the band a few times over the years, and Trevor was one of the nicest guys you could ever meet.

Of course it's hard to lose people you know, but I look at it in a different way. The reason you think about people so much after they die is because they made a mark on your life. Whether it's Jesse or Phil or Mieszko or anyone else, in a weird way it feels like they're still there.

I love the band Rush, and their drummer Neil Peart wrote one of my favourite ever lyrics in the song 'Dreamline': "We're only immortal for a limited time." Sometimes I feel I should reach out more to the people I know while I can, but it's hard not to get caught up in the cogs of life. You're making records, playing shows, just grinding away and it's all great. It's easy not to notice time slipping by, but then you lose someone you're close to and it stops you for a second. I hate to be morbid, but I'm in my 50s now. I love Napalm Death, but I've got my family and my kids. It's hard not to think, "How long have I got on this planet? Who am I going to spend it with?"

That's not to say I'm going to quit Napalm tomorrow, because it's been part of me since I was a teenager, but maybe there'll come a point where my priorities start to shift. On the other hand, I never expected to still be in Napalm Death when I was in my 50s, so who the hell knows what the future holds?

2007

"After a rocky few years in the early 2000s, things felt like they were looking up for Napalm. Our last two albums had gone down well, things were good with our new label Century Media and the worst of our financial worries seemed to be behind us, thanks mainly to Barney really getting a handle on that side of things. We were also starting to tour a lot again, which was good and bad.

It was good because touring is what bands have to do to survive, plus we always had a good time... except when we were all crammed together in an RV with no bunks to sleep in. But the downside of it was that I wasn't able to go to Japan as much to see Madoka. So we talked and she decided that she would come and live in the UK and we'd get married.

I met Madoka when Napalm played in Tokyo in 2004 with Nasum, Pig Destroyer and Anal Cunt. That was a romantic bill if ever there was one. She was at the gig – she was a Napalm Death fan. I saw her and thought, "She's nice", but I'm dreadfully shy when it comes to going up to women and talking to them. Back when me, Mitch and Jesse used to go out and get pissed at clubs in Birmingham in the early 90s, they'd never have any problems pulling. If I saw a girl I fancied, I never had the balls to go up to her and say anything, so I would just focus on getting more and more drunk then go home at the end of the night and listen to the Cocteau Twins and feel sorry for myself.

Luckily, the singer from Nasum, Mieszko, jumped in. He introduced us: "This is Shane from Napalm Death..." We hung out and got on really well. She was born in Japan but had lived in America between the ages of eight and 16, so she spoke really good English – which is a good job because my Japanese was non-existent.

We liked each other, but I didn't think it would go anywhere. I wasn't sure if I wanted a long-distance relationship – I'd had one before, and I wasn't sure if I was ready for another. Plus, I was still a bit of a wild bastard, even though I wasn't drinking at the time.

But she reached out to me when I got home. We started to keep in touch and things developed from there. At first we communicated by email, then we started speaking on the phone more and more. Madoka was commuting in and out of Tokyo, so she was getting up at 7am and not getting back until 11 or 12 at night. At one point, I was spending a bit of time in Los Angeles with Brujeria, and there's a 17-hour difference between there and Tokyo so I'd set my timer to wake her up for work.

We were getting on well, and the relationship was starting to develop. I began going across to Japan whenever I could – I loved the place ever since I'd first been there with Napalm in 1989, and it just felt right being there. At one point, she came over to the UK very briefly and stayed in the Napalm House for a few days. That wasn't the best idea – that house is great if you're a pissed-up musician, but it's not exactly conducive to a romantic relationship.

We were in Barcelona when I proposed. I've got friends out there, and we did the whole tourist thing – the cathedral, La Rambla, the Gaudi museum. Obviously I was a little nervous beforehand, but I was chuffed when she said yes. Then 10 minutes later she said, "So what are we going to do?" I hadn't thought any further than asking her, let alone what the actual wedding would entail.

We got married in a registry office in 2007. Madoka came over earlier than we'd arranged, which wasn't great because Napalm were just about to go on tour for three months. Thankfully she stayed with a friend of mine while I was away – the idea of her being stuck in the Napalm House for three months was not appealing.

I imagine it can be quite tough being married to a musician. I'm not at home all the time because of touring, and I can disappear down a rabbit hole when I'm working on music. And I can be a lazy bastard at times in terms of wanting to do stuff. She'll suggest we go somewhere for the day, and I can't be bothered. Then when we've been, I'll say, "That was really good," and she'll say, "Yes, I told you so." She can force me out of my comfort zone.

Since we've married, we've had two fantastic kids. Sometimes I wake up and I can't believe that I'm a dad. I never wanted children when I was younger – I was so petrified of the responsibility and just doing the right thing. My mom and my nan brought me up but my role models were Bon Scott and Ozzy Osbourne, which shows the attitude I had to actually being a responsible adult. There was definitely an arrested adolescence thing going on.

I try to be a good dad. I'm a child of the 70s, and things were different when I was growing up. Times were hard for my parents back then, there wasn't always a lot of money around, and my mom and dad would argue. I think back to the lack of money and wonder if some of that has rubbed off on me. I'm not money-driven, but having a family has made me realize that it is important. A friend of mine says, "Money is energy" – meaning you need it to live. That's especially true when you have a family.

My dad was very much a product of his time. When he was growing up, there was a distance between sons and fathers, and some of that carried on when I was growing up. He'd be down the club with his mates, which is where he got his camaraderie – I suppose that's not a million miles away from me being in a band.

I don't mean to sound horrible, but I don't want to be my dad. We made our peace and we got to know each other when I was older, but I want to be around for my kids as much as possible. It's difficult sometimes because of the band, but I try and spend as much time as I can with my children, just watching them grow up.

Madoka is really creative, and my daughter likes to draw – she's said she wants to be an Anime artist one day. My son's still fairly young, but he loves the keyboards. I think I'm secretly hoping he'll follow me into music, and there'll be some cross-generation Aphex Twin/Napalm Death-style mash-up one day. Or maybe he'll see sense and not go into the music business at all.

My wife's family are great. Her dad's mega-cool. He doesn't understand grindcore at all, but he understands what Napalm do. Sometimes I'll get a bit stressed and he'll say, "Look Shane, your job is to entertain people and make them happy." That's a nice thing to hear.

Madoka is supportive of what I do, but she doesn't let me forget that I've a life away from the band. Occasionally, a complete stranger comes up and says, "Are you the guy from Napalm Death, can I have a photo?" It happened once in Piccadilly Circus in London when I was with Madoka. She just rolled her eyes. As she often tells me, "You're not the bass player from Napalm Death when you're at home."

Every couple has their ups and downs and we're no exception. It's too easy to go, "Fuck it, I'm off, I've had enough" when things get tough. You have to stick at it and think about all the positives: what you have versus what you wouldn't have if you weren't married. If I wasn't married, I'd probably still be sitting in the Napalm House playing Nintendo, which is fine when you're in your 20s but not when you're 50-something.

When I look at my life in 2023, I'm married, my kids are at school, I've got some property. The part of me that's still headbanging to Venom in a graveyard in 1982 is thinking, "How the hell did this happen?" But then it's all linked. If I hadn't been that kid, I wouldn't have started tape trading, which wouldn't have led to me join Napalm Death. And if I'd never joined Napalm Death, then I ultimately wouldn't have been in Japan and met my wife.

EYE WITNESS: SVEN ATLE KOPPERUD (AKA SILENOZ)

Dimmu Borgir guitarist / bassist / songwriter

There was a rule within the Norwegian black metal scene of the early 90s not to show any admiration for bands like Napalm Death. The movement's unofficial godfather, Mayhem guitarist Øystein 'Euronymous' Aarseth, decreed that occult-themed nihilism and irreligious iconoclasm was more important than hero worshipping the "old guard".

"You weren't allowed to like anything that wasn't black metal," says Silenoz, aka Sven Atle Kopperud. "If you liked Napalm Death or Pantera, you kept quiet about it. Of course, that didn't stop Euronymous selling Napalm Death vinyl in his record shop Helvete, because it gave him money in his pocket."

Before he became involved in the black metal scene, Silenoz was a regular teenage metal fan. He became aware of Napalm Death around the time of the British band's 1990 album *Harmony*

Corruption after seeing the video for the song 'Suffer The Children' on MTV.

"Before I started Dimmu Borgir with my bandmate Shagrath, I had a death metal band," he says. "We were definitely fans of bands like Napalm Death. It was only later when I dug back into their history that I realized how different they sounded when they started. I didn't appreciate how unique Shane's bass sound was back then – it's like a tractor that ploughs over everything in its way."

Silenoz was certainly impressed one afternoon in 1992 when, as a 15-year-old, he saw Embury outside Oslo's Rockerfeller club, where Napalm Death were due to play later that night. "I saw him walk across the street, and obviously, he's really recognizable," says Silenoz. "I thought, 'Oh shit, that's Shane.' But I was too starstruck to go up to him and introduce myself…"

After forming Dimmu Borgir in 1993, Silenoz immersed himself in the black metal scene and the musical drawbridge came up. "I missed a couple of Napalm's albums because I was so focused on black metal," he says. "As I grew older I realized those restrictions were kind of stupid."

The two men got two know each other via their mutual friend Nick Barker, who played in Dimmu Borgir in the late 90s. Memorably, Silenoz celebrated the turn of the millennium with Shane and his friends in Birmingham. "That was quite a night," he says. "Well, about three nights. Then when Lock Up played at the Inferno festival in Norway, we let them use our equipment and our warehouse to rehearse in. They stayed at my house. It was an ongoing party."

It was inevitable that Shane and Silenoz would end up in a band together. "We had many drunken early morning conversations when we talked about writing some songs together. We came from pretty much the same background when it came to music – we both had that love of old-school bands like Dio, Saxon and Judas Priest."

In the end, it was Silenoz who asked Shane to join his band, Insidious Disease, a throwback to the death metal groups he'd grown up loving in the early 90s. To date, they've released two albums, 2010's *Shadowcast* and 2020's *After Death*. "He's a 110 per cent type of guy," says Silenoz. "When he goes into the studio, he's usually well prepared. And even if he's not prepared, he still wants it to be right, so he won't leave until everybody's happy."

Silenoz says the best piece of advice he was given by Shane came in the mid-2000s, when Dimmu Borgir played the UK's Bloodstock festival.

"Personally, it was one of my worst shows," he says. "Bad sound, I didn't play well, I made so many mistakes and I was sloppy. I came offstage and I was about to smash my guitar into pieces. Shane was there, and he took me to one side and said, 'Look, I've had days like that in the past, but now I go onstage to enjoy it. If I make a mistake or two, so what? I'm there to play in front of people and enjoy myself.' That stuck with me. You go onstage and do your best and enjoy yourself, because that's all you can do and there's no point beating yourself up about it."

2008–2010

"There were three years between *Smear Campaign*, which came out in 2006, and our next album, *Time Waits For No Slave*. It was the longest gap between Napalm records to that point. It wasn't that we were being lazy bastards, it's just that we all had different things going on.

I'd married in 2007, and was still getting used to it. I'd spent most of the previous 15 years living in the Napalm House, and although I'd moved in with Madoka after our wedding, I probably took a bit of domesticating. We did keep the Napalm House on, though. I still spend time down there even these days, especially if I need some space to work on music.

We recorded *Time Waits For No Slave* at Russ Russell's studio in Kettering. In his quest for heaviness, Mitch decided to use six guitar rhythms on every song – they were all slightly different, but that's still a lot. Years later, when we played some of the songs from that record, me and our then guitarist Johnny Cooke were trying to work out how Mitch had done it: "What fucking riff is that? It's not possible. You can't have your fingers in these two places at the same time."

We did promo shots for the album in a clock shop in Bromsgrove. It was full of all these antique clocks and old timepieces. I know the album title was about time, but we were really going overboard on the clock thing. I remember seeing Barney walk in there with a look on his face that said, "What are we doing here?"

Photo sessions can be great, but sometimes you look back and go, "What were we thinking?" In the early days, we'd get one of our mates with a decent camera to take a picture of us just sitting there and that was it. But then you start to get a bit more professional about it. We've done some strange ones. Mickey Harris was crazy about baseball bats, so we ended up doing one where Barney was holding this baseball bat and wearing these dark shades. It was fine at the time, but you wouldn't get him doing that now.

Sometimes you get to do shoots in cool places. Back in the 90s, we did one out in the desert in Nevada, mainly because Mitch had wanted to. Jesse was moaning because he hadn't been to bed, and Danny wasn't too chuffed either – he's the only Californian I know who hates hot weather. I sometimes wish we'd done photo shoots in a lot more extravagant locations, but we could never really be arsed at the time.

The best shots are the ones that aren't posed or gimmicky. There have been some great pictures of us just after we've come off stage and we're sweating and laughing. I'm sure some people see Napalm as a bunch of miserable, serious bastards, but photos like that show what it's really like. They say more about the band than us waving baseball bats around or standing in a clock shop.

Time Waits For No Slave is a very heavy album, which people seemed to like. We had a release party for it at a club called The Asylum in Birmingham, which wasn't far from where we rehearsed. We played the whole of the new album from start to finish, which was something we've never done before or since. It was interesting doing that. Sometimes songs can get forgotten about after an album comes out, so at least we've played everything from that record at least once.

There was a bit of fuss because the album leaked on the internet before it came out. That kind of thing happened all the time back then, and labels especially saw it as a real problem. There was a brief moment years earlier when Metallica started complaining about Napster and I thought, "Yeah, that could be quite damaging", but I stopped worrying about it pretty quickly. I came from the tape-trading scene – we were doing what Napster did 20 years earlier, and that's how I discovered so much great new music.

I'm not saying leaking albums is a good thing, but I don't lose too much sleep over it. I don't think that stuff affects Napalm too much. Barney was on top of it a long time ago. He figured that people who really love your band want to support you, so they'll want a physical copy of the album anyway. We have fans that go out and buy multiple variations of albums on vinyl and CD.

On the back of *Time Waits For No Slave*, we toured Europe with Immolation, Waking The Cadaver and Macabre. There was a great spirit on that tour. It was a bunch of bands crammed together on the same bus. It was like the travelling house from *The Addams Family*, with the big black thundercloud following you constantly.

We'd known Macabre for years. Me and Mickey Harris used to tape-trade with them years ago. All their songs are about serial killers, but they're real characters – it's like Frank Zappa meets death metal. They had a song I loved called 'Ed Gein', which was inspired by the serial killer. They never played it live, so I said, "Would you do it if I sang it?" I'd sung backing vocals on various Napalm Death songs, though I'm not a proper singer like Barney. Still, I gave it a shot. Lance, the singer from Macabre, had this demented screech, so I was trying to do that. I'm sure there were people there thinking, "What's this twat doing?"

I'm getting more confident as a singer. I sing on some tracks with Dark Sky Burial. I started off with a fairly standard hardcore tone, which mutated into more of a homage to Jaz Coleman from Killing Joke. I'm planning on doing some Dead Can Dance-style crooning at some point, which will be interesting to try – and to see how it goes down.

Weirdly, around that time we ended up appearing in an episode of the British TV series *Skins*. It was basically a show about a bunch of teenagers taking drugs and shagging each other, but it was massively popular at the time.

The guy who was directing that particular episode was a huge Napalm Death fan. The storyline involved this boy who was a metalhead taking a girl he liked to a club, and Napalm were the band playing. We went down to Bristol, which is where they filmed it. We turned up and there's an insane amount of food and drink – It would have kept Napalm going on the road for about three weeks.

They'd advertised that we were playing, so a load of Napalm fans turned up. We ended up hanging out with them, which was a nice thing to do. We played 'Strong-Arm', the first track on *Time Waits For No Slave*. Because it's TV they make you play it over and over again while they get all these different camera shots. I'd love to say we were brilliant but I don't think I've ever watched it, though I know my mom and dad were pretty excited when it was on TV. I do remember passing some Lock Up CDs on to the director: "If you're doing anything like this again, I've got this other band…"

You don't expect to appear on a show like *Skins*, but then again it wasn't completely out of the blue. Ever since we did the

BBC *Arena* documentary and the kids' TV show *What's That Noise?* back in the late 80s, we've appeared on television a few times over the years.

There was a show we did around the time of *Enemy Of The Music Business* called *The Priory*, which was a mix of music, guests and comedy. They'd get bands in to do stupid stuff, and they gave us a call. One of the things we had to do was go head-to-head with some pop band to see who could put a kids' play-set up quickest – I'm pretty sure Barney point-blank refused to do it.

The other thing we did on *The Priory* was that thing based on a famous scene from a 70s kids' TV show with cub scouts eating on a rollercoaster and got it all over their faces. They asked us to recreate the original clip, which seemed like a laugh. The only problem was that Mitch decided to throw his milkshake all over me before we even moved. So I had to go around this rollercoaster twice absolutely covered in milkshake.

We appeared on TFI *Friday* around the same time. It was this really popular early evening show presented by the DJ Chris Evans. People watched it between getting in from work and going to the pub on a Friday. They wanted us to come in and play three short tracks, 'Lowpoint', 'The Kill' and 'Dead'. It was a good time, they treated us well, though I do remember the presenter Chris Evans seemed a bit miserable.

Part of me thinks people in the mainstream media see us as a novelty band because we always get asked to play the shorter songs and never the longer ones. But then I think back to having my mind blown by The Exploited on *Top Of The Pops* when I was a young kid. If one person is watching us play 'The Kill' on a TV show at 6pm on a Friday evening and it opens them up to this kind of music, then that's our job done.

Because the gaps between Napalm albums started to get longer in the late 2000s, I had even more time to work on music for various other projects I had on the go. I think I'd convinced myself that I needed to keep as busy as I could. We reactivated Lock Up around 2009 and played a handful of gigs. It was me, Nick Barker on drums and Tomas Lindberg from At The Gates on vocals. Sadly, Jesse Pintado wasn't around anymore so we got in guitarist Anton

Reisenegger, who had been in a couple of really influential underground metal bands from Chile called Pentagram and Criminal.

I never stopped writing, and I'd got a ton of different riffs to use on the third Lock Up album, *Necropolis Transparent*, which eventually came out in 2011. We did a few shows, but I think a couple of the guys in the band wanted Lock Up to be more than it was in terms of playing live – they wanted it to be a full-on touring band, but there was no way I could do that, because of Napalm. I saw Lock Up as the perfect festival band – come on mid-afternoon, blast through a few songs then enjoy the rest of the night.

I look back now and I think that need to be doing things all the time was partly a reaction to my lack of understanding of what a marriage actually entailed. When you get married, you have to change your own behaviour in some ways because there's a responsibility to the other person. You don't always realize that at first, especially if you've been living a certain way for years and years.

Music has always given me a chance to escape. I'm someone who is happiest when I have solitude to make music and let my mind drift. It goes all the way back to me sitting in my nan's back garden as a toddler, hitting her buckets with whatever I could get my hands on. Writing stuff for Lock Up, or all the other projects I had on the go at the time, gave me that solitude. That hasn't changed, even now. Sometimes I just need to step away from the realities of life and lose myself in my music.

2011

"Me and Simon Efemey had been talking about doing a proper old-school heavy metal album for years. We come from the same musical background. We'd head-banged our way through the same gigs at the Birmingham Odeon when we were younger. That music was in our blood.

When we reconnected in the late 90s, we'd hang out, get drunk and talk about heavy metal. We came up with the idea of putting together something that was a love-letter to those bands we'd grown up listening to as kids: Dio, Priest, Accept, Riot, early Tygers Of Pan Tang. Of course, when I get an idea in my head, I have to do it no matter how much other stuff I've got on my plate. That's how Absolute Power was born.

While the concept behind Absolute Power was fairly tongue-in-cheek, we were deadly serious about the music. We actually started recording songs for it around the time of Napalm's *Order Of The Leech* album – that's how far back it went. Our label at the time were into the idea to start with but then they changed their minds and went cold on it. They wouldn't pay for any more studio time, so the songs just sat on Simon's hard drives for a while. But neither of us wanted to abandon it, so we'd go back to it whenever we had a bit of time. We spent ages properly crafting the songs – we wanted them to stand up next to the bands that had influenced us.

Simon decided that he'd be the singer, rather than get an outside vocalist in. He's actually got a killer voice and a great range – he can sing those kinds of songs better than a lot of singers in old-school metal bands could at the time. We roped in a few of our mates to help out – Russ Russell, Mitch from Napalm, John Walker from the band Cancer, and a friend named Paul Harrington played guitars on various songs, and Ian Treacy from Benediction was on drums. We even got Brian Tatler from Diamond Head to do a proper old-school solo on one song.

One of the tracks we'd written was called 'Raging Pursuer'. A journalist I knew named Paul Elliott came up with that title. What the hell is a 'Raging Pursuer'? I had no idea, but it made us laugh. It was exactly the sort of song title Judas Priest would have come up with in the 80s, so I wrote some lyrics with a Priest vibe. Then I realized that it was crying out for some Rob Halford-type screams. We were never going to get Halford himself so I asked Tim 'Ripper' Owens, who had replaced him in Priest for a few years in the late 90s. I'd got to know Ripper when he was singing in the band Iced Earth. Simon was doing one of their albums, and we ended up taking them out for a curry around the corner from the Napalm House.

Ripper was totally into the idea of singing on 'Raging Pursuer'. He sent over his vocals via email while we were on tour in America. It came through at about 4 o'clock in the morning and I remember sitting in the back of the tour bus while everyone else was asleep, listening to it and pissing myself laughing because he'd absolutely nailed it.

There was one person I really wanted to get for the album: Ronnie James Dio. In my opinion, he's the greatest heavy metal vocalist ever, and some of the albums he made with Rainbow, Black Sabbath and his own band Dio are my favourite records of all time. Me and my mates in Broseley once had a famous headbanging competition to Rainbow's 'Stargazer' in one of our bedrooms, which of course I won. Another time, I came second in a school talent competition by miming to Dio's 'Rainbow In The Dark'. I won £2. It would have been one of the greatest moments of my life if my mom hadn't just cut my hair off.

Dio was a big hero of mine for more than one reason. His voice was incredible, but it was his lyrics too – they were fantastical, but they had meaning. They were full of rainbows and dragons, but they were metaphorical: he was singing about the struggles of life and relationships. As quite a shy kid who liked his own company, I related to what he was saying. He recognized the outsiders in life. I always connected to heavy metal on a different level to the way I connected to punk. With punk, it's nice to go, "Fuck this and fuck that", but I like something a bit more multi-dimensional.

I only met Ronnie once, years later. That was a moment that I'll never forget. He was playing with Tony Iommi and Geezer Butler from Black Sabbath in the band Heaven & Hell, which was Dio-era

Sabbath in all but name. They were doing a gig just before my birthday in 2007, so I went along with my wife and Simon Efemey.

At one point, Simon said to me, "Do you want to come backstage and meet someone?" Ronnie was there with a glass of wine, and somebody said, "This is Shane from Napalm Death." I'd heard he was a big fan of Indian curries, and he started asking about where I was from in Birmingham. When I told him I lived in Sparkhill, he said, "When we were rehearsing with Heaven & Hell, there were some excellent curry houses there."

That blew my mind for starters, but I'll never forget what happened next. Barney had interviewed him years before and he said that Ronnie had told him he was a fan of Napalm Death. That's the sort of thing that makes me think, "Hmmm, I bet he was just saying that." But I was talking to Ronnie and he said to me, "You know, I really like Napalm Death." Then he put his hand on my shoulder. "Listen man, never give up. Never give up." I had to go and sit down, because I had a tear in my eye. My wife was laughing at me. I said, "You don't realize, I've been touched by the hand of god here." It wasn't just that he knew who Napalm Death were, it was a connection to my younger self, the kid who had grown up listening to his records.

When me and Simon were doing the Absolute Power album I thought, "Why don't we see if Ronnie James Dio wants to sing on it?" So being a bit cheeky, I emailed his wife and manager Wendy to ask if he wanted to appear on it. I got a very polite reply: "Ronnie thanks you for your email, but he can't participate." What I didn't know at the time was that he'd been diagnosed with cancer. He passed away a little while later. It was a sad day when he died.

The influence Dio has had on my life has been huge. Musically, he helped shape me so much when I was a kid. But the way he behaved and carried himself around other people was an inspiration. Everybody who knew him says how down-to-earth he was, which is really admirable in the music business. Everybody has an ego, it's normal. Sometimes when you're in a band, it can go to your head.

There was a brief period after I joined Napalm where I got really cocky. That lasted about 10 seconds, until a *Kerrang!* journalist named Mörat called me out on something I'd said. I can't even remember what it was, but I deserved it. That was the point where I thought, "I can't go around behaving like this."

Sometimes you come across rock star bullshit first-hand. Years ago, Napalm did a show with a fairly big American punk band who I loved when I was younger. We'd opened for them in the 80s, and it was all fine. But then we played with them again in 1997. We were on before them, and we were halfway through our last song when they turned the PA off. It was one of the guys from the band. I just thought, "Really? Are you that insecure?" I'd rather a band go on before us and blow everyone away and make me think, "Right, we've got to up our game and be better than those guys." Unplugging someone's PA while they're playing is just bullshit.

I'd like to think Napalm are really down-to-earth as people. We have a good relationship with other bands, we have a good relationship with fans and some of them have become really good friends over the years, almost like part of an extended family that we have around the world.

The Absolute Power album took the best part of a decade to come out. It was finally released in 2011. Some people didn't get it: "Why has the guy from Napalm Death done this cheesy heavy metal record?" Maybe they thought it was some jokey, ironic thing. It was to a certain extent, but musically it was totally serious. Me and Simon wanted to make a record that our 14-year-old selves would have been headbanging to in our bedrooms. A lot of people our age loved it. I got a text from Bill Steer at 5 o'clock in the morning to tell me he was playing a track called 'Land Of Steel' at full volume.

Absolute Power only played live once, at the Download festival in 2012. I was gutted that I couldn't do it, though they went down a storm. But a few years later, Napalm were playing Paris with Carcass, Voivod and a couple of other bands. There had been the horrible shooting at an Eagles Of Death Metal gig at the Bataclan theatre two weeks before and people were understandably para-noid about playing Paris. Me and Barney thought, "Let's do it, a gig might be what they need."

The venue we were playing was sold out, but the atmosphere was quite nervy. We decided that going onstage to play an Absolute Power song might alleviate a bit of the tension. So before the show, we spent a bit of time learning 'Land Of Steel', which is the track from the album that everybody loved.

After Carcass came off, we trooped onstage. No one knew who the hell this band was – Simon Efemey's singing, I'm on bass, we've got Voivod's guitarist and one of Carcass's techs up there. But the crowd had the chorus nailed halfway through the song – there's 1,500 people singing along to this epic heavy metal song that most of them had never heard before. It was a joyous moment.

Absolute Power have become a legend in our own lunchtime over the years. People still ask me if we're going to do another album. Simon and me have plenty of ideas, and we plan on ploughing ahead with it at some point. It's our chance to scratch that heavy metal itch we both have, and have a laugh doing it as well. Because if you don't have fun, what's the point in doing something?

2012–2013

❝ Things have changed a lot since Napalm Death's early days on Earache. Back then, we'd put out albums every year or two. When you're young, you have that energy and that drive. But things are simpler too. You might be single, you probably don't have kids, so you can focus all your attention on music and on getting drunk, and not always in that order.

But as you get older and move through life, all these other factors come into play. Relationships and kids, different commitments, different pressures. That's what was happening with Napalm. It was understandable – Madoka and I were starting a family, Mitch already had kids. You just can't do everything all at once like you could when you were younger.

There had been three years between the release of *Smear Campaign* and *Time Waits For No Slave*, and another three years between *Time…* and our 14th album, *Utilitarian*. But while it might have looked like we were slowing down from the outside, we were all busy, whether it was with side projects or personal stuff. Plus Napalm were still touring like crazy – we did something like a hundred gigs in 2010.

Utilitarian was an enjoyable record to make. There was a good feeling in the band at the time, especially compared to the way things had been at a few years earlier, and our relationship with Russ was super-productive – he was up for trying different approaches. Being in the studio was a chance to step away from our day-to-day lives at home. I remember at one point me and Mitch getting drunk after one session and just piling on all these ridiculous extra ideas. When we sobered up, we realized there were a few too many things going on, and we had to dial some of the more unnecessary vocal effects back.

We got the avant-garde jazz saxophonist John Zorn to appear on the song 'Everyday Pox'. Napalm and Zorn go way back – I remember Mickey Harris totally vibing off him back in the 80s, and I think Zorn was fascinated with the whole grindcore thing and

Mickey's drumming in particular. We did a split flexi-disc single together in 1990 and Mickey and Zorn had a mad jazz/grindcore band called Painkiller. I'd stayed in touch with John over the years, so it was great to finally get him on a Napalm Death album.

There was a little bit of butting of heads over the album title. Barney wanted to call it *How Revolting*. In typically blunt fashion, I just went: "Nah". Mark, who worked at MAD Agency, agreed with him. I still wasn't having it: "What else have you got?" One of the other names on the list was *Utilitarian*. There you go, one word, brilliant – plus it reminded me of an old punk band I liked from Denmark called Totalitär. Though with hindsight, maybe I should have been a bit more diplomatic when it came to telling Barney I didn't like his original title.

The cover for *Utilitarian* is interesting. It's designed by a friend of ours named Frode Slythe who is an old-school Napalm fan. He based it on some of the old albums. The businessman from the *Scum* album is there, which I never clocked at the time. There's a guy in the middle who's getting a kicking, which is inspired by the Rodin statue *The Thinker*, which was Barney's idea.

Ever since *The Code Is Red… Long Live The Code*, we'd always written way more songs than ended up on the actual album. You need tracks for digipacks, bonus discs, Japanese editions… sometimes you just end up writing songs without any proper idea of where these songs are going to end up, you just know they'll come out somewhere. It was like that with *Utilitarian*. We had so many songs that we ended up holding some over until the next album. I amassed all the extra tracks we've done over the last 20 years for a compilation album called *Coded Smears And More Uncommon Slurs*, which came out in 2018. It was a double album. I remember listening back to it, and I'd forgotten about half the songs.

Around that time we began to change the way we toured. Mitch, especially, didn't want to go out on these long tours that lasted weeks on end. When your wife is having to hold the fort at home, it can be incredibly stressful for her. So Mitch suggested that we play at weekends instead – we could fly out on a Thursday, play gigs on Friday, Saturday and Sunday, then come back. Now I've got kids myself, I understand why he was stressing out. Life gets more complicated the older you get, and it becomes more and more difficult to balance all the different things you've got going on.

The only downside for me was that I'd got back into the habit of drinking. I'd given up alcohol for a few years after I ended up in hospital with pancreatitis in 2002, but the booze had started to creep back in and things were starting to get crazy again. There were a couple of things that happened on the 2012 tour that made me look at my relationship with alcohol again.

That summer, Napalm were due to play Hellfest, which is a massive French festival. Brujeria and Lock Up were on the same bill, and I was supposed to be playing with them as well, plus I said I'd get up with my mate Mick Kenney's grindcore band Anaal Nathrakh – four bands across the whole weekend. I did the Anaal Nathrakh gig one night, then Brujeria another night, and then Napalm on the Saturday. But by the Sunday night, I was such a mess that I couldn't play the Lock Up set – Dan Lilker from the band Brutal Truth had to cover me.

It came to a head a couple of months later. I was doing a lot of weekend festivals, not just with Napalm but with Lock Up and Anaal Nathrakh too, just going crazy and not looking after myself. I got back home from one festival and had curry that night. I remember feeling pretty rough afterwards, so I went to the local hospital the next day. They did their tests, and I was having problems with my pancreas again, so they kept me in there for six days.

This was right before a Japanese tour with Napalm. Barney was panicking a little bit, worried whether I'd be OK in time for the tour. I said, "Look, I know what's going on, I'll be out in time to go to Japan, we'll be good to go." He wasn't having any of it: "No, you can't come out to Japan, what if something happens." I think he thought I'd be straight back on the beer and that would be it.

That pissed me off. I'm stupid at times but even I know that ending up in hospital for six days is a sign that you need to change what you're doing. But they weren't budging. They said they'd do the Japanese shows with our sound guy AK filling in on bass, even though he didn't have enough time to practice properly.

Lo and behold, I was out of hospital two days before the Japanese dates, feeling right as rain, but it was too late. I ended up staying at home and getting 10 or 12 T-shirt designs together for the next tour, which was in the States was with Municipal Waste, who were a real party band. I remember Barney saying to Mitch, "Be careful around Shane, in case he wants to start drinking again." I'd had another warning sign, so that wasn't going to happen. At least not for a few years.

Towards the end of 2013, Napalm got invited to do another pretty unusual event by an artist named Keith Harrison, who specialized in ceramics. He had this idea for a performance which involved us destroying a wall through the power of our music. Keith was originally from Birmingham, and I think the idea behind it was to represent the industrialization of the city. We were really up for it. Barney described himself at the time as "a bit of an art wanker", and we all thought it was a chance to do something totally out of the ordinary.

The plan was to do it at the V&A Museum in London. Keith talked them into letting us do it there, but somewhere along the line somebody must have thought, "What if they don't just destroy the wall, what if they destroy some priceless piece of antique art while they're doing it?" So the V&A plan was nixed, and we ended up doing it at a place near Hastings instead.

We were really up for the challenge and we took it seriously. Keith had embedded speakers into the walls and one of his mates had tiled over them. We started playing and it was punishing. We were doing songs rather than just blasting out random noise, and Russ Russell had brought this noise generator, which was loud as fuck too. We kept cranking up the volume until there was so much noise, but all that happened was that three or four tiles flew off. Keith was looking over at his mate, going, "It's his fault, he stuck them on too strong." Eventually, some guy just jumped over and started trying to kick the wall down himself.

It was so funny, though I did feel a bit embarrassed for poor Keith: "Sorry we couldn't knock your wall down, mate." What can I say? You win some, you lose some.

EYE WITNESS:
ANTON REISENEGGER

Guitarist, Pentagram / Criminal / Lock Up

Being a young heavy metal fan in Chile in the 80s could be a dangerous business. When Anton Reisenegger was a teenager growing up in Santiago, he would meet up with like-minded friends at a local record shop to exchange tapes, swap records and sell his home-made fanzine. But the country was governed by General Augusto Pinochet, the dictator who seized power in a 1973 coup and had led the ruling military junta ever since. Under Pinochet, there was no room for dissent or deviancy – and that included people who liked anti-social music like metal and punk.

"It became quite a big thing," says Reisenegger of those ad hoc swap-meets at the record store. "But eventually the police would show up and start dispersing people with batons. I was arrested once for just standing there with a bunch of records in my hands."

"They saw metal fans as Satanic drug addicts who went around beating people up," he continues. "Many times in the 80s, the police would turn up at concerts and close things down. They'd beat everyone up and arrest half the audience."

That institutional brutality didn't stop Reisenegger from forming his own band, Pentagram. By 1987, they were playing to 2,000 people in Santiago. "There was no security, the PA system was rudimentary, everything was very basic," he says. "But the energy was incredible."

He also immersed himself in the international tape-trading scene, writing to people around the world. Inevitably, Napalm Death's music came onto his radar early on. "They were one of the bands who caught my attention, even though I have to say that I wasn't a big fan back then," he says. "It was a bit too much for me. I liked things to be a bit more technical. But their sound and imagery and raw energy gave you a feeling that you were an outsider, and that there were other people like you."

By 1988, Pentagram had fizzled out. A couple of years later, Reisenegger saw a photo of Napalm Death in a metal magazine. "Their guitarist, Mitch Harris, was wearing a Pentagram T-shirt," he says. "My mind was completely blown. We'd closed the book on it, but it had taken on a life of its own."

In 1991, Reisenegger formed a new band, Criminal. The Pinochet government had fallen at the start of the decade, and metal fans weren't quite the pariahs they had once been. In 1997, Criminal's label suggested staging a special show in Santiago to mark the release of the band's second album, *Dead Soul*. Reisenegger suggested that Napalm Death, who were touring South America at the time, play the show too. Criminal's label agreed, but with one caveat: Napalm Death had to open for them.

"I thought Napalm were never going agree, but they didn't have a problem with it," says Reisenegger. "When we played the show, it was obvious to me and everyone else that Napalm Death were the main act and that Criminal were only billed as the headliner because our record company were paying for it. I thought it was cool of the band not to have a problem with it: 'Fuck it, we'll just play.'"

The show marked the first meeting between Reisenegger and Shane Embury and the rest of Napalm Death. "Mitch was the one who was the complete Pentagram freak in Napalm, he was the one I had more contact with," says Reisenegger. "But we went to a party at a friend's apartment, which is where I talked to Shane properly for the first time. There was a lot of alcohol involved, but I remember we talked about horror movies and music for a long time. They were only in Chile for one or two days, but we established a friendship."

That friendship was fuelled by a mutual admiration. In 1999, Napalm Death covered Pentagram's 'Demonic Possession' on their *Leaders Not Followers* mini-album. Shane contacted Reisenegger to get hold of the lyrics. "For some reason I didn't send them to him, so they worked them out on their own. Did they get them right? Close enough."

Reisenegger himself eventually moved to the UK in 2001, briefly joining Extreme Noise Terror on guitar. "One of the first things I did as soon as I landed in the UK was to go to Sparkhill and spend the weekend with the guys at the Napalm House," he says. "We'd drink beer and watch Bill Hicks videos all day. They'd introduce me to people as 'Anton from Pentagram', and people knew who I was."

His stay in Britain was ultimately temporary, though he ran into Shane at various European festivals over subsequent years. When Shane re-activated Lock Up at the end of the 2000s, he enlisted Reisenegger to play guitar, replacing late Napalm Death member Jesse Pintado.

"I had never played music that intense and demanding before," he says. "It wasn't complex, it was just so fast. When we toured, we'd sit in the back of the van, drinking and listening to Mercyful Fate and Slayer. There was a lot of alcohol back then. Sometimes we'd take a flight at 7 o'clock in the morning, and we'd go to the bar and drink beers. At that time, it seemed normal."

Reisenegger admits that he worried about his bandmate's state of mind. "We played one festival and we got there a day early so we went to this beer garden," he says. "We were pounding the beers. When we left the place, Shane missed the step and fell flat on his face. He looked really bad. We had to take him back to the hotel. I remember having to use a wet towel to clean him up and everything. He was in shock.

"A lot of fun was had, don't get me wrong. But when he started doing stuff in public, like dropping his trousers backstage at a festival and people start taking pictures of him, I felt I had to step in and protect him a little bit.

"There was one particular time when Lock Up played Hellfest and he had a real meltdown. Shane was a mess at the time. He ended up going to hospital, and the doctors told him he had to stop drinking. I think that was the best for him."

Reisenegger still plays with Shane in Lock Up, with the guitarist steering 2017's *Demonization* album. In the mid-2010s he also joined Brujeria.

"There are many sides to Shane," he says. "He's an inspiring person to be around because he does so much. At the same time he also has a temper. He can be short-fused. When something isn't to his liking, he'll let you know, or he'll just walk out and say, 'I can't deal with this, I'm out.'

"But he's loyal to his friends – he sees them as his extended family. I wouldn't be where I am today if it wasn't for him. He put his trust in me, and that opened a lot of doors for me."

2014–2015

" When I think about it now, I was definitely a control freak in the 90s. It wasn't an ego thing, it was because I was passionate about what I was doing, whether that was Napalm Death or any of the other projects I'd got going on. With hindsight, it was good and bad. Every band needs somebody to beat that drum, but I know now that it pissed people off sometimes. Barney and Danny have both told me that I was way too blunt with the way I spoke to people.

By the mid-2010s, I was trying to be more relaxed about all of that stuff. Not that I didn't care, but it can be quite draining on your energy. Around the time of *Utilitarian*, we made a decision to start playing two or three shows every weekend rather than go out for weeks on end. Fifteen years earlier, I would have pushed back, but at that point I was happy to go with it, even though it meant the length of time we would tour would be extended. Back in the early 90s, you could do a two-month tour, then come home and sit on your arse for two months. But now we were playing every weekend for months on end.

It was mainly Mitch who wanted to do it that way because of his family situation, but I think he found this new way of touring quite stressful too. I love Mitch, and we're still really close, but he had a lot going on in his life at that time. He had his family, and his stepfather back in Las Vegas was unwell – it can't have been easy juggling all that and doing the band as well.

I think at that point me and Mitch had different views of what we wanted out of Napalm. A couple of years earlier, I'd come bounding in, saying, "I've had an idea, Jacob from Converge wants to do a split with us, I'm so chuffed about it." And he'd go, "Really, that's what's exciting for you right now? I'm not excited by that." I can see now where his head must have been at, but at the time it bummed me out.

With the *Apex Predator – Easy Meat* album, it became more and more difficult for Mitch to give his time to Napalm. I got some songs together with Danny, but Mitch was leaving it to the last minute.

He was always prolific when it came to writing riffs, but around that time the arranging side of things was tougher. He'd play his songs and I'd say, "That one's amazingly structured, but that one's not so good." I'm not exactly Mozart, but I ended up working on some of his arrangements, which I think made him frustrated.

There had always been a little bit of underlying competition between me and Mitch. We both laugh about it now, but at the time Mitch would always fight for the first track on the album. I didn't really care, as long as it was a good track. I never got jealous of other people's riffs. If someone came up with a great riff, I'd be quite open about it: "Fucking hell, that's good, I wish I'd written it."

Because of the way we'd scheduled our touring we were still playing shows in support of *Utilitarian*, so we were trying to put *Apex Predator* together in between that. It was all a bit disjointed and back-and-forth. Mitch wasn't always around because of everything he had going on in his life. He'd come in for a few days, record his guitar tracks, then leave again while we carried on recording Danny's drums, though full credit to Mitch because he was always focused on getting his parts done brilliantly. Barney is never around until the music is done and it's time to do his vocals anyway, so often it was just me, Danny and Russ Russell.

During the process of making the album, Mitch decided to leave the UK and move back to Las Vegas to look after his stepfather. I completely understood why he did it, but it was a strange situation because we were so close – we'd literally lived under the same roof for years.

Even though the situation around the band had made things more complicated, I was really happy with the album. The song 'Apex Predator – Easy Meat' itself opens the album, which I was really pleased with. Barney and I were talking about introducing a record with solitary vocals, and he came up with this deep, slow, spoken word intonation which started out sounding like some monk's chanting, but then gave way to this crazy ranting which Barney said was influenced by the way Johnny Rotten used to spit his words out. I had a lot of fun with the percussion on that track, just bashing out rhythms on iron and metal tins, which Russ then put into some sort of shape.

We'd never started an album like that before and the label were worried that people just wouldn't get it and they'd turn the album off before it even started. I didn't want to compromise – if they didn't like it, people could skip it and go straight into the next track, 'Smash A Single Digit', which was a proper Napalm rager. If any band should be challenging people 14 albums into their career, it's Napalm Death.

At the end of 2014, two or three months before the album came out, we played a short US tour. The last show was at the Knotfest, which was this big festival organized by Slipknot. We were head-lining one of the smaller stages, and Mitch came down from Vegas for the show. We did photos for the album the day before we were playing, and Mitch was moaning his tits off that he had to be there a day early. I get it now – he was stressed by the whole situation.

The Knotfest gig was Mitch's last show with Napalm. We got our friend John Cooke in to play guitar on the next tour, and he's been with us ever since. But it was never a case of Mitch leaving Napalm or us getting rid of him. He had his own life to live, and that door was never closed. We made it clear he could always step back in when or if he wanted to. He played on some songs on Napalm's *Throes Of Joy In The Jaws Of Defeatism*, which came out in 2020.

There was a point where Mitch talked about playing live with us again. Napalm finally got to tour with Slayer in 2018. That was a big deal for me. Mitch wanted to come back for that tour, but I wasn't going to kick Johnny Cooke out after everything he'd done with us in the past few years. I told Mitch we could do it with a two-guitar line-up. He didn't seem too happy about that, but he'd been away for a while – what about all those other tours we'd done without him?

It's interesting, at one point during that whole period, Mitch had suggested that Napalm should think about going away for a bit. We'd seen other bands do it. Carcass, who we'd known for years, had split up in the mid-90s then reunited 10 or 11 years later and became way bigger than they were first time around. Mitch's idea was that we should disappear for a few years then come back and do a reunion.

I could see the logic behind doing it, but there was no way it was happening. I'm a musician – what else would I have done? I suppose I could have focused on some of the other projects I'd got going on, or I could have started something new. But then I think, no, it would have been the wrong decision to make. Even after all this time, Napalm has so much to prove.

2016–2017

66 There was a lot going on in and around Napalm Death after we released *Apex Predator – Easy Meat*. Mitch had moved back to America, and we were uncertain of what he wanted to do when it came to Napalm. Plus it was the last album we were contracted to do for our label, Century Media, so that stuff was going on in the background.

I've always got some ideas left over from each album which become a stepping stone to the next one, but it was difficult to actually start work on the follow-up to *Apex Predator* because of the situation with Mitch. I wanted to get the ball rolling, but because we don't do demos, we were waiting to see what was happening with Mitch. Barney was insistent that he should play on the album, but I said, "I don't think he really wants to."

I wasn't fazed at the thought of taking on the songwriting myself. I had some songs that were finished, but I wanted to get in there and add percussion and samples and weird noises. I had an idea for a track with no guitar on it. All these various crazy ideas that I thought we should try, just to keep pushing things forward. One of the things I'm proud of is that no Napalm Death album has sounded exactly like the one that came before it.

We started working on the new album properly in 2017. There was still some debate at that point as to whether Mitch wanted to be involved. Communication was very, very distant and a little bit weird. At one point, he said, "Well, why don't you come to Vegas to record?" I told him that wouldn't have worked. Me, him and Russ would have just been out on the town all the time, which would have been enjoyable but really just a paid vacation.

I got the sense that Mitch didn't really want to submit his songs for whatever reason. Maybe he wanted to keep them for a project of his own. It was frustrating to me: "You're still in the band, you're still in Napalm Death, way more people will get to hear these songs on a Napalm record than they would anywhere else." But we didn't end up doing any of his material.

I know Johnny Cooke was frustrated, he wanted to play on the album. We did an amazing cover of the Sonic Youth song 'White Kross' during that time, which eventually came out as a bonus track, and Johnny was instrumental in helping us put that together. But it was a case of, "Is Mitch in or is he out?"

It was just me and Danny in most of the early sessions.

Barney has his own way of doing things. He gets all the music and then he works out the words to go with it. What he comes up with is always brilliant, but I can't imagine working like that. Getting 18 or 19 songs and having to write lyrics for them all? No chance.

Danny and me always work well in the studio, but he'd get frustrated with me, because we'd record in the day and then I'd write something else in the evening and say: "I've got this idea, let's do something with it...", which meant doing more stuff. I played drums on a couple of the songs during those sessions, not because I didn't think Danny could do it, just because my head was going so fast.

We recorded a song called 'Resentment Is Always Seismic', which ended up as the opening track on a mini-album we put out after *Apex Predator*. We were at the stage where it was just a riff, and Danny said, "I'm tired, I've done 10 hours, you play it." So I put a click track on and went in and did it. I wasn't being an asshole about it, I was just in this whirlwind of wanting to get stuff done.

The album took a while to make, and Mitch did end up playing on some of the songs. I said, "Look, we're going to do the guitar tracks on this date, it'd be great if you came over to do them, but if you're not there then Johnny Cooke is going to record them." He came over and contributed to a couple of things, did some backing vocals. It was great having him there. We hung out and had a laugh. He had a few drinks and we ended up singing late at night like we always did in the past. It was like old times.

Mitch went back to Vegas full time, and I understand why. But even now, it sometimes feels weird that he's not around like he used to be, just because we were all so close for so long.

Making that album was quite a slow process. There were the delays because of the situation with Mitch, but we were also touring and playing festivals at the same time. We played more than 70 shows in

2017. Maybe that was too many, but Napalm Death isn't some huge band who can afford to take months off to make an album. And it did mean that we got to play Glastonbury for the first time.

The first time I went to Glastonbury was in 1989. It was a completely different festival back then. Suzanne Vega was headlining and All About Eve played the same day, who I liked because I'm a bit of a goth on the inside. Napalm's singer at the time, Lee Dorrian, had given me the task of babysitting the Japanese band S.O.B.

There were just two problems. One was that someone had given me a joint the week before, and I'd done some stupid jump and fucked my leg. The second problem was that S.O.B. had all dropped acid. My main memory is of them leaping over these hippies' bonfires. So my first Glastonbury was spent limping around, in charge of this Japanese hardcore band off their nuts on LSD.

The next time I went, it wasn't as chaotic. It was June 2017, and Napalm Death had been booked to play, which was a pretty big deal. The organizers seemed to be a bit sniffy about certain kinds of metal and hardcore, but Dan Tobin persuaded them to book Napalm and a few other groups. We were the first grindcore band to ever play there, which is something to be proud of.

Glastonbury was way bigger than I ever remembered it, though it was definitely easier not having to deal with a busted leg and a bunch of manic Japanese musicians. I saw a few bands I liked. Goldfrapp were playing, who I'm a big fan of. The Foo Fighters were headlining, and I heard that they wanted us to play on the same day as them so that Dave Grohl could come down and get onstage with us during our set. I'd met Dave years before when Nirvana played the Hummingbird in Birmingham, and much later Lee Dorrian had appeared on a record by Grohl's side project, Probot. I don't know how close it came to happening, or even if it was only rumour, but for whatever reason it never materialized. It's a shame, though I'd still love to do something with Dave Grohl at some point.

The organizers originally had the idea of us playing inside a converted railway carriage that they had on the site. I'm not sure they'd thought that through properly – it would have been carnage. In the end, we played on the Shangri-La Stage. There was a massive crowd, an interesting mix of people too. Some of them definitely knew who Napalm Death were, and given the kind of people who go to Glastonbury, I'd say there were probably a couple who saw the band back in the days of *Scum* and *From Enslavement To Obliteration*. But there were a lot of people who were there out of curiosity – they probably knew us as the band that do these insane one-second songs.

There was a great vibe. Barney, especially, is really plugged into the same kind of ethos as Glastonbury, which connected with a lot of people in the crowd. At one point afterwards, I remember talking to the snooker player Steve Davis, who was there to do a techno DJ set with a guy I know named Kavus Torabi. Steve Davis said, "I saw you play, I really enjoyed it." He's a massive fan of crazy prog rock, so we ended up chatting about that. That was pretty surreal – I'm talking to this guy who I watched playing snooker on the telly in the 80s about Napalm Death and Magma.

It was great that Glastonbury asked Napalm Death to play, but I don't think it should have taken so long for them to put on a band like us. It's easy to marginalize this kind of music because it's extreme, but it's as relevant as anything else out there. Napalm Death have been around in one form or another for 40 years – you don't last that long if you're irrelevant.

Personally, I feel quite comfortable in that world. I love playing metal festivals, but it's good to step out of your comfort zone. We've done all kinds of mad gigs and festivals over the years. We played a small jazz-reggae festival where we were the only grindcore band on – 3,000 people, really happy to see something like Napalm Death. Then a few days after that, we did Hellfest in front of 100,000 raging European metal fans. I love doing stuff that a lot of other metal bands would turn their noses up at. It keeps things challenging, plus we just like meeting people we wouldn't otherwise get to talk to.

I sometimes wonder why Napalm Death seems to cross over to these other areas of music. We are on the fringes, but somehow we've become part of mainstream culture without ever trying to. There was an initial notoriety around the band at the start, but that only gets you so far. I hope there's a kind of respect or admiration for what we do, and for having done it for so long. But whatever the reason, it feels like Napalm is part of something bigger, even if that was never something we intended.

EYE WITNESS:
RUSS RUSSELL

Engineer / producer

The first time Russ Russell worked with Napalm Death, he was doing their live sound at a gig in France. The guy who normally did the job couldn't make it, so they asked him if he would step in.

"It was this big sports arena, a terrible venue for Napalm Death," says Russell, who became the band's long-time producer. "The PA wasn't powerful enough and I was about half a mile from the stage. At the end, I thought, 'Did I do a good job or not?' I had no idea."

Some old friends of the band who were veterans of Napalm Death gigs were backstage after the show. "They said, 'We must tell you about the sound,'" remembers Russell. "And I thought, 'Oh god, here we go.' And they said, 'That's the best we've ever heard them.' That's when Shane said, 'Do you want to carry on the rest of the tour?'"

On the ferry back to the UK, Russell and Shane began talking. They soon realized they'd attended several of the same gigs in the late 80s and early 90s, when Russell would make his way across to Birmingham from his native Kettering.

"It was the usual thing: 'What's your favourite band?'" says Russell. "I said, 'You've probably never heard of them, but my favourite band are Cardiacs.' He went, 'You're fucking kidding me, that's my favourite band in the world.' We instantly had this rapport."

"He was a little wilder, but he's the same guy as he is now," says Russell. "We're very similar in a lot of ways. When I first meet people, I tend to be quite quiet and try to suss out the situation. I don't open my mouth too much. We're the same like that. We're both Sagittarians, so maybe it's because of that."

Russell had met Napalm Death at a gig in 1998 at long-gone venue The Falcon in Camden, London, where he was introduced by their then manager Rudy Reed, who he'd known from art college. He'd been aware of them at least a decade earlier, and his reaction was similar to many other people's.

"My teenage years were a mix of punk and psychedelia," he says. "When I was at art college in '87 or '88, a guy I knew who was always into interesting music played me this tape. I put the headphones on and it was like this wall of noise. I said, 'Holy fuck, what's that?' And he said, 'It's Napalm Death.'"

Russell got to experience that wall of noise first-hand in the studio when he began working as the engineer alongside producer Simon Efemey on 1999's *Leaders Not Followers* covers E.P. and 2000's follow-up *Enemy Of The Music Business*.

"*Enemy Of The Music Business* was definitely the most extreme thing I've been involved with," says Russell, who had previously worked with West Midlands indie band The Wishplants and Kettering alt-rockers The Junket. "It sounds pissed off, but it wasn't just a bunch of angry people sitting around raging in the studio. It was pretty comical. Shane invented a character called The Doctor. He had a pair of psychedelic sunglasses and a headband, and he'd try to sell you things like he was on one of those late-night shopping channels: 'Here's the doctor, he's gonna sell you this for $9.99 a month for the rest of your goddamn life.' Any time there was a moment of stress, Shane would pop up as The Doctor and completely alleviate all the problems."

By 2005's *The Code Is Red... Long Live The Code* album, Russell had taken over production duties from Simon Efemey with the latter's blessing. He got to see the dynamic of the band up close, particularly when it came to Shane Embury and Mitch Harris.

"Shane and Mitch were so close, they were the best of friends, but they were also hugely competitive," says Russell. "For the most part it was really positive, but there were times when they'd fight to get one extra track on the album, and if one got it then the other would want his track on it as well.

"Sometimes they'd hide what they were doing from each other. One of them would come up to me and say, 'Check this out, I've got this idea for a new song.' Quite often they'd come up with similar ideas. I'd think, 'Wow, have you really not heard what the other one is doing? You need to talk to each other more often.' It got quite heated at times, but mostly it was a healthy competition."

Like many in the band's orbit, Russell spent a lot of time at the Napalm House in Birmingham over the years. "It was beyond carnage at times with the booze, but there was such a buzz going on there all the time," he says. "Every time I went up, we'd start a new side project."

One of the projects that began life during that period was Russell and Embury's darkly psychedelic Tronos collaboration.

"Me and Shane were both massively into the Cocteau Twins and Celtic Frost* in equal amounts," says Russell. "We'd spent years sitting drinking on tour buses going, 'We should do something that fuses those two things together, with a bit of Cardiacs and Jane's Addiction.' One day we just said, 'We've been talking about this for too long, let's just do it.'"

Tronos began with a two-and-a-half-day session at Russell's home studio in 2012. "Shane was still drinking at the time," he says. "I remember clearing up the cans at the end of it. There were 80 cans of Fosters. I know it was him because I don't drink Fosters, I can't stand the stuff."

It took another seven years before the pair completed Tronos's debut album, *Celestial Mechanics*. By that point, Shane had already released several more albums with Napalm Death as well as with Lock Up, Hicks Kinison and Blood From The Soul. The bassist's epic Dark Sky Burial project was also taking shape in his mind.

"His mind never stops thinking about music," says Russell. "He's already got a dozen things stacked up in his brain, and he's desperate to get them out before they fizzle away. It's the same when he's in the studio. We'll be working on a song and we'll get to a section that we're stuck on. He'll go, 'Hang on a minute…', and pull up some piece of music from five years ago that works perfectly."

Russell's relationship with Napalm Death endured. He produced 2020's *Throes Of Joy In The Jaws Of Defeatism* album.

"Shane does know what he wants, and sometimes that can make him a little bit impatient," he says of the bassist. "When he's got 10 ideas and he wants them to all appear at the same time I have to say, 'Hang on, we'll get there, it just might take a minute.'"

2018

"I stopped giving a fuck a long time ago about what people think of what I do. You can let that stuff get to you. I did it with Napalm Death in the 90s. One negative review sent us off down a completely different path, which changed the course of the band in many ways.

But you can't be afraid of trying new things. When you first start creating music, you do what you do because you're driven by passion and energy. The music you're making is who you are. But as you progress, you get more comfortable and you can find yourself becoming a little bit scared of deviating from the path, and so you play it safe. You have to continually challenge yourself.

I'd wanted to do an electronic project for years, but it took me until 2018 to actually start working on it properly. That was the beginning of Dark Sky Burial.

It wasn't for want of trying, because I've always been a fan of electronic music, from Skinny Puppy and Coil to Aphex Twin and Squarepusher. I originally planned to do something along those lines in 1993 or 1994. I had an Atari ST computer back then, which I dabbled around on, but a mate borrowed it and I never got it back. Then Napalm became really busy, so I just put off doing it. It's funny, the mate who borrowed my computer ended up moving to LA and working on music for movies.

A few years ago I was touring with Brujeria and I decided to check out the GarageBand app. I ended up really getting into it and creating all of these loops, which reignited my interest in doing something more electronic. I'd sit there for hours, making these pieces of music and getting lost in my own head.

Dark Sky Burial slowly took shape over the next few years. I wanted to create something that was built around loops, but also had a feel of soundtrack music to. It's influenced by the electronic bands that I love, but also bands like the Cocteau Twins and some at the gothier end of things. There's an eerie edge to it.

If I had to describe Dark Sky Burial, it's me. It's more than just another side project. It's a chance to express what's going on in my head. I can do that with Napalm, but there are other people involved, who all have their own input to one degree or another. With Dark Sky, it's just me and whoever I choose to collaborate with. I've gone from being really controlling when I was younger to being more collaborative in recent years. I really enjoy the spontaneity of just going in and seeing what happens, but that's never been the Napalm way. That's what Dark Sky Burial gives me. I can spend hours working through the night on it.

The name Dark Sky Burial has spiritual connotations. It was partly inspired by the Tibetan Sky Burial ritual. Rather than being buried in the earth or cremated, the bodies of the recently deceased are taken to a Tower Of Silence and laid out on the top for vultures to eat. It sounds grisly, but there's something beautiful about it – it's seen as your last gift to the universe. I was attracted to it partly because I like the esoteric side of things, but I think part of it is going deeper.

I recorded and released four Dark Sky Burial albums between April 2020 and December 2021, and I decided to get Russ Russell involved. I didn't want to just cobble them together and chuck them out, I wanted them to have the same level of quality as a Napalm album, even though they sound completely different.

I see those first four Dark Sky Burial albums as a kind of audio diary of everything that happened to me during those years, one of which was my dad passing away. Growing up, I wasn't as close to him as I was my mom. There were the usual father-son tensions, but he started to understand what I was doing when he saw that I was making a living from the band. He was definitely proud of me. Apparently he used to go down the club and say, "My son's doing this, my son's doing that."

In some ways, he was probably living his life through me. I think he was a bit of a thwarted musician and always got the feeling he would have loved to have carried on playing after he left the Army. It's funny, right towards the end of his life, he told me that he could read musical notation. I said, "Why didn't you tell me? You could have taught me!" Even now, I don't know anything about the theory behind music. It's a shame, I wish we'd talked more when he was around.

By the time he died, we'd grown closer. I think I understood more of what's involved in having a family and being a father. On the day he passed away, I went home and wrote a song. I haven't released it yet. I'm thinking of using it as a ritual at some point, something to finally say goodbye to him. The feelings were all there, but I struggled to let them out.

I'm not sure I was conscious of it at the time, but some of what I was doing with Dark Sky Burial was influenced by my dad passing away. I ignored that side of it for a long time. I thought, "It can't be that, it's too obvious." But now I think, "Why wouldn't that have shaped what I do and who I am?"

But Dark Sky Burial is more than just about losing my dad. The last few years have been weird and difficult for all manner of reasons, and those records are a diary of where my head was over that period. There have been dark times and struggles, and I've used the stress and depressions of everyday life to inspire it. There's a track called 'Beware Your Subconscious Destroyer', which is about the idea of fighting your inner demons.

Because Dark Sky Burial is sound-based and loop-based, I find myself entering a trance when I'm working on music for it. I can start on it at 10am and I'm still going at 6pm. I've been finding things recently that I have no recollection of recording, all these unfinished pieces of music. I want to use them all somehow.

In many ways, Dark Sky Burial is me returning to my child-hood. The influence of *Doctor Who* and *The Tomorrow People* and the BBC Radiophonic Workshop is in there, horror and sci-fi movie soundtracks – all these things that take me back to when I was a kid. There's a therapeutic element to it for me. It's the idea of escapism. The older I get the more I realize that's something that's been there my whole life.

But there's also a freedom to Dark Sky Burial that there isn't with Napalm Death, purely because everybody in the band has their own schedules that we all have to work around. That's one of the things I love about DSB – it's just me. The great thing about experimental music is that I can go and do a gig and not have to play anything off an album I've just released. That freedom is really liberating.

I played my very first Dark Sky Burial gig at the Underworld in London in 2021 and it was a pretty daunting experience. It was just me and my friend Carl Stokes, who I've known since the 80s, on drums. There were only 30 people there, which I was thankful for in a way – it was easing myself into it. I was sitting down with my bass which was unusual for start, and I was actually performing vocals on these songs, doing it in different tones. It wasn't perfect in any way but it gave me more confidence about doing more things vocally with DSB.

I'm thinking way ahead with Dark Sky Burial. The plan is to release the material in quadrilogies – sets of four albums, with all the albums in each set linked in some way, even though they're all going to be different. I've got seven or eight covers for records that I haven't even made yet, which could shape what they sound like.

I'm interested to see where Dark Sky Burial leads me. It's an ever-evolving path with no set rules to it. I can do electronic albums, I can do heavier albums, I can do soundtrack work. I don't care if people don't like what I'm doing with it, either. I'm at the stage in my life where I'll make the records I want to make, no matter what it costs.

It's a chance to do the kind of things we'd never do in Napalm. If I want to mix some Cocteau Twins-type guitar with electronic music, then I can do it without having to go and start another band. And it gives me the chance to collaborate with people I've not worked with before, and see what we can come up with that's different. I'm working on the next set of Dark Sky Burial albums, and there's some very tuneful singing on some of the songs. Not the kind of thing that people would expect from me. The great thing about Dark Sky is that it can be what I want it to be.

Napalm Death will always be a huge part of me, but Dark Sky Burial has become just as important. It's going to take time to be what it will be.

2019

" My ambition is to make a hundred albums by the time I'm 60. I'd done around 50 at the time of writing (and I'm 55)– that's Napalm Death albums plus all the other bands I've been involved in. It'll be a challenge to hit that target, and it doesn't mean just chucking out albums for the sake of it, but I think I can do it.

My friend Mitch Dickinson once asked me why I had to do all these other things. The only answer I have is that I have to make music, that's who I am. I do create my own chaos sometimes. Something will pop into my head and I have to make it happen. I've sometimes woken up in a sweat at 3 or 4 o'clock in the morning because I'd had an idea for another band in my mind but I hadn't had the chance to start recording it yet. It feels like there's so much I have to do before my time is up.

Sometimes it's a chance to work with my mates outside of the context of Napalm Death. Me, Mitch Harris and a singer called Simon Orme had a band named Little Giant Drug, and we released an album called *Prismcast* in 1998. That was us indulging our love of the Cocteau Twins, the Smashing Pumpkins and The Wonder Stuff. I'm pretty sure Napalm Death fans heard it and went, "What the fuck are they doing?"

The other reason I do all these other projects is that they give me the chance to work with musicians I admire. Blood From The Soul was a collaboration with Lou Koller from the hardcore band Sick Of It All. I finally put out a second album in 2020, with Jacob Bannon from Converge singing on it, who I'm a big fan of. It's the same with Venomous Concept and Buzz Osborne – I never really plan these things, they just tend to happen.

Sometimes projects come together really quickly and easily, like Venomous Concept or the Brujeria albums I've worked on, and especially Dark Sky Burial. Other times, they take ages to reach fruition. Tronos is one of those.

Tronos stemmed from some really spiritual conversations that me, Russ and Mitch Harris had years ago about life after death and déjà vu and alternate realities. We'd often sit down to do something then find ourselves wandering off at all these different tangents.

Russ and I had been talking about doing something together for a while outside of recording Napalm Death albums. It was originally going to be more of an industrial-style project, but Russ was really into a band called Triptykon, who had been founded by Tom G. Warrior from the band Celtic Frost*, so it became a bit more doomy. We had no agenda for it. We decided to do what we felt came naturally.

We started work on the Tronos album at Russ's home studio in 2012, but it wasn't until we got Dirk Verbeuren in to drum that it started to take shape properly. Dirk's most famous these days as the drummer in Megadeth, but I've known him for years. He's a massive Napalm Death fan. Russ and I had sent him the music we were making and he literally came up with something overnight.

Tronos still took years to evolve into what it became, but that meant I could ask some musicians who I admire to be involved. I didn't want to play bass myself, I wanted it to have a different feel. My friend Billy Gould from Faith No More played bass on a few tracks, Dan Lilker from Nuclear Assault and Brutal Truth is on there, Troy Sanders from Mastodon too. We got Snake from Voivod, a band I'd loved since the 80s, to come and do some vocals, and also Erica Nockalls, who's an amazing violinist and plays with The Wonder Stuff.

We finally released the first Tronos album, *Celestial Mechanics*, in 2019. The title says it all. It's an exploration of outer and inner space. It gets deep – how long do we have on earth and where do we go afterwards, why you connect with certain people and why you don't connect with others? With Tronos I can explore feelings that I can't with some of the other bands I'm in. Lyrically, Napalm Death has a clear social conscience, whereas Lock Up and Brujeria are more escapist. Tronos lets me look into myself, but keep it abstract enough for other people to relate to.

One of the songs on the album is called 'Premonition'. I started writing it on my birthday in Portugal. I was thinking about this road we're on that only leads to one destination and how we shouldn't have regrets about the lives we've lived. I'd just had my daughter, and there's a line in there that goes: "I clench this tiny hand for hope." Sometimes when you feel lost, you hold your kid's hand and it doesn't feel so bad.

Having a young baby around the time we started Tronos actually gave me the confidence to sing vocals on a record for the first time. I'd sing and hum to my daughter all the time, which seemed like a good way of building vocal strength. When it came to getting a singer for Tronos, we didn't have much joy finding anybody who felt right so I thought, "Fuck it, I'll have a go." I've sung backing vocals on Napalm songs, and I got up with Macabre onstage in Germany to sing 'Ed Gein' with them, but I'd never wanted to put myself in the spotlight like that before.

It was one of the most nerve-wracking things I've done. Doing hardcore-style backing vocals is a world away from what we wanted to do with Tronos. Me and Russ started building up vocal ideas whenever we had the time. I didn't have much confidence at first, but we gave ourselves the time and freedom to explore, which built confidence. I'm still more Jaz Coleman than Ronnie James Dio, but I like the challenge of singing more than I did when I started.

Things like Tronos and Dark Sky Burial are where my head is at a lot these days. I enjoy writing music for Napalm, but it takes a lot of time and it stresses me out at times. I'm at a point where I want to focus my attention elsewhere, not just on the band. That might mean not doing as much Napalm in the future. Then again, I've never been great at planning. I could wake up tomorrow with a dozen ideas for Napalm in my head.

2020-2021

66 Napalm Death's 16th album, *Throes Of Joy In The Jaws Of Defeatism*, was released in September 2020, five years after *Apex Predator*. It was a frustrating record to make because of the uncertainty and the delays, but then I'm always frustrated about some aspect of making a Napalm record. I really enjoy just going in and seeing what happens, but that's not been the Napalm way since the early days.

It took a long time for Barney to do the vocals. He has his own reasons for that, but it turned out brilliantly. He brought something completely different to the album, just in terms of how willing he was to try different things. Barney loves all kinds of different music, though he's sometimes been a bit more cautious about bringing it into Napalm in the past. But in recent years, it feels like he's been much more open to incorporating those influences, whether it's Swans or Public Image Limited or something else. He really pushed the range of things that he had at his disposal this time.

There was a lot of experimentation happening all across that album. One of the songs, 'A Bellyful Of Salt And Spleen', is a really grinding, almost tribal track with lots of strange effects. That was basically me doing weird guitar slides and banging on tin pots and big buckets for percussion. It was like being back in my nan's back garden when I was a young kid. I got shivers down my spine when Barney came in to do his vocals, because I love it when he breaks the mould vocally and he absolutely nailed it.

There's another song on *Throes Of Joy*… called 'Amoral', which is more of a mid-paced song, but really stark and doomy. People have said, "Oh, you're just ripping off Killing Joke." Yeah, there's a bit of Killing Joke there, but it's really a nod to very early Napalm Death – songs like 'Abattoir' and 'What Man Can Do' which were on the pre-*Scum* demos and never got properly released. 'Amoral' is me paying tribute to Nik Bullen and all the guys who were in the band back then.

When the album came out I said I wasn't going to do any interviews for it, which I think frustrated Barney. It's the first time I'd ever said that, but they were his lyrics and his concept, so I wanted to let him speak for them. I sometimes feel uncomfortable when people ask me questions about things he's written, not because I disagree with him but because they're his words and his opinions. He's way more knowledgeable than I am about the state of the world. I don't want to half-ass an answer because people will see that I don't know what I'm talking about, and what's the point in that?

I never take Barney for granted. He has a lot to bear being the singer in Napalm Death and I know that he's an essential part of what makes the band what it is, but I think I sometimes forget to show it. Everybody wants a pat on the shoulder from the people around them just to let them know they're valued, but that's not always an easy thing to remember to do.

Me and Barney are both very passionate about Napalm. He has his vision of what it should be, and I have mine. I'm always questioning myself and my surroundings. I want the best for Napalm, but I don't always express it the right way, which has repercussions. With Barney, sometimes it's been a case of, "If it isn't broke, don't fix it." And he's right to think that too.

I can be hard to keep up with. Some days I can sit there with a guitar and come up with three or four riffs, and I'll think, "That's the start of another Napalm track." I could go in the studio next week and make an album, but it would flip other people in the band out, and I understand that. Barney has his method of working. He likes to lock the door, draw the curtains and be completely isolated. And it works for him – what he comes up with is brilliant. You just have to work around these things and try not to hurt each other's feelings while you're doing it.

That's easier said than done sometimes. Me and Barney are better than we were when it comes to communicating with each other, but we still have our moments. One of our co-managers gets frustrated. He says, "You'll both email me to moan, but you won't talk to each other about it." I think it's because we're both afraid of saying something in case we end up getting angry.

We did have a proper fight in Ireland a couple of years ago. It was during a time when I was back drinking. We'd played a great gig and I had a couple of beers, which I think pissed him off because he wanted me to get healthy. And mine and Simon Efemey's sense of humour was winding him up. We went at it for a while, then it just blew over. It was a storm in a teacup. The next day we apologized to each other and we hugged. We never used to be able to do that.

How do we get through it? It's been said before, but a band is like a marriage. You have your ups and downs. But at the end of the day, me and Barney are great friends. Most of the time when you see us in Napalm Death, we're laughing. We're not these stern, po-faced, socially conscious people 24/7.

We released *Throes Of Joy…* in the middle of the pandemic, which was weird. Normally we'd be touring around it, and one of the hardest things I found about that whole period was not being able to do that. I've been playing solidly since the late 80s, and it's been a large part of my life ever since. When all that suddenly vanishes and you don't know when it will come back, it becomes hard to deal with sometimes. My wife would ask me why I was freaking out about it. I didn't really have an answer, other than something I was so used to doing had been taken away and I didn't know if it was coming back.

When shows started getting postponed and pushed back and then postponed again, I realized I needed to keep my mind occupied. I was a bit lost for a while without touring. And what always helped get through the tough times, ever since I was a kid, was music. It was always reliable and safe and let me escape from everything. If I'm left to my own devices, I'll just sit there all day and make music.

With hindsight, I should have used the pandemic to take a breather and put the brakes on. But in many ways, I intensified my life. Having a break from touring with Napalm Death gave me the opportunity to make more music. In the space of about two years, I put out four Dark Sky Burial albums, we recorded a new Lock Up album, we did the fifth Venomous Concept album and recorded demos for a sixth. When I wasn't doing that, I was doing family stuff – moving house, home-schooling the kids, trying to be present for them.

People have told me I should mellow out, but I find it difficult to. This sounds pretentious, but if you're a creative individual it's hard to switch it on and off. Everybody invests their time and energy into something they love. For some people it's buying and selling houses, for some people it's setting up a business. For me it's making music and having these bands and projects on the go.

After 10 years of not drinking, I fell off the wagon during the pandemic. I started drinking a bit again, then when touring restarted properly I was back in the full swing of things. I'd never describe myself as an alcoholic, but with booze, I binge. It's not healthy, but in some ways, it can be very inspirational. When I drink, lyrics suddenly come pouring out, or a piece of music I'm working on sounds great. Most of the guitar tracks on the Tronos record were done while I was pounding cans of beer. I'm not ashamed to say that I wrote some of the Dark Sky Burial songs while I was on cocaine.

It's wrong to say there's a romance to it. There's no romance to ending up with pancreatitis, believe me. But sometimes being in that frame of mind unlocks creativity in different ways. The question I ask myself is, do I really need to use those tools to unlock that, or is it just an excuse? All these things go through my head. I still don't know the answer.

There have been periods with my drinking, especially when I lapsed during the pandemic, when people around me have been worried for me. Like everything, it's trying to find a balance between what works for you and what doesn't.

When I think about it, it's mad that we can make an album like *Throes Of Joy In The Jaws Of Defeatism* after all this time. When Mickey Harris left in 1991, it was partly because he wanted to push Napalm forward. I thought it would have been too much at that point. I said to him, "I'm all up for what you want to do, just wait and be patient." *Throes Of Joy In The Jaws Of Defeatism* is what I meant. It's a Napalm Death record, but it encompasses all these other things: alternative music, industrial, indie… all these influences we had back in the early days. We didn't know how to channel them back then, but by the time of *Throes Of Joy…* we'd worked it out.

Even now, there are differences in how we do things with the band. After *Throes Of Joy In The Jaws Of Defeatism*, we released an EP called *Resentment Is Always Seismic* featuring tracks we wrote at the same time. We were out of contract with our label, and I wanted to put it out via Bandcamp ourselves, just as an experiment. I'd released the Dark Sky Burial stuff that way and it had done well. I wanted to see how Napalm Death's music would do. It wasn't about how much money we could have made, it was just trying something different. But nobody else wanted to try it, and I just gave up on the idea after a while.

Things like that can be frustrating, but then you have to remember that a band is a democracy and not everybody sees things the way you see things. Everybody has their own view on how to do things, whether that's musically or in terms of business. There's no right or wrong in the end, only your opinion.

At the end of the day, we're still trying to push the boundaries of what we can be. *Throes Of Joy...* has so many different things on it. I'm really proud that we're still able to do something like that this far into our career. It's an accumulation of our experiences over the last 30-odd years. That's the reason you don't go away for a decade then reunite. You miss out on that journey.

EYE WITNESS: JOHN COOKE

Napalm Death guitarist

Napalm Death have been in John Cooke's life since he was 13 years old, first as a fan, then as part of their crew and then as the band's guitarist. His entry point was 1996's *Diatribes* album, a record that balanced extremity with a growing sense of experimentation.

"I was a huge Metallica fan, but I'd been looking for faster and faster stuff," he says. "That led to The Exploited, Minor Threat, Black Flag, loads of old punk bands. Then I heard a Napalm Death song on an Earache Records compilation, and that was it. There was nothing else around at the time that sounded like them. I didn't know anything about their history at that point, but I started digging back and I got the *Mass Appeal Madness* EP, which is one of my favourite records ever."

He first crossed paths with Shane Embury on the tour for Napalm's *Enemy Of The Music Business* album in 2000. At the time,

Cooke had his own two-piece band, Evade. "It was just me and my mate making really noisy, fast music," he says. "I gave him a demo tape of my band. He says he doesn't remember it, but it was a long time ago so that's fair enough."

Cooke entered the band's orbit in the mid-2000s after getting a job at the rehearsal rooms they used in central Birmingham. He mostly worked as a van driver, delivering PA systems to wherever they were needed. Then he got a call: could he drive Shane and Napalm drummer Danny Herrera to a session for their other band, Venomous Concept?

"I was kind of nervous going because I was a huge Napalm fan, but we got on really well," says Cooke. "We ended up chatting about *Star Wars* and old punk records."

When the band needed someone to sell T-shirts on a lengthy UK tour in 2007, they decided to ask Cooke. Over the next few years, he ended up not only selling merch but becoming their tour van driver, ad hoc roadie and occasional tour manager. One time the band spent 26 hours driving to Germany in blizzard-like conditions, with Cooke and Napalm's Barney Greenway splitting the driving duties between them.

By the end of the 2010s, Cooke was living in the basement of the four-storey Napalm House, at least until he was forced to move out after a torrential flood. Still, his closeness to the band meant he was the logical choice to play guitar on a 2010 US tour with Shane's punk side project Venomous Concept. It was a less than luxurious experience, with the band sleeping on people's floors. There was also the occasional run-in with the law.

"We were playing the Viper Room in LA, which was Johnny Depp's club," says Cooke. "It's a shithole and there's no backstage, so we were sitting in the parking lot. Suddenly three or four cop cars turn up and accuse us of being something to do with these guys who were smoking weed across the other side. The next thing, we've all got our hands behind our backs, bent over the hoods of the cars, and Shane is taken away because they think he's got an outstanding DUI. It turns out he gave the wrong birth date – in America they have the month first."

Two years later, he got to stand in for Shane at a handful of

German festivals after the bassist was taken ill. "I got an emergency call from Mitch Harris, so I had 24 hours to learn the whole set," he says. On another occasion, Cooke assumed temporary singing duties during a Napalm set when Greenway was suffering from laryngitis. "I've basically done everything but play drums," he says.

The shift from occasional helping hand to regular stand-in came in 2014 when Cooke was asked to deputise on guitar for the absent Mitch Harris, later becoming the band's full-time touring guitarist when Harris elected to stay in Vegas. Cooke added a guitar to the song 'Hierarchies' on 2015's *Apex Predator – Easy Meat* album; he also contributed parts to 2020's *Throes Of Joy In The Jaws Of Defeatism*.

"It was strange, I wasn't sure what my position was," he says. "Musicians aren't always good at communicating. There's a lot of things that don't get addressed, but everything gets placed to one side just to put the best show on."

Cooke realized early on that being a member of Napalm Death carried some physical risks. He's had two teeth knocked out by a stage diver and suffered concussion at a gig. Then there was the show in Paris in 2018 where the venue was so hot that the band members nearly passed out onstage.

But it's also given him a chance to get to know Shane Embury. As well as playing with Napalm, Cooke has been involved with several of the bassist's other bands, including Blood From The Soul, Absolute Power and Dark Sky Burial.

"We've known each other for a long time now, so it's easy to play with him," says Cooke. "Even though he can be pretty blunt. Sometimes you'll be working on something for ages and you'll take it to him and he'll go, 'Nah, that's shit.' I don't mind. I'm used to it. But the flipside is that he's a big softy really. We played a gig where there was a kid at the front who didn't have headphones on to protect his ears, and Shane was worried about the kid."

As befits someone who came of age in the 90s, Cooke remains a staunch defender of the divisive run of Napalm Death albums that spans 1994's *Fear, Emptiness, Despair* to 1998's *Words From The Exit Wound*. "They started out fast, then got weird," he says. "It was all about the groove and the power. It was ambiguous – you had to piece it together yourself."

But as someone who has been in their orbit for close to two decades, he's seen first-hand the desire in the band, and Shane in particular, to push things forwards. "He's always got 20 things on the go, whether it's Napalm Death or Dark Sky Burial, which is the most personal thing he's done. He's still got music to make, and he's always interested in finding new ways to make it."

2022

66 The hardest time of not only the last few years but of my whole life came in August 2022, when my mom passed away. She was getting on, and a little bit frail, but I wasn't expecting it. It was different to when my dad died, just because I was closer to my mom. All the emotions flooded out, and I have to admit, it sent me to a dark place for a while. I think the people around me were worried for me, but it was something I had to process in my own way.

My mom, and my nan before her, were both a huge influence on me. They were really compassionate people. My mom used to work at the local chip shop and eventually got fired because she gave away free chips to the kids from families who couldn't afford to eat. She couldn't bear to see them go hungry. My mom was a battler in that way.

A friend of mine named Rob used to work with my mom. He had piercings and tattoos. The other people there would always give him shit about his appearance, but Rob told me my mom would always defend him. She'd call them out on how they judged people on the way they looked: "You see these people with their tattoos and bright coloured hair and you look down on them, but they're better than most of you people." I always remember that. She stood up for people.

Maybe she was a bit over-protective of me when I was a child, but that's just the person she was. She worried about others a lot.

One of the things I'm proudest of is that I managed to buy my mom's house for her before she died. We'd been living there since I was six years old, so there was a real connection to it. It was a council house, and her and my dad had the chance to buy it before then, but for whatever reason they never did. I thought buying it would give her some security and it did.

Losing my mom really got me thinking about what happens after you die. Most of the time I think there's nothing. But then weird things happen that make you wonder. Two or three days after my dad died, my sister got a text message from him even though his phone was turned off – it had obviously been sent before he died and had got delayed for some reason, but it was still spooky. When I went to clear out my mom's house, I went upstairs and her walking stick fell over as soon as I walked through the door. I think part of me was looking for a sign, even though I know it was really just coincidence.

Dying doesn't scare me, but the thought of not being around does. I want to have enough time to see my kids get to a good age, especially as I started pretty late as a father. I really don't know what happens after you die. No one does. We're here for now, so let's do it while we can.

In the last couple of years I've become interested in something called Jungian individuation. It's based around the works of Carl Jung and deals with myths and archetypes. I've been regularly speaking to a Jungian analyst, who has become a kind of mentor to me.

It's all part of getting myself healthy, mentally and physically. I'm trying to balance out who I am – the good bits and the bad bits, trying work out who I'm meant to be. I'm aware of how destructive I can be within myself. Like everybody, I have my ups and downs. I don't think I'm a bad person and I have a reasonable sense of humour, but there's a dark side to me. What's that dark side? That's what I'm trying to find out.

One of the ideas Jungian Individuation deals with is the labyrinth. The labyrinth is your life. Sometimes you come across things that are immoveable, that you can't negotiate with. Sometimes it becomes a spiral – you think you're OK then, boom, you're back down here again.

The labyrinth, for me, is addressing grief. Not just my mom and dad's passing, but grief from a long time ago – even something like being bullied at school. People who are bullied can become bullies themselves, which is something I'm really aware of and has made me think about how I interact with other people. But it's also about being aware of your own needs, and trying to make time for yourself.

Jungian Individuation has influenced my work with Dark Sky Burial. When I began DSB, I was becoming attracted to symbols –

alchemical symbols, pagan symbols, pentagrams. Even the idea that my albums had to be released in series of four is a symbol. My mentor tells me that symbols represent something you haven't worked out to express yet, so you're searching for meaning within them.

It's also a way of exploring your inner self, this creative impulse you have. Musicians are shamans in a way – it's their way of expressing emotion through music. I've found that difficult at times in the past, but with Dark Sky Burial in particular it seems to be easier.

I sometimes wonder if this is purely a creative infatuation, and that I'm only really into the metaphors and the symbolism of it. Even if that's the case, there's nothing wrong with it, but I think there's more going on. Back when I was a teenager, I'd carry around Venom albums to scare off the local vicar. There was a symbolism that I probably wasn't fully aware of, but it feels like I always knew there was something deeper to it even then.

I think the whole idea behind Jungian Individuation for me is to work out who I truly am and to accept myself, the good and the bad. Some people have told me, "Be careful what door you open, you might not like what you find." But that's the whole point of it. You have to fail and face your failures,you have to admit your guilt but not carry it around for the rest of your life, you have to forgive your-self to move forwards. It's not about being perfect. People have this idea of perfection as something to strive for. You can never be per-fect, but you can be good enough.

In recent years, I've tried to keep the chaos of my life under con-trol. Sometimes people look to me when it comes to certain bands, but I've started pushing things back. A new Lock Up album called *The Dregs Of Hades* came out in 2021, but I wasn't as involved in that as I have been in the past. It's the same with the *Pocho Aztlan* Brujeria album – I wrote a couple of songs for it, but let my friend Anton Reisenegger take the reins.

What I like about doing my own thing is that I'm not dependent on other people. I can book a studio and just go in and do something without having to worry about anyone else. Right now, I'm focusing on Napalm Death and Dark Sky Burial, but who knows what else could come along and grab my interest?

The Future...

66 There have been times in the last few years when I've felt that I was done with Napalm Death. The band is a big part of me, but it's not all of me. I fought against settling down for years because I wanted to make music and have a good time. Now I'm married and we have kids but I still go away for long periods of time. Family is more and more important to me, and if I'm away on tour for six or seven weeks at a time, some of that connection with my family gets lost. I can speak to them via Facetime, but it's not the same as being there with them, especially as children grow.

Recently, I woke up in a strange mood and wrote on my Facebook page that no one is going to be prepared for the next Napalm Death album. I'm not sure myself exactly where it's going to go, but I believe in a kind of universal destiny. I said that for a reason, and now it's my duty to make it happen.

I sometimes count myself lucky to have joined the band, but then there was more to it than luck. It was lucky that we went down to see Napalm at The Mermaid in Birmingham after Mitch bumped into Justin Broadrick. But to be honest, it wasn't luck that they asked me to join, or that I've been in this band for more than 35 years.

When I look back, I'm proud of what Napalm Death have achieved. I don't just mean what we've done since I joined the band, but what those guys who started it in the early 80s achieved. I do feel like I'm carrying on the legacy of Napalm, and so are Barney and Danny.

But I'm proud of what I achieved myself. I've made albums with all kinds of weird and wonderful people, I've seen the world in ways that I wouldn't have done otherwise, I've become friends with people I would never have met, it's given me a better education than school ever did. Sure, it's stressed me out at some points, but those highs and lows are part of life.

I still go down to the Napalm House a lot. It's got so many memories embedded in those walls – all the crazy drunken nights we had, piling home after the clubs had shut and listening to the Cocteau Twins or some old heavy metal band. It's hard not to miss those days, but then I remember that I'm in my mid-50s and my life is completely different now.

I think I'm still running away from real life in some ways. Part of me is still that kid in his own little world. I never realized it at the time, but I think a lot of what I've done with Napalm Death and all the other stuff I've been involved with was partly an attempt to prove something to those people who said I'd never have a career in music, or even those kids that bullied me at school. It's not an arrogant, "Fuck you, look at what I've achieved", but it is about leaving a mark of some kind, even if it's a small one.

Can I imagine a point in my life where Napalm is no longer in it? Sometimes. I imagine myself with the house paid off, hanging out with my kids, making some noise and just being balanced. Then I'll sit down with a guitar and three or four riffs will come out and I'll think, "That'll work on the new Napalm album."

There'll be plenty more Napalm Death albums, and plenty more Dark Sky Burial music, and whatever other crazy ideas come into my head. I sometimes tell myself to slow down, but I never do. I always go back to the lyric Neil Peart wrote for the Rush song 'Dreamline': "We're only immortal for a limited time." I love that line. Life isn't forever, so be who you are.

Roll of Honour

The publishers gratefully acknowledge the contribution of everyone listed below, whose generous support helped bring this project to fruition.

Elijah Nathan
    Abbott
Vents Aboltins
Jenson Abraham
Rikkert Achtereekte
Mike Ackermann
Mariusz Adamczyk
Alessandro Adamou
Dan Ahern
Tapsu Ahola
Chris Aidonopoulos
Danne Åkesson
Rob Alderman
Chris Alexander
Tommy Alexander
Didier Almouzni
Hendrix Alomar
    Martinez
Nick Ambroson
Jean-Luc Ammar
Lars Ammonsen
Emma Anderson
Noah Anderson
Jonas Andersson
Michael Andersson
Robin Andersson
Knut Andiel
Yuriy Andiel
John Andrews
Anton

Rock Ape
Apo e Gioia
Santiago Ares de Blas
Claes Argårds
Simon Arnold
Frank Arriola
Dave Arsey
Iván As the world
    keeps turning!
Johan Asp
John Aston
Hendrik Attema
Lee Attenborough
Paul Audino
Bob Augsburger
Andrew Aversionline
Ainara Azkoaga

Tymofii Baga
Shaun Bagley
Sean Baillie
Alfred Bakker
Jordi Balagué i
    Linares
Firat Balci
Tomek Baniuszewicz
Marco Barbieri
Nick Bareham
Alessandro Barisone
Lars Barkholtz

Jason Barmash
Simon Barrington
Antonio Barrote
Jeremy Bartelt
Oliver Barth
Greg Bartle
Greg Bartlett
Graeme Barton
Robert Bassar
Scott Batrick
Cyril Baudlet
Marc Baumann
Stefan Baumgartner
Guillaume Bay
Rev. Paul Bearer
Andy Beaveridge
Kevin Beck
Ad Beekenkamp
Carl Bennett
Dan Bennis
Zoltan Berente
Johan Berglund
JS Bergstrom
Vincent Berkey
David Bessler
Adriano Bestetti
Aaron Bevins
Joel Bianco
Gareth Bidder
Ralph Bidner

Sascha Bieber
Frank Bijnens
Tom Bill
Bilos
Povilas Bingelis
Buster Nykjær
  Björkman
Matthew
  Black-Bryson
Jan Blanch
Zdeněk Blažek
Jodie Block
Geoff D. Blogg
Sebastiaan Bluemers
Kyle Bockelman
David Bohn Stoltz
Boris Boitieux
Hugh Boland
Dallas Bolen
Örtschi Bollock
Nathan Bolt
Mikey 'FOH' Bolton
Tim Bond
Gabriel Borg
Jacek Borowy
Dieter Heavy-D
  Bossaerts
David Boston
David Boulogne
Captain Bourko
Manu Bouziat
Phil Bowden
Stuart Bowditch
Scott Boyd
Justin Brecese
Gretha Breuer
Laura Brigden

Jason Briggs
Gareth Brindle Jones
Martin Brindley
Britta
Lee Broadmore
Johan Brom
Sebastien Brosseau
Cara 'Grind on!'
  Brown
Jasper Brown
Susan Brown
Duncan Bruce
Joshua Buffin
Vincent 'Quintangle'
  Buisson
Tim Burkland
Guy Burman
Todd Bush
Vaughn Byrd
Cathy Byrne

Dominic C-B
Eddie C
Greg Cadu
Chip Calhoun
Matthew Hoo Hah
  Campbell
Steve Campbell
Manuel Campistany
Franck Camus
Laura Candy
Chris Cannings
Elliot Capper
Seany Carey
Bob Carey-Grieve
Jose M. Carnero
Pascal Carpe

Mitch Carpenter
Scott Carpentier
David Carr
Claudio Carrasco
Antonio Manuel
  Carrero Rodríguez
Stuart Carson
Adam Caruana
N. Casio Poe
Chris Casket
Mikey Castillo
Jim Cattron
Tiffany Chalmer
  'themagickcat'
Lynda Chalmers
Dan Charge
Gordon Chase
Laurent Chaulet
Jose Chavez
Andres Chávez
Manuel Chávez
Clint Chiarella
Alexey Chirkov
Lars Christiansen
Aleš Chytil
Giorgio Cifuni
Horia Ciocan
Graham Clamp
Ian Clarkson
Adolfo Clavo
Bryn Clegg
Simon Cleverly
Ryan Cockram
Matt Cole
Matt Commoner
Stephen Conlon
Daniel Connelly

Declan Connolly
Adam Cook
John Cook
John Grizloch Cook
Mean Gene Cook
Shane 'Red' Corcoran
A.T. Coulter
Patrick Crashbang-
  wallop666 Meuris
Shaun Crawford
Mark Creevy
Alan Cresswell
Critch
John Cromar
André Crombach
Mark Cronin
Bing Crowell
Chad Cruthers
Giuseppe Cutispoto

Stefan Dahlberg
Niklas Dahlin
Doug Dalton
Michael Daly
Björn Danneman
Kristopher Dass
Noel Davies
Brad Davis
Rob Day
Dave De Buysscher
Patrick De Francisco
Dimas De La Cruz
Tim de Lang
Frank De Leeuw
Michael De Lorenzo
David De Ridder
Laurens de Rooij

Death By Derrrick
Dan Debling
Sean DeChant
Matthew Decker
Friso Dekker
Eric Dekkers
Peter DeLuycker
Andreas Demarmels
Gryffyd Dempsey
Mike Dempsey
Lionel Deroche
Florian Deubel
Fernando Di Donato
Jeffrey Diaz
Carlos D. Díaz
  Moracho
Steve Dickson
Ulf Diel
Berend Dijk
Simon Dillon
Mike Diorio
Rob Diziki
Terence T. D. Doak
Frank Doc Albers
DollGarm
John Serrated
  Donegan
Scott Downes
Glenn Downing
Tim Doyle
Dr anger
CMS Dreizehn
Conor Droney
Pete Drysdale
Michel Dumats
Chris Dunn
Jason Dunstan

Daniel Dürrfeld
Derek Durward
Ryan Dusseau
(Mad) Frank
  'HeavY'
  Düwel-Janke
Dennis Dyer

Trevor Earis
Christopher Eccles
Irfaan Edoo
Elena
Ari Elo
Thomas Buthler
  Emanuelsen
Joe Embleton
Nick Emde
Stephen Emerel
Conny Enstrom
David Erbe
Roberto Ernst
Joshua Ervin
Mike Esposito
Stuart Eyre

Fabio
Scott Fairfax
Alex Faisst
Steven Falconer
Roozbeh Farzanmehr
Fatherdude
Michael Fehder
Mario Feichtner
Dave Felstead
Jay Felton
Brian Ferguson
Jae Warren Ferrer

Asher Ferri
Jan Fessore
Kevin Fetus
Joost Fhij
Metal Mark Fields
Erika Figabomba
Rudi Filej
Mike Filth
Marco Fiffy Fiscus
Marc Fisher
Paul Fisher-Stokes
Brian Flynn
Hans FM
John Foley
Nathan Foster
Norbert Fournier
Christian Foust
Steve Francis
Moritz Frank
Veith Franke
Daniel Fransson
Franz
Mike Frey
Ollie Fröhlich
Milan Fuchs
Milan Fuchs
Anthony Furlong
Michal Furtak
Ivan Fusi
Fuska

Dr. Robin Gallagher
Kyle Galloway
Rob Gange
Chris Gardner
Cristoforo Garigliano

Matthew
   Gaskill-Jones
Adam Gauntlett
Jürgen Gayer
Rainer Gehrke
Ted Genz
C & R Geoghegan
Doug Geyer
Greg Gibb
Yvan Gillioz
David Glading
Tim Glennie
KT Glitz
Alexander Glockner
Jason Fuller
   Goatsound
Dave Goddard
Andrew Goldstein
Julián Gomariz
   García
Mateo Gomez
Hugo Alberto
   Gonzalez
Devon & Finn
   Goodrich
Bryan Goon
Marcin Gotfryd
Kristof Grabowski
Paul Graham
Deron Grams
Carl Granehult
Alisa Grant
Dave Grant
Simon Grapes
Terry Green
Eric (303Eric)
   Greenfield

Damon Greenhalgh
Niall Gregory
Marc Grewe
Diogenes Grief
Trevor Grigg
Olivier Grisvard
Edwin Groenewold
Joseph Gruber
Marco Gruhn
Halli Gudmunds
Javier Guerra
Johan Gummesson
Andrew Gunn
Gunshot!
Lewis Gurd
Anders Gustavsson
Gerardo Gutierrez
Gerson Gutierrez
Miroslaw Guzik
Matej Gyarfas
Jeroen Gysen

Jim H
Rob Hakemo
Ian Halliwell
Juha Hamalainen
Neil Hancock
Pistol Pete Hancox
Disinterested
   Handjob
Johnny Hanke
Cory Hanson
Michael & Owen
   Hanson
Nic Harding
Carleton Hardy
Matt Hargrave

Richard Harper
Steve Harries
Jason Harris
Kees Harrison
Ian Hart
Bob Harvey
John Haskett
Rasmus Hastrup
Paul Haug
Tim Havard
Eloy Haya García
Brenden Healey
Frank 'Dirt bird'
    Healy
Matthew Heath
Erik Hedin
Isaak Heemskerk
Greg Heerdt
Wouter Heetesonne
Kristjan B.
    Heidarsson
Johannes Heinonen
Marco Hemming
Andrew Henderson
Stewart Henderson
Ian Heran
Peter Herbert
Scott Herkaler
Chris Herrera
Raymond Herrera
Carl Heuschmidt
Brant Hewelt
Patrick Hienckes
Harry Hilland
Steve Hinan
Will Hinkle
Maciek Hirsebrei

Mikko Hirvonen
Mike Hodges
Ashleigh Hodgkin
Graham Hodis
hofee
Markus Hofmann
Sean Hogan
Jeremy Holcombe
Jack Holloway
Magnus Holmgren
Peter Kompripiotr
    Holzknecht
Dan Horton
Marc Horton
Gareth Alan
    Houghton
Frederic Houriez
Yannick Houtmeyers
Bogroll Howard
Scott Howard
Paul Hoyle
David Huggele
Simon Hulbert
Sebastian Hull
Smoo Hull
Rod Hunt
Iain Huntley
Trev Hurley
Gareth Hutchins

David Ince
Barkingboy
    Inhackney
Ipp
Gregor Iwanoff
Enzo Izzi

Andy Jackson
Cyril Jaffré
Anders Jakobson
Stanislaw
    Jakubowicz
Gert Janssen
Mykul Japhet
Stewart Jardine
Eduardo Jarry
Kari Järvinen
JCRASH!
Valérie Jean-Marc
Mike Jeffries
Ryan Jelf
Adam Jenkins
Paul Jenkins
Paul bassmonkey
    Jenkins
Peter Jenkins
BigMetalDave
    Johnson
Lee Johnson
Ben Johnston
Ben Jones
Karen Jones
Mark Jones
Jefe Miguel Jorge

Martin Kah
Mike Kanahn
Oliver Kannegiesser
Marlon Kasberg
Jayme Keglor
Martin Kellermann
Paul Kellett
Kelly & Daf
Leonard Kelly

Mike Kelly
Daniel Kelly Kelly
Lyndon Kennedy
Adam Keranen
Terry Kerns
Urs Kersten
Martin Ketzer
Daniel 'Decay'
  Killgore
Lemmy Kilmister
Stephen King
King Peat 1895
Hannupekka
  Kinnunen
Tony Kirby
Tony Kirby
Antti Kivilahti
Jens Kleinert
Jens Kleinert
Helmut Kleve
Georg Klingenbeck
Jason Knecht
Thomas Kneer
Carsten Koch
Marcellus Koch
Aljaz Kocjan
Thomas Konrader
Jesper Kornerud
Eirini Kouka
Benjamin Krause
Paulie Kraynak
Cam Kroetsch
Leo J. Kryger
Paweł Kubiś
Konsta Kukkonen
Adam Kwiecień

Richu Lall
Marts Lambert
Gordon Lancaster
Marcel Lang
Tim and Nick
  Langridge
Arthur Lara
James Laraway
Steve Larosa
Christopher Larson
Guðmundur
  Lárusson
Imperatrice Laurent
Kai Lavila
Stephen Lawton
Sébastien Le
  Martelot
Laurent le Morellec
John Lebiatowski
Geoffroy Lefebvre
Calvin Leick
Simon Leiser
Andreas Lejondahl
Alessio Leocadia
Phil LeQua
Massimo
  Librodicarta
Eric Lide
Sean Limbert
Frank & Alix
  Linguelet
Ruben Link
Michal 'Mick666'
  Lipinski
Ian Lipthorpe
Aaron Livingston
Allan Livingstone

Jim Lloyd
Brett Locking
Till Löhrmann
Alvar Loog
Albert Lopez
Joanne Love
Stewart Love
David Loveless
Kevin Re LoVullo
Khaled Lowe
Marc Loyseau
Jason Lueck
Lunkan 2000
Nick Luty
Scott Lyall
Daniel Lynch
Steve Lynch

Henning M.
Matthew Mabbott
Alexander Macrow
Tony Maddison
John Madsen
Gunther Maes
Ingvar Magnusson
Jason Maher
Patrick Maier
Charlie Makin
Perttu Makkonen
Daniel Malcovsky
Eetu Manninen
Anders Månsson
Lasse Marhaug
Lennon Marie
Chris Marijs
Colin Marquardt
Kimberly Marquez

Marre
Erik Marshall
Chris Marston
David Martin
Cesar Martinez
Norberto Martinez
Rodrigo Martinez
Marissa
    Martinez-Hoadley
Matthew Mason
Danny Massey
Freud Massicotte
Craig Mather
Luc Matthyssen
Ian Maxwell
Abelardo Mayoral
Gavin McAllister
Michael McCabe
John McCallom
Derek McCarthy
Paul S McCartney
Leland McClure
Jon McCollum
Jason McGuigan
Jarrod McIntosh
Robbie McKeeve
Henry McKelvie
Kyle McLellan
John McMeiken
Colly Meade
Mick Meagher
Meandean1970
Adrian Medhurst
Albert Meijer
David Meister
Carl & Melanie
Paul Mele

Andy Mellors
Rob Mells
Mark Mengerink
Allen Mercer
Justin Mercer
Janine Michno
Gérald Micou
Alan H. Middleton
Bruce Milian
Kryss Milla
John Miller
Matthias Miller
John Mincemoyer
Carlos Kazuo Missao
Ed Mitchell
Jeff Mitchell
Justin Mitchell
Peter Mitchell
Jonathan Mizzi
Per Arne Mohr
Cristiano Monga
Andrew Monteverde
David Montour
Shauna Montrucchio
Adam Moore
Kenneth Moore
Tim Moore
Eduardo Moreno
Huw Morgan
Graham Morris
Andrew Morrish
Andrew Mortensen
David Moucha
Xavier Mouthon
MP 1910
Samir Mulalic
Kent Mulcahy

Falko Müller
James Munyon
Jouni Murtomäki
Christian Muschiol
Temgesic Mustonen

Kevin Nacey
Paul Nash
In memory of
    Shaun Neary
Bill Needham
Christophe Neixkens
Michael Nelson
Elliot Newman
Craig Nicholls
Dave Nicholls
Gallo Nicolas
Zakk Nicolson
Thomas Nielsen
Rei Nishimoto
Peter Nolan
Isac Nordgren
    Jonasson
Andrey Novikov
Andreas Nusko
Peter Nygaard
Morten Nyutstumo
Darren O'Connell
Ethan O'Connell
Dave O'Neil
Casey O'Neill
Niall O'Neill
David O'Ryan
Čurby Obscene
Thomas Ødegaard
Erik Odeldahl
Zachary Ohler

Ryan Olive
Frans Oomen
Sait Ortac
Susana + Oscar
Robert Osgood
Stefan Ott
Ian Over

David Paganotti
Alan Palfrey
Thomas Palm
Stu Palmer
Arturo Palomo
Oleksandr
   Panteleimonov
Brody Parker
Daniel Parra
Sean 'Beast' Parry
Jarvis Paul Samat
Will Pedley
Frank Pellegrin
Erno Pennanen
Steve Pepper
Martin Perdin
Allan Perez
Jon Andoni Pérez
   Simón
Landon Perry
Karim Peter
Melcher Petermann
Chris Pether
Tyler Phelps
Josh Piagno
Steve Picazio
Clemens Pierer
Emma Pintado
Tom Pinto

Antonio Pisanu
Plattsie
Aleks Polanski
Filippos Polatsidis
Ivan Poliakov
Andrejs Pomarnevskis
Andy Pope
Roman Porubec
Matt Potter
Claus Poulsen
Pete Povey
Chris Powell
Edouard Prat
Jean-François
   Pratlong
Michele Premi
Alessandro Prenci
Stuart Prickett
Matthias Prill
Mark Pringle
Jeremy Pritchett
Thais Danilo Prohlis
Pol Pujals Garriga
Igor Purgic
Ivo Půst

Nicolas Quintana
   Zunino

James Radcliffe
Keith Radcliffe
Sanjey Rai
John A. J. Ramsay
Patrick 'Swissman'
   Ramseier
Aiden Ramsey
Marko Randell

Ari Rannanpaa
Cyrus Rashvand
Helen Rasmussen
Jakob Rasmussen
Jason Rathman
Peter Raub
Gareth Rees
Philipp Reichart
Neil Reid
Dehuman Reign
Robert Reilly
Michael Restle
Phillip Anthony
   Reyes
Brian Reynolds
Dario Ricca
Damion Rice
Glen Rice
Marklew Rice
Erik Riemer
Jack Riley
Austen Rivas
Darren Robb
Tony Robertson
Shawn Robinson
Alan Rodgers
Michael Rogers
Chris Rohde
Sting Roll
Artem Romashov
Mika Ronkainen
Michael Roop
Hayden Roszczewski
Jason Roth
Gunter Roth
Chris Rotsias
Dan Rozenblum